Living and Working
in the
Gulf States
&
Saudi Arabia

A Survival Handbook
by
Bob Hughes & Graeme Chesters

SURVIVAL BOOKS • LONDON • ENGLAND

First Edition 2003

Survival Books Limited, 1st Floor,
60 St James's Street, London SW1A 1ZN, United Kingdom
☎ +44 (0)20-7493 4244, 🖨 +44 (0)20-7491 0605
✉ info@survivalbooks.net
💻 www.survivalbooks.net
To order books, please refer to page 412.

British Library Cataloguing in Publication Data.
A CIP record for this book is available
from the British Library.
ISBN 1 901130 21 5

Printed and bound in Finland by WS Bookwell Ltd

ACKNOWLEDGEMENTS

The authors wish to thank all those who contributed to the successful publication of this book, in particular the many people who provided information and took the time and trouble to read and comment on the draft versions. We would especially like to thank Joanna Styles, David Hampshire, Trish Dodds (an invaluable researcher), and Joe and Kerry Laredo (editing and proof-reading) for their invaluable help. Also a special thank you to Jim Watson for the superb illustrations, map and cover.

Bob Hughes would also like to thank His Excellency Abdulnabi Al-Sho'ala, now Minister of Labour and Social affairs (Bahrain), and his former business partners Khamis al Muqla and Hasan Al-Jishi, who first introduced him to the region and showed much warmth and generosity during many happy years of association. He would also like to thank his family, Patricia, Melanie and Tempe, for shared experiences in the Gulf, and Captain James Dunk, a prime navigator.

OTHER TITLES BY SURVIVAL BOOKS

Living and Working Series

Abroad; America; Australia; Britain; Canada; France; Germany; Holland, Belgium & Luxembourg; Ireland; Italy; London; New Zealand; Spain; Switzerland

Buying a Home Series

Abroad; Britain; Florida; France; Greece & Cyprus; Ireland; Italy; Portugal; Spain

Other Titles

The Alien's Guide to Britain; The Alien's Guide to France; The Best Places to Live in France; The Best Places to Live in Spain; How to Avoid Holiday & Travel Disasters; Retiring Abroad; Rioja and its Wines; The Wines of Spain

Order forms are on page 414.

WHAT READERS & REVIEWERS

When you buy a model plane for your child, a video recorder, or some new computer gizmo, you get with it a leaflet or booklet pleading 'Read Me First', or bearing large friendly letters or bold type saying 'IMPORTANT – follow the instructions carefully'. This book should be similarly supplied to all those entering France with anything more durable than a 5-day return ticket. It is worth reading even if you are just visiting briefly, or if you have lived here for years and feel totally knowledgeable and secure. But if you need to find out how France works then it is indispensable. Native French people probably have a less thorough understanding of how their country functions. – Where it is most essential, the book is most up to the minute.

LIVING FRANCE

We would like to congratulate you on this work: it is really super! We hand it out to our expatriates and they read it with great interest and pleasure.

ICI (SWITZERLAND) AG

Rarely has a 'survival guide' contained such useful advice. This book dispels doubts for first-time travellers, yet is also useful for seasoned globetrotters – In a word, if you're planning to move to the USA or go there for a long-term stay, then buy this book both for general reading and as a ready-reference.

AMERICAN CITIZENS ABROAD

It is everything you always wanted to ask but didn't for fear of the contemptuous put down – The best English-language guide – Its pages are stuffed with practical information on everyday subjects and are designed to complement the traditional guidebook.

SWISS NEWS

A complete revelation to me – I found it both enlightening and interesting, not to mention amusing.

CAROLE CLARK

Let's say it at once. David Hampshire's **Living and Working in France** is the best handbook ever produced for visitors and foreign residents in this country; indeed, my discussion with locals showed that it has much to teach even those born and bred in l'Hexagone. – It is Hampshire's meticulous detail which lifts his work way beyond the range of other books with similar titles. Often you think of a supplementary question and search for the answer in vain. With Hampshire this is rarely the case. – He writes with great clarity (and gives French equivalents of all key terms), a touch of humour and a ready eye for the odd (and often illuminating) fact. – This book is absolutely indispensable.

THE RIVIERA REPORTER

HAVE SAID ABOUT SURVIVAL BOOKS

What a great work, wealth of useful information, well-balanced wording and accuracy in details. My compliments!

THOMAS MÜLLER

This handbook has all the practical information one needs to set up home in the UK – The sheer volume of information is almost daunting – Highly recommended for anyone moving to the UK.

AMERICAN CITIZENS ABROAD

A very good book which has answered so many questions and even some I hadn't thought of – I would certainly recommend it.

BRIAN FAIRMAN

A mine of information – I may have avoided some embarrassments and frights if I had read it prior to my first Swiss encounters – Deserves an honoured place on any newcomer's bookshelf.

ENGLISH TEACHERS ASSOCIATION, SWITZERLAND

Covers just about all the things you want to know on the subject – In answer to the desert island question about the one how-to book on France, this book would be it – Almost 500 pages of solid accurate reading – This book is about enjoyment as much as survival.

THE RECORDER

It's so funny – I love it and definitely need a copy of my own – Thanks very much for having written such a humorous and helpful book.

HEIDI GUILIANI

A must for all foreigners coming to Switzerland.

ANTOINETTE O'DONOGHUE

A comprehensive guide to all things French, written in a highly readable and amusing style, for anyone planning to live, work or retire in France.

THE TIMES

A concise, thorough account of the DOs and DON'Ts for a foreigner in Switzerland – Crammed with useful information and lightened with humorous quips which make the facts more readable.

AMERICAN CITIZENS ABROAD

Covers every conceivable question that may be asked concerning everyday life – I know of no other book that could take the place of this one.

FRANCE IN PRINT

Hats off to **Living and Working in Switzerland**!

RONNIE ALMEIDA

THE AUTHORS

This book is a collaboration between Bob Hughes, who provided the detailed information on the region (including valuable input from Trish Dodds), and Graeme Chesters, who composed the text.

Bob Hughes has lived and worked in the Gulf region for the past 20 years, based at various times in Bahrain, Dubai, and Jeddah in Saudi Arabia. As a senior director of one of the world's leading advertising and marketing agencies, he has gained extensive experience of the Gulf States and Saudi Arabia, including their business environment, culture and people.

Graeme Chesters Graeme Chesters was born in the north-west of England in 1963, obtained a degree in philosophy at Bristol University and worked in the City of London for ten years. He has lived in Spain since 1995. He's a columnist for a Spanish newspaper, contributes to British newspapers and magazines, and writes wine, travel and children's books. He's the author of *How to Avoid Holiday and Travel Disasters* and *The Wines of Spain*, both published by Survival Books (see page 416).

CONTENTS

1. FINDING A JOB 21

2. WORKING CONDITIONS 53

3. PERMITS & VISAS 71

14. FINANCE — 225

15. LEISURE — 251

APPENDICES 377

INDEX 403

ORDER FORMS 412

NOTES 417

IMPORTANT NOTE

The Gulf is, not surprisingly, a strange and alien region for many newcomers, with numerous restrictive rules and regulations (often based on religious law), which it would be foolish or risky to ignore. The rules and regulations concerning expatriates are liable to change at short notice and without warning; it's therefore important to check with an official and reliable source (not always the same) before making any major decisions or undertaking an irreversible course of action. However, don't believe everything you're told or read — even, dare I say it, herein!

To help you obtain further information and verify data with official sources, useful addresses and references to other sources of information have been included in all chapters and in Appendices A to C. Important points have been emphasised throughout the book in **bold** print, some of which it would be expensive or even dangerous to disregard. **Ignore them at your peril or cost!** Unless specifically stated, the reference to any company, organisation, product or publication in this book *doesn't* constitute an endorsement or recommendation. Any reference to any place (real or fictional) or person (living or dead) is purely coincidental.

Authors' Notes

- Opinions differ as to whether Saudi Arabia is one of the Gulf states. However, all references to the Gulf states in this book include Saudi Arabia, unless otherwise stated.

- Costs and prices are shown in local currency where appropriate (with US$ equivalents) and otherwise in US$ (with GB£ equivalents). They should be taken as guides only, although they were correct at the time of publication.

- Times are shown using the 12-hour clock, e.g. 10am and 10pm.

- His/he/him also means her/she/her (please forgive us ladies). This is done to make life easier for both the reader and (in particular) the authors, and isn't intended to be sexist.

- British English and not American English is used throughout (or should be).

- Warnings and important points are shown in **bold** type.

- Arabic words are shown in *italics*. (Note that the English transliteration of Arabic words varies, although we have attempted to be consistent.)

- The following symbols are used in this book: ☎ (telephone), 🖹 (fax), 🖳 (Internet) and ✉ (e-mail).

- Lists of **Useful Addresses, Further Reading** and **Useful Websites** are contained in **Appendices A, B and C** respectively.

- For those unfamiliar with the metric system of weights and measures, imperial conversion tables are included in **Appendix D**.

- A map of the Gulf region is shown in **Appendix E**.

INTRODUCTION

Whether you're already living or working in the Gulf or just thinking about it, this is **THE BOOK** for you. *Living and Working in the Gulf States & Saudi Arabia* is designed to meet the needs of anybody who needs to know the essentials of life in the region, including temporary workers, business people, tourists, transferees and even extra-terrestrials. However long your intended stay, you'll find the information in this book invaluable.

General information isn't difficult to find about the Gulf States and Saudi Arabia, and a number of guide books are published for tourists and short-stay visitors. However, reliable and up-to-date information in English specifically intended for foreigners living and working in the Gulf isn't so easy to find, least of all in one volume. Our aim in publishing this book was to help fill this void and provide the comprehensive practical information necessary for a relatively trouble-free life. You may have travelled abroad on holiday, but living and working in a foreign country for an extended period is a different matter altogether; adjusting to a different environment, culture and language, and making a home abroad can be a traumatic and stressful experience.

You need to adapt to new customs and traditions and discover the local way of doing things, for example, finding a home, paying bills and obtaining insurance. For most foreigners, overcoming the everyday obstacles of life has previously been a case of pot luck. **But no more!** With a copy of *Living and Working in the Gulf States & Saudi Arabia* to hand, you'll have a wealth of information at your fingertips — information that derives from a variety of sources, both official and unofficial, not least the hard-won personal experiences of the authors and their researchers, families, friends, colleagues and acquaintances. *Living and Working in the Gulf States & Saudi Arabia* is a comprehensive handbook on a wide variety of everyday subjects and represents the most up-to-date source of general information available to anyone planning to live, work or do business in the region.

Adapting to living in a new country is a continuous process and, although this book will help reduce your 'beginner's phase' and minimise the frustrations, it doesn't contain all the answers (most of us don't even know the right questions to ask). What it will *do* is help you make informed decisions and calculated judgements, instead of uneducated guesses and costly mistakes. **Most importantly, it will help save you time, trouble and money, and will repay your investment many times over.**

Although you may find some of the information a bit daunting, don't be discouraged. Most problems occur only once and fade into insignificance after a short time (as you face the next half dozen . . .). The majority of foreigners living in the Gulf would agree that, all things considered, they enjoy living there. A period spent in the region is a great way to enrich your life, broaden your horizons and, with any luck, also please your bank manager! I trust this book will help you avoid the pitfalls of life in the Gulf and smooth your way to a happy and rewarding future in your new home.

Good luck!

1.

FINDING A JOB

The countries of the Arabian peninsula – Bahrain, Kuwait, The Sultanate of Oman, Qatar, the Kingdom of Saudi Arabia, and the United Arab Emirates (UAE) – are among the most affluent in the world and should remain so for many years with large export surpluses from their oil revenue and high per capita incomes (the UAE boasts the highest per capita income in the Arab world). The region's financial resources have funded major expansion and building programmes, and for the past three decades, hundreds of thousands of foreign workers have flocked to the Gulf, where most find that the region offers better opportunities than do their home countries.

It wasn't until the oil boom of the early 1970s that the world's gaze fell on the Gulf. Before then, little was known about the countries sitting on the world's largest oil reserves. Their economies were positively backward by western standards, and their people tribal, insular and sometimes nomadic. The boom meant that the economies of the Gulf states were transformed almost overnight, with massive oil income allowing rapid and major changes to the countries' infrastructures (roads, hospitals, airports, etc.) and major progress in the fields of telecommunications, general industry, construction and health. The Gulf states' small populations and lack of people with professional experience and technical skills in many areas meant that they were unable to service these new businesses. They looked to the west for managerial expertise, to the Indian sub-continent and Far East for manual and semi-skilled workers, and to North Africa for teachers, lawyers and doctors able to speak Arabic. This resulted in an employment boom, which made the region a focus for foreigners seeking well-paid work and an exotic expatriate lifestyle.

Since then, the Gulf states have become thriving centres for a variety of trades and industries, having successfully diversified from their oil base, and now require and attract workers from a wide range of industries, with a variety of skills and experience. Tourism is growing rapidly (with a consequent increase in employment opportunities for hotel and recreation staff) while the welfare sector, telecommunications, personnel, banking and financial services also offer plenty of new jobs. The situation is changing in the early 21st century, with more local people qualified to do some of the jobs that only foreigners had been educated enough to undertake in the 1970s. Nevertheless, the region is affluent and provides countless opportunities for many hundreds of thousands of foreign workers.

Note that, as a foreigner, your only access to living and working in the region is by finding a job, securing a work visa (see **Chapter 3**) and by staying in the area for the duration of your work contract. Except by marrying a native or otherwise under exceptional circumstances, you won't be permitted to become a citizen of any of the Gulf states (see **Citizenship** on page 334).

The Gulf governments allow plenty of foreign workers into the states, but almost exclusively on a temporary basis. Expatriates aren't generally allowed to become part of the permanent population. Foreign workers are dealt with in a fair but controlled way, paid and treated well, and at the end of their time in the region, thanked and rewarded for their efforts. On the other hand, the region's governments are conscious of the need to provide decent jobs with career paths for their own young people, who are increasingly educated and aware of the attractions of the outside world – many attend universities in the USA or UK. Having made major investments in education and social welfare, they hope that eventually the Gulf states will become almost self-sufficient in terms of labour.

A majority of outside observers, however, believe that expatriates will have a substantial role to play for many years to come, and it seems likely that expatriates will continue to be important for the next two or three decades, although there will undoubtedly be changes in the number of people employed and the type of skills required. For example, the vast construction projects currently found throughout the region (e.g. road systems, airports, ports and trading zones) will become less numerous, with a resulting decline in the number of manual workers required. Commercial development, however, will lead to further building programmes as the Gulf economies continue to grow. Managerial, professional and particularly technological experience will still be in strong demand for many years to come. But there will be none of the mass immigration and resulting demands for citizenship that have been experienced in western societies, or the current trend of economic refugees looking for a better way of life. The Gulf states will simply not allow it. Foreigners cannot become citizens or own land and property, although there appears to be some lessening of the restrictions, certainly as regards owning one's own business.

There are other general issues to consider: you're contemplating a move to a culture that's almost certainly different to your own; will the way of life, and particularly the restrictions imposed on you, suit you?

Will the relocation benefit your long-term career prospects? Will your family (especially any children) cope with and benefit from the move? What impact will it have on their education and employment prospects? If you aspire to be your own boss, as many people do, be aware that starting a business in the region can prove difficult and that you will almost always be required to have a local partner who has a majority holding. Is that acceptable to you?

The Middle East has been the scene of considerable conflict and unrest in recent decades, although the Gulf states are generally safe places to live and work (see **Crime** on page 337). **However, before travelling anywhere in the Middle East, it's wise to obtain advice from your country's foreign office.** Note also that homosexuality is regarded as a criminal offence throughout the region.

The following notes may be helpful if you're deciding which of the Gulf states to look for work in. Further information can be found under **Climate** (on page 334), **Legal System** (on page 341) and **Population** (on page 351).

Bahrain

The Kingdom of Bahrain is an absolute monarchy (although its head is an emir) and the only Gulf state with strict primogeniture (the principal by which title or property descends to the eldest son) in the royal family. With a population of around 620,000, Bahrain is the smallest of the Gulf states but has an influence that belies its size. Bahrain was the site of the first discovery of oil on the Arabian peninsula side of the Gulf. This occurred at an opportune time, coinciding with the breakdown of the global pearl market, which was previously a crucial part of Bahrain's economy. Since then, Bahrain has shown foresight by diversifying its economy away from an almost total reliance on oil production. This has been necessary because, in comparison with the other Gulf states, Bahrain has limited oil resources, with an output of around 50,000 barrels per day, although it also receives around three times that amount daily, from coastal offshore fields shared with Saudi Arabia. Oil production now accounts for only 10 to 15 per cent of the gross domestic product, the latter around US$6 billion annually.

The state controlled companies Bahrain National Oil Company (BANOCO) and Bahrain Petroleum Company (BAPCO) located at Awali control the oil resources and have extensive development plans, including the production of refined unleaded fuel. BAPCO at Awali is in effect a small town, with extensive on-site amenities for its employees and their families. Other energy industries include BANAGAS, which provides gas services.

Aluminium Bahrain (ALBA) is the largest aluminium smelter in the Middle East, although it has a strong competitor from DUBAL, which is based in Dubai. ALBA's Bahraini ownership has Saudi Arabian and German companies as minority partners and it provides a significant portion of Bahrain's non-oil based exports. It has bred many downstream industries, such as a large rolling mill and an aluminium extrusion company, BALEXCO, manufacturing products for industrial and home use, including for export.

The Gulf's largest ship repair yard, Arabian Ship Repair Yard (ASRY), operates at Sitra and employs a large workforce, both national and foreign, to cater for ships using the region's busy oil routes. Bahrain originally aimed to become the centre for service industries in the Gulf, but that crown has been claimed by Dubai (see below). The exception to this is the financial services industry, in which Bahrain reigns supreme, having taken the position that Beirut originally held, before the conflict in the Lebanon. Banks from all over the world have established branches in Bahrain, with retail, investment and off-shore operations. Today, Bahrain has almost 200 international banks and financial institutions, all under the control of the Bahrain Monetary Agency (BMA), which also has also overseen the Bahrain Stock Exchange since it opened in 1989. Banking and finance is now the second-largest sector in the economy, accounting for over a quarter of the GDP, and the service sector is the country's largest employer, followed by general commerce and then government occupations.

The Bahrain Telecommunications Company (BATELCO) is a national company that was formed in 1981 after the take-over of the country's telecommunications system, previously operated by the UK's Cable & Wireless. BATELCO provides first-class satellite telecommunication links and cellular and internet services, advanced telecommunications being a pre-requisite for the operation of Bahrain's financial services. Evidence of BATELCO's efficiency is provided by the fact that many of the world's leading financial institutions choose Bahrain as their regional base. Bahrain also boasts two 'free zones': Mina Sulman and North Sitra.

Tourism is growing rapidly in the Arabian peninsula, and Bahrain is a popular destination. It has long benefited from being at the crossroads of east and west and has been a stopping-off point for international airlines for many years. This has led to an openness and acceptance of foreigners visiting and working in the country, and might account for the genuine hospitality of the people in this friendly little country. Small it might be, but Bahrain's political influence and goodwill in the region outweigh its size.

Bahrainis have a reputation for being astute and occupy many positions alongside their foreign counterparts in the state's financial institutions. In recent times, more have been reaching positions of power, encouraged by the programme of 'Bahrainisation', which has been designed to encourage the local population to take full-time employment, develop their skills and at the same time reduce the risk of local unemployment.

Kuwait

Kuwait is the third-largest oil producer in the Middle East, after Saudi Arabia and Iraq. It has great wealth and is of tremendous strategic importance, as was shown by the world's response to the Iraqi invasion of 1990/91. The Iraqi invasion had a significant impact on the Kuwaiti economy, both in terms of damage to the oil industry and exports and because of the cost of paying the military forces called in to eject the Iraqis. Kuwait and its people also lost a significant portion of their wealth through its unlawful 'confiscation' by the Iraqis. In spite of this, however, much of the country's assets were safely invested overseas and the government in exile managed to retain control of these vital resources.

Since the war, the economy has gradually recovered, and recent oil price increases are allowing further expansion. (Kuwait's financial assets were greatly, if momentarily, diminished by the decision to compensate its people for losses suffered as a result of the Iraqi conflict.) Foreign investment has increased, largely as a result of a decree of 1999, which approved the 100 per cent foreign ownership of certain companies registered in the country, a significant departure from the original ruling of a maximum equity holding of 49 per cent. These companies will be those that contribute to a more diverse economy and the provision of advanced technology and industry.

Oil production and associated downstream industries, including refining and petrochemicals, account for around 90 per cent of foreign earnings and nearly three quarters of Kuwait's gross domestic product, which is estimated at around $30 billion annually. Kuwait has tremendous reserves of oil, with an estimated 90 billion barrels in the Burgan area alone. Oil production is estimated to be around 1.8 million barrels per day, with the majority of oil exports sent east. The Kuwait Petroleum Company (KPC) controls the country's oil interests, including many overseas downstream assets, in addition to home production. Kuwait Petroleum International has several refineries in Europe and the Far East, and operates the thousands of Q8 petrol service stations in those regions.

The petrochemicals industry has recently diversified and produces polyethylene, polypropylene, fertilisers and other products for export to Kuwait's neighbours and international markets. A free trade zone in the port of Al-Shuwaikh (see page 47) is expected to encourage further diversification of the overall economy and the development of trade with neighbouring countries and the Far East. Local and international investors in the industrial, service and commercial sectors are encouraged by the 100 per cent foreign ownership concession, with no corporate taxes or currency restrictions and the free movement of funds (see **Commercial Taxation** on page 244). New highways and the modern shipping port at Shuaiba add to the attraction of the zone.

Kuwait has a healthy financial and banking sector, with commercial banks owned by the government or by wealthy trading families. The National Bank of Kuwait is the main retail bank, with over 35 branches. Other banks, such as the Commercial Bank of Kuwait and The Credit and Savings Bank, also offer full service banking facilities. The Industrial Bank of Kuwait deals mainly with the funding of industrial, manufacturing and agricultural programmes. The Central Bank of Kuwait is responsible for regulating the financial industry as a whole. The Kuwait Stock Exchange was successfully reopened in 1992, after experiencing major problems following its initial formation in 1977 and the suspension of trading during the Iraqi conflict. Other significant financial institutions include (ARIG) the Arab Reinsurance Group, which deals with major insurance such as aviation and shipping.

Kuwait's telecommunications network is state-of-the-art, well able to meet the demands of the rapidly developing economy. Agriculture and fishing, on the other hand, which are among the country's traditional industries, contribute relatively little to the gross domestic product, and Kuwait relies heavily on food imports.

A downturn in oil prices in 1998/99 prompted the Kuwaiti government to to reduce the dependency on state subsidies by moving towards the privatisation of its consumer utilities, electricity, health etc. This process continues, with proposals to privatise the airline and telecommunications industries and to encourage foreign investment.

Kuwait is a significant member of the GCC (see **Gulf Co-operation Council** on page 34), enjoys vast resources and has largely overcome the serious problems experienced as a result of the Iraqi invasion. The repatriation of foreign workers at the start of that conflict allowed the authorities to adjust the volume and nationalities of foreign workers permitted to return when the conflict was over. (Workers from countries or groups of people whose sympathies were believed to lie with Iraq — notably Palestinians and Yemenis — weren't allowed to return.) The expatriate work force is concentrated in oil-related activities and the service sector.

Sultanate of Oman

Oman is strategically important — part of its territory overlooks the Straits of Hormuz at the entrance to the Arabian Gulf — but until 1970 suffered under a backward, repressive regime, a large number of Omanis being forced to leave the country to seek opportunities elsewhere. (Many established themselves in nearby Zanzibar, awaiting more favourable times.) The country began a much-needed modernisation programme in 1970, when Sultan Qaboos took over from his father in a bloodless palace coup (the deposed Sultan spending his last years in England), and used the country's resources wisely to build a sound infrastructure, with modern road systems and a programme for building new hospitals and schools.

In common with its neighbours, Oman relies heavily on the export of oil to support the economy, and oil-related industry accounts for over 75 per cent of gross domestic product. However, the country's reserves, which are controlled by the state owned Petrol Development of Oman (PDO) in partnership with Shell, TOTAL and Partex and are estimated at around 4 billion barrels, are smaller than those of its neighbours, and a decline in oil prices in the late 1990s prompted diversification of the economy, which is now well under way. The production and export of LNG (liquefied natural gas) is due to begin soon, and other industries include fertiliser production and light manufacturing industry. This last, which includes the production of textiles, detergents and wood products, is as yet modest, generating around 5 per cent of gross domestic product, but several projects are planned, such as the manufacture of chemicals and fertilisers, a major partnership to set up an aluminium smelter and a joint venture for the production of ethylene and polyethylene.

The container port of Port Raysut was opened in 1998 in the hope of attracting business away from Dubai, which is higher up the Gulf and the other side of the Straits of Hormuz, as well as from Jeddah on Saudi Arabia's Red Sea coast. The government has also devoted considerable effort to encouraging the agricultural sector, and it's hoped that fishing will eventually become an export industry. At present, however, most of the country's food is imported.

In the financial sector, the Central Bank of Oman encourages mergers with the commercial and retail banks of its GCC partner countries, as well as with other foreign banks with interests in the region. Foreign investors are allowed to own majority shareholdings in Omani companies and can have 100 per cent ownership of certain major concerns, when approved by the Development Council.

For many years, foreigners wishing to visit Oman on business had to negotiate a tortuous series of administrative hurdles, but this has eased considerably. The previous restrictions were designed to inhibit the arrival of foreign materialism and consumerism while Oman's resources were being directed towards building the country's infrastructure. Today, tourism is being encouraged and it's hoped that it will become an important part of the economy. Oman has much to offer visitors and expatriate workers, with a variety of beautiful landscapes and hospitable people.

Qatar

Qatar has a fast-growing economy, a GDP of around US$9 billion and, like its neighbours, relies heavily on its hydrocarbon resources. The Qatar General Petroleum Corporation (QGPC) is responsible for oil production and exploration, and the Qatari government has full control of oil resources. The country also has the third-largest reserves of liquified gas (LNG) in the world, after the states of the former Soviet Union and Iran. The north gas field is thought to contain the largest individual concentration of natural gas on earth. Qatar has devoted a great deal of investment to these reserves and expects to earn a considerable revenue from them in the future.

In the field of industry and manufacturing, Qatar produces steel, iron, cement, petrochemicals and fertilisers. Unlike most of its neighbours, Qatar exports a major proportion of its steel production.

The Qatar Industrial Manufacturing Company (QIMCO) encourages the support of small-to-medium-sized commercial activities in the country. Agriculture and fishing are tiny contributors to the economy and the country relies heavily on food imports.

The Central Bank of Qatar controls monetary policy and regulates the banking system. There are a number of commercial and retail banks doing business in Qatar, including local and foreign owned banks. The Qatar stock exchange is active and has recently been boosted by government privatisation schemes. Foreign companies and joint ventures are subject to variable levels of corporate tax, although those that are wholly foreign-owned are allowed corporate tax 'holidays', specifically designed to encourage such businesses (see **Commercial Taxation** on page 244). Minority foreign investment is allowed in specified key sectors such as steel and petrochemicals.

Qatar is still seen as a rather secluded country and little is known about it. Therefore, it isn't widely regarded as a tourist destination. In fact, Qatar has much to offer those seeking rest and recreation, with fine beaches, great watersports facilities, a world-class golf course and many superb, modern hotels in the capital city of Doha. Having seen the success of other Gulf states in this regard, the Qatari government is now beginning to promote the country as a tourist destination. The state of Qatar is rather insular (although it shows support for the USA by allowing that country an airfield on its territory) and displays its individuality by not always toeing the line with the other GCC States. It's a generally safe country and is quieter than Dubai and Bahrain.

Kingdom of Saudi Arabia

As the most powerful and important country in the region, the Kingdom of Saudi Arabia is recognised as the major influence on the states of the Gulf Co-operation Council (see page 34). In addition to this, the religious significance that Saudi Arabia has as the geographical and spiritual centre of the Islamic world cannot be over-emphasised. Muslims regard Mecca (Makkah in Arabic) as the birthplace of Islam, and the faith demands that every Muslim who can afford it make a pilgrimage to the holy sites. Saudis feel honoured that their country is the centre of the religion.

In the past, the Kingdom was financially dependent on the massive influx of visitors for the annual pilgrimage (*Haj*) to Mecca and the many other religious occasions that constitute the faithful's duties in visiting the birthplace of the Islamic religion. However, increasingly since the 1970s, Saudi Arabia has been a major oil producer, and it now dominates the sector. It's estimated that around a quarter of the world's oil and gas resources are situated in the Kingdom, and oil exports account for 90 per cent of its total earnings.

The 1970s and 1980s saw vast spending programmes incorporated into Soviet-style five-year plans. However, with the drop in oil prices in the late 1990s, Saudi Arabia's income was reduced and the country's ambitious development programmes restricted. Spending cuts were introduced to some public sectors, although not to those that would radically affect people's everyday lives, such as health and education. The Kingdom is currently finishing its sixth five-year plan, which called for expansion of private investment and industry, including the important financial sector. Recent oil price rises will increase revenue again but, because most of the numerous expansion projects have been completed and hordes of foreign workers have departed, the demand for imports has reduced.

One of the most notable government institutions, with part-private ownership, is Saudi Basic Industries Corporation (SABIC), which operates across a wide field of activities with many foreign companies. Its main ventures are the production of petrochemicals, plastics and fertilisers. Mining is also being actively developed in Saudi Arabia, whose wealth of natural resources includes phosphate, copper and gold ore, and it's expected that in the future, mining might become the country's second source of revenue, after oil. The Kingdom also produces iron, steel, cement and processed foods. Employment is concentrated in construction, industry, and consumer and government services, and major industrial expansion centres are located at Jubail in the eastern province and at Yanbu on the Red Sea coast.

As a result of industrial development, massive power generation has been needed, and this is provided by the Saudi Electric Company (SEC). Water is a vital resource, for human consumption and commercial use, and has always been in short supply, but the Kingdom's needs are now met by numerous desalination plants on the coast.

The Saudi financial sector is important, and its banking industry is the largest in the region. The Saudi Arabian Monetary Agency (SAMA) controls and regulates finance in its role as the central bank, and many foreign banks operate in the country. The Saudi stock exchange is a leading new bourse.

Despite Saudi's harsh climate, there has been an expansion in agri-business as the government has sought to become self-sufficient in foodstuffs. Large milk-producing farms supply much of the Kingdom's needs. Wheat production originally allowed for some exports, but this has ceased, the high cost of irrigation having made it unviable. There's an export market in fish, particularly to neighbouring Gulf states, but also to some parts of Europe.

Apart from religious pilgrims visiting the Kingdom's holy sites, general tourism was, until recently, discouraged in Saudi Arabia. This is now slowly changing, partly for economic reasons. Although Saudi Arabia has vast tracts of empty desert, it also offers many places of great beauty, from mountains to lush fertile plains and a huge coastline. In recent years, European cruise ships have been calling at the port of Jeddah on the Red Sea, a previously unheard-of occurrence. However, a visit to Saudi Arabia is unlikely to suit the average fun-loving holidaymaker, and the annual pilgrimage (*Haj*) to Mecca is still by far the country's largest 'tourist' event. Quotas of visitors to Mecca are now allocated to each country in order to keep the crowds to manageable levels, and countries whose pilgrims have caused major disturbances have had their quotas reduced.

United Arab Emirates

The UAE is a conferedation of Emirates (see **Ruling Families** on page 356) comprising Abu Dhabi, Ajman, Dubai, Fujairah, Ras Al-Khaimah, Sharjah and Umm Al-Quwain, of which Abu Dhabi and Dubai are the two main partners and subsidise the other Emirates. As with the other Gulf states, oil and gas underpin the Emirates' economy. The Emirates, as the confederation is usually called, is the third-largest oil producer in the Middle East, with a reported daily output of around 2.5 million barrels, and it claims to have the world's third-largest known reserves of oil. (Oil reserve projections estimate that Abu Dhabi has enough oil in the ground to last 100 years or more at the current rate of extraction.) The UAE's natural gas resources are also abundant, and shrewd overseas investments by the International Petroleum Company (IPIC), particularly in the area of oil refining and petrochemicals, have added value to the energy resources of the UAE.

As elsewhere in the Gulf, economic diversification has been encouraged, to the extent that non-oil business now accounts for over half of gross domestic product. Major projects include petrochemicals, downstream oil refining, telecommunications, aviation and tourism. The UAE has the highest per capita income in the Arab world.

Dubai has had a more urgent need to diversify than the other Emirates and it has responded by developing a wide portfolio of industrial, manufacturing, construction and service interests. DUBAL is a major aluminium smelting operation, with increasing capacity and a progressive export programme to the countries of the European Union and others. The Jebel Ali Free Zone Authority (JAFZA) port has contributed greatly to the economy, highly preferential trading conditions attracting many international manufacturing and distribution companies, who are allowed 100 per cent ownership. A second free zone, Um Al-Qain, is situated around 50km (30mi) north of Dubai within the Ahmed Bin Rashid port, where Dubai Drydocks is one of the world's largest ship repair yards and competes with Bahrain's ASRY yard.

Sharjah, one of the smaller Emirates, has the largest non-oil industry and is currently developing two new free zones, at Sharjah airport and Hamriyah, to complement its purpose-built zone at Al-Rostamani. There's also a free zone in Fujairah. The smallest of the Emirates, Ajman is virtually integrated with Sharjah and Dubai and serves as a dormitory town for these, with its lower rents and living costs. Fishing and dhow-building are its main industries.

In the financial sector, the UAE has the largest number of retail banks in the GCC, including national and foreign banks. Banking in the Emirates had a major and well documented setback in the 1980s, from which it has now recovered, and is regulated by the Central Bank of the UAE. With industrial and commercial expansion projected to continue vigorously, the banking sector is set to flourish. The government of the UAE is keen to see more nationals employed in the field of finance and is encouraging them to acquire the appropriate qualifications.

The major agricultural crop is dates (others include vegetables and dairy produce), and agriculture accounts for around 3 per cent of GDP. Tourism is also a major industry in the Emirates – especially in Dubai, which, along with Bahrain, can claim to have led the development of tourism in the region. Dubai boasts 70 per cent of the hotels in the Federation and also has superb, well-maintained beaches and excellent weather for tourists from October to March. The UAE's internationally-renowned golf courses attract players from around the world and are probably responsible for starting the tourist revolution. Another attraction is the new Dubai International airport, which must rank as one of the most exciting and luxurious in the world. The UAE's hotels range from five-star, super-luxury, international chains to more modest accommodation. With its buoyant economy and world-class facilities, the Emirates is certainly one of the most attractive places in the Gulf for expatriates, who can enjoy a high standard of living in a fairly liberal environment.

GULF CO-OPERATION COUNCIL

Although independent, the six Gulf states co-operate on trade, economic, political and cultural matters that affect them jointly. This co-operation was formalised by the formation of the Gulf Co-operation Council (GCC) in 1981. The rulers of the Gulf states meet annually to discuss matters of mutual concern and to plan for the future, and the GCC is concerned with defence, education, foreign affairs and civil and commercial issues, such as welfare programmes, inter-state trade, customs regulations, education and employment. The GCC also encourages harmony between the states by settling disputes, such as those relating to border demarcations. Although it doesn't manage to resolve all the region's problems or have all its policy proposals accepted unanimously — for example, with regard to defence — it has enjoyed success in many areas.

Nationals of all GCC countries have the right to enter, live and work in any of the member states, provided they have the necessary supporting documentation, such as a passport or national identity card, and also that they comply with the member country's laws and regulations.

The GCC has stated its intention to promote the development of its own nationals through education and training, so that they might play a greater role in their own countries' economies and development. This means that the Gulf states should eventually become less reliant on foreign workers, but this will probably be a long process and the dependence on expatriate workers looks set to continue for many years, particularly in high-tech industries.

WORK FORCE

The make-up of the local work force is heavily influenced by the cultural tradition of the extended family, which is patriarchal and close-knit.

The male is regarded as the provider for the family and the protector, while the female is the nurturer. Men work; women tend the home. A hierarchy extends down from the Ruling Families to the rich traders and then to the establishments employing the majority of the work force.

Until recently, many locals worked in agriculture, fishing, pearling and other traditional activities, as well as the production of oil, which was discovered in the 1930s. The economic changes of the 1970s resulting from oil exploitation saw the growth of a modern work force, employed in trade, industry, communications and the service sector, together with the arrival of major multi-national companies. As well as attracting hundreds of thousands of foreign workers, these developments have encouraged the appearance of more local women in the work force, notably in Bahrain and the UAE. However, although women have broken away from their traditional jobs in education and medicine into banking, marketing, advertising and other areas, the vast majority of expatriate employment is for men, and many locals in the region still regard the home as a woman's rightful place (see **Working Women** on page 44).

EMPLOYMENT PROSPECTS

Of particular benefit to the potential western expatriate in the Gulf are the region's strong links with the USA and Europe, especially regarding defence construction, armament sales and military training. A good example of this is the massive joint venture project undertaken by the Saudi Ministry of Defence and British Aerospace for the assembly of Tornado aircraft in the Kingdom. The influence of the western powers in the region is still considerable – despite occasional misunderstandings – and this helps expatriates coming from the west.

You should ideally have a firm offer of employment before travelling to any of the Gulf countries; in the case of Saudi Arabia, it's extremely difficult to enter the country for the purpose of employment without one. Speculative visits are *occasionally* successful, but you need to be notably lucky and have high-grade qualifications and experience to stand any chance. In addition, you will almost certainly need knowledgeable local contacts and have done some research into the types of company which would most value your experience.

UNEMPLOYMENT

There is unemployment in the Gulf. This is partly because the region has a strong tradition of social welfare and because the oil revenue earned over the last three decades has paid for a comprehensive system to support those who don't work, which can obviously be a disincentive to those who prefer not to. In general, Arabs tend to avoid manual labour and jobs that require them to work long hours. Moreover, the region has a young, increasingly educated population with high salary expectations, and some of them aren't prepared to start at the bottom and work their way up. Because of this, many firms prefer to employ expatriates for certain jobs. Foreigners have also been regarded as easier to dispense with than local workers when they're no longer required. When oil prices drop, as they do periodically, there's a tendency to cut the level of foreign staff and employ more locals, which obviously reduces unemployment rates. Recently, however, some employers (often with the encouragement of their government) have begun to recognise that they have a long-term responsibility to their employees, wherever they come from. Unemployment, however, isn't an option for the expatriate worker: he either finds another job or returns home.

In general, unemployment in the Gulf isn't the major issue that it is in other societies, because levels are low and therefore unlikely to lead to public discontent. Low unemployment – and generous social security payments – also mean that local people feel little, if any, resentment to the presence of so many foreign workers.

AGE DISCRIMINATION

Employment programmes in the region are a balancing act between the necessity of hiring foreign expertise and the desire to find rewarding work for nationals. For this reason, the Gulf states aren't keen to issue new work visas to those aged 50 or over. As with all matters, however, if your sponsor (see **Sponsorship** on page 37) deems that your experience and skills are irreplaceable, and if he's powerful enough, he can overcome this hurdle. Another way round it is to call you an 'adviser' rather than an employee; within reason, an adviser can be any age!

When you're employed – as opposed to seeking a new contract – most companies have a retirement age of either 60 or 65, in line with the rest of the world. Age can in fact be an advantage in the Gulf: Arabs equate advancing years with the acquisition of wisdom and it's part of their culture to treat elders with respect, this belief deriving from the custom of the extended family. Therefore, the older employee might be treated better by his employer than he would in the west.

There's no age limit for those wishing to start their own business (see page 46).

QUALIFICATIONS

It's unnecessary to be able to speak Arabic (although it's a distinct advantage) but it's essential to be able to communicate fluently in spoken and written English, which is the common business language in the region as well as being the *lingua franca* among the many nationalities who live in the region. As for academic and professional qualifications, standard international attitudes are current: degrees from western universities and experience in western companies are more highly regarded than those obtained elsewhere. Managers are expected to be educated to college or university level, and the local Ministry of Labour usually requires supporting documentation to this effect before issuing work visas. The importance to an expatriate of having a high-quality education and/or relevant experience cannot be overstressed. Like most countries, all the Gulf states give job priority to their own citizens, and you need to demonstrate that you have qualifications that most nationals lack in order to find work in many industries and businesses.

SPONSORSHIP

All foreigners require a local sponsor in order to visit the Gulf (whether on holiday or business) or live and work there. Whereas in the west the word 'sponsor' is commonly used of individuals or businesses paying to have their names associated with an artistic or sporting event, in the Gulf it has a quite different meaning: a sponsor acts as a sort of guardian as well as guarantor and must undertake all administrative work (i.e. paperwork) on behalf of the foreigner, including applying for a work and residence visa, opening a bank account and signing a rental accommodation contract. A sponsor can be an individual, a company or an institution. In the case of employees, your employer usually also acts as your sponsor; visitors may be sponsored by a business partner or associate or by the hotel in which they're staying (see page 73). Those aiming to do business or set up a business in the Gulf should research the local business environment, establish contacts and find an individual or company with a good reputation and experience in the relevant field to act as your sponsor, who will expect remuneration for his services (see **Self-employment** on page 45).

The sponsorship system is an effective form of immigration control. As your sponsor is responsible for you and 'takes the rap' if you misbehave or contravene any regulations (which will also involve him in loss of 'face' in the community), he automatically checks that you're reliable and trustworthy, as well as ensuring that you don't inadvertently step out of line. For this reason, your sponsor is an important source of help and advice and a valuable 'ally'. Note that there is talk of the sponsorship requirement being waived in some states, particularly for foreigners wanting to set up businesses in the free trade zones (see page 47), but this hadn't happened at the time of publication.

GOVERNMENT EMPLOYMENT SERVICE

The Gulf states have no equivalent of the nationally-organised job centres found in western countries, and it's the responsibility of the Ministries of Labour and Social Affairs to deal with employment.

Bahrain: Ministry of Labour and Social Affairs, PO Box 32333, Manama (☎ 973-687 800);

Kuwait: Ministry of Social Affairs and Labour, PO Box 563, Safat, 13001 (☎ 965-246 6300);

Oman: Ministry of Social Affairs and Labour, PO Box 560, Muscat 113 (☎ 968-602 444);

Qatar: Ministry of Labour, Social Affairs and Housing, PO Box 201, Doha (☎ 974-321 955);

Saudi Arabia: Ministry of Labour and Social Affairs, Riyadh 11157 (☎ 966-1-477 14800;

UAE: Department of Economic Development, PO Box 13223, Dubai (☎ 971-4-222 9922).

All the region's states are trying to balance the need to import foreign labour with the interests of the local population, and companies are strongly encouraged to take on local nationals where possible. This 'encouragement' can be quite robust, and the Ministries are able to restrict the number of work visas issued or renewed to a company in order to comply with a quota of local intake.

RECRUITMENT AGENCIES

Recruitment consultants or agents play a major role in the placement of workers in a host of occupations in the Gulf states. In view of the distance between the Gulf and the countries that supply many of the region's employees, it's necessary for agents to act as middlemen. Private recruitment consultants and headhunters in western countries (and particularly in London and New York) deal with most managerial jobs in the Gulf states, while agencies in India (particularly Bombay), Sri Lanka, Pakistan, Korea, the Philippines (Manila) and Thailand (Bankok) supply most of the enormous number of manual labourers employed in the Gulf's numerous construction projects.

Agencies tend to specialise in particular areas of work, e.g. medical and nursing staff, computer personnel, accountants, construction managers, executive and office staff, engineering and the technical trades. Agency and consultancy fees are paid by the employer, with no charge to staff. Fees are usually a percentage of the annual salary, ranging from 10 to 20 per cent for most jobs but lower for those with high salaries. Regular customers are often offered preferential rates.

Recruitment agencies in the Gulf itself are sometimes used for placing expatriates in temporary work or for expatriate wives wishing to take up local employment (although recruitment agents are rare in Saudi Arabia). There are numerous regulations controlling the employment of spouses, and separate work visas are needed (see page 73); the agent handles the details. Local agents are also used if expatriates change jobs. This, however, is uncommon, as expatriates are normally sent to the Gulf under contract and job changes are restricted by their employers. You might under certain circumstances be allowed to break your contract, in which case a local agency might be of use. Otherwise, at the conclusion of your contract, a local agency might find you another job.

CONTRACT & FREELANCE JOBS

There are plenty of contract and freelance jobs in the region, many in the construction industry, shipbuilding and ship repairs, and the oil industry, including offshore installations. However, the majority of contract and freelance appointments are made outside the Gulf, and it's rarely possible to arrive in the Gulf without a job and find one locally. Many expatriate workers in the Gulf are contracted either on a fixed-term contract (usually a year) or for a particular project, but many sub-contracted workers have managed to stay in the region for a number of years, having first arrived on a single, one-off, short-term contract. Work visas are still required (see page 73), and it's often a matter of who you know rather than what you know. But you're helped by the fact that the expatriate community is close-knit and newcomers are sometimes surprised by the amount of help they're offered.

SEASONAL JOBS

The Gulf has traditionally had little in the way of a seasonal job market. This might change as the tourist industry takes off, notably in the UAE, Bahrain and Oman; more seasonal work should become available during the peak season, which runs from October to April. Jobs in this bracket include tour company representatives and bar staff (in some states). Hotel and restaurant staff are often brought from the Philippines or India.

TEACHING ENGLISH

The majority of general teaching staff in the Gulf states come from Egypt, Syria and Jordan. Although the national curriculum of most of the Gulf states requires English to be taught as a second language, native English-speakers are rarely found in the state education system, cultural differences accounting for this. There is, however, a constant demand for English teachers in the region, as English is the lingua franca between locals and expatriates, and staff in hotels, airports, hospitals and other service businesses are required to speak English. Jobs are usually advertised in the teaching profession's publications and national newspaper supplements.

Private Schools

There's a large number of private schools in each of the Gulf states, catering mainly for the needs of the expatriate population (see **Chapter 9**). English is generally the language used for all lessons. There are some French schools, which hold lessons in that language, but these usually also teach English.

Language Schools

As well as being popular with Gulf nationals, private language schools are sometimes used by expatriate workers from various countries to improve their English. If you choose to work in one, remember that the hours can be long and anti-social because the schools are teaching pupils who can only attend after their working day. Foreign international language schools, such as Berlitz and Linguarama, have branches in the Gulf. They often require that their teachers attend their own teacher training courses to learn the particular teaching methods of that language school.

Private Tuition

Private English lessons are popular in the Gulf and therefore a significant source of employment. Many of the teachers offering them are 'moonlighting' from their full-time employment in schools and colleges, private lessons being a lucrative way to supplement their income. The demand for private English lessons is to some extent seasonal, more people wanting them in the run-up to the examination season. There's another peak of demand when exam results are published, from those who have failed and need to improve their skills for exam retakes. Study advertisements for tutors in local newspapers, the yellow pages and on notice boards in clubs and sporting institutions, or post advertisements yourself.

The British Council

The British Council recruits English language teachers for placement in its centres. It requires a recognised qualification, such as an RSA diploma or PGCE in Teaching English as a Foreign Language (TEFL), and also a minimum of two years' teaching experience for most of its positions. For more senior jobs and those with managerial responsibilities, postgraduate qualifications and a minimum of five years' experience are required.

For further information, contact The British Council Recruitment Section, Central Management of Direct Teaching, 10 Spring Gardens, London SW1A 2BN, UK (☎ 020-7389 4931). The British Council also recruits English teachers and teachers of other subjects for British International Schools. For information, contact The Overseas Educational Appointments Department, British Council, 65 Davies Street, London W1Y 2AA, UK (☎ 020-7389 7660). The free publication Teaching Overseas is also produced by the Council.

Translators & Interpreters

Those who are fluent in Arabic and English can find work as translators and interpreters. Translation work is particularly required for legal and contractual documentation, and technical papers. Interpreters are often needed at seminars and on management training courses. Both types of work are usually part-time or short-term.

AU PAIRS

The concept of the au pair is largely unknown in Arab societies. Most reasonably affluent families and individuals, whether local or expatriate, can afford to hire live-in or part-time housemaids, nannies or general servants. Cleaners and people who do the laundry, ironing and other household chores are widely available. Direct employment of staff will involve sponsorship, fees and all the costs associated with having employees. Many states have minimum salaries, and no one can legally employ people for less. There are a few families in the region who use the services of au pairs, but servants are more common, most villas providing servant quarters.

TEMPORARY & CASUAL WORK

Owing to the number of expatriate workers on short-term contracts (see above), there isn't much casual and temporary work available, and you shouldn't travel to the Gulf with the purpose of finding temporary or casual work. Over the last few years, however, increasing numbers of young westerners on a gap-year have managed to find temporary work in the Gulf states – particularly in the more liberal Bahrain and UAE – before travelling on to south-east Asia, Australia and New Zealand. If this is your intention, bear in mind that you're up against workers from Asia who might be prepared to work for lower wages than a westerner would expect. Temporary and casual work might be available in the following areas:

- office administration, secretarial work and work in recruitment agencies;
- retail work during the height of the tourist season;
- bar staff in restaurants and nightclubs*;
- various jobs in ports such as crewing or making deliveries;
- market research street interviewers, but not in Saudi Arabia;
- nursing, for those with the qualifications;
- courier services with international companies;
- driving for companies offering desert tours.

* Note that there are also 'vacancies' for women to act as hostesses in nightclubs; this work involves talking to male customers and encouraging them to run up large bar bills.

Temporary jobs tend to be advertised in English-language newspapers, on club notice boards and occasionally with recruitment agencies.

TRAINEES & WORK EXPERIENCE

Ministries of Labour and Social Affairs in the Gulf states are active in helping their nationals to find employment. As a result, expatriates trying to obtain access to traineeships or work experience are unlikely to be successful. A well placed individual in a company may be able to find you a temporary position, but in general it isn't worth pursuing.

VOLUNTARY WORK

There are numerous organisations in the Gulf working for the benefit of the disadvantaged and needy, and volunteers are welcome. Archaeological projects and digs in the region sometimes also seek volunteers to help. Voluntary work is, of course, unpaid but it can be rewarding and is a good way for spouses, who aren't usually allowed to undertake paid work, to meet people.

WORKING WOMEN

In Arab countries, men have traditionally been the providers, women the homemakers. This concept is slowly changing, however, as the attitudes of the outside world permeate Arab society. This process is hastened by the influx of foreign women to the Gulf. For some time, Arab women have worked in teaching and nursing, but they're increasingly also found in other fields, especially banking, finance and the service sector. The exception is Saudi Arabia, where women aren't allowed to work in offices (except women-only banks) and may be employed only in the medical profession or teaching. In the other states, the majority of expatriate female workers are employed in the service sector as doctors, lawyers, hotel administrators, in advertising, public relations, nursing, education and as stewardesses for the many national airlines.

More local women are entering the work force in the Gulf and some employers view them as harder-working and more reliable than the average local male worker (and invariably cheaper to employ). Women rising to positions of power and influence tend to come from middle and upper echelon families. Indeed, for a woman to rise to a position of influence at work she needs the support of her family, especially the male members.

Most expatriate workers — whether western or eastern — are male. Their wives often have a restriction in their passport which prohibits them from working. Should the wives wish to work, they must obtain their own sponsorship and work visa, but employers tend to be biased against giving work visas to women. Women are often offered work (illegally) and, while this isn't a major crime, it can result in the company being fined and the woman losing her job.

Women are generally safe in the workplace, with little sexual harassment because of the severe punishments for this. The influx of female 'tourists' (i.e. prostitutes) from eastern Europe in recent times, however, has reduced the level of respect that foreign females hitherto enjoyed. Women should also be careful not to be too friendly towards Arab men in the workplace, because this can be misunderstood as flirtatiousness.

SALARY

Salaries in the Gulf are usually similar to or greater than those paid in western countries. But because the region has no personal taxation, net income is usually much greater, which is one of the major attractions of working in the Gulf. In the past, remuneration packages were split into various elements: basic salary, car provision or allowance, housing provision or allowance, medical cover, education for children and air tickets for home visits. Today, however, employers tend just to pay a salary, which covers all these expenses, although in some cases there are performance or other bonuses.

In addition to their salary, contract workers are awarded an 'indemnity' at the end of the contract period (see page 62). Different states have slightly different labour laws, but the indemnity is usually based on basic salary excluding any bonuses; only Saudi Arabia legislates that the indemnity is based on the value of the entire remuneration package. The indemnity can be a significant amount of money if you've been working in the Gulf for a long time, and many people manage either to accumulate a reasonable financial cushion or to live the high life. If you're clever and disciplined, you should be able to do some of both.

SELF-EMPLOYMENT

If you wish to be self-employed in the Gulf, your major hurdle is to find a sponsor. When you've found one, you will experience few further problems with bureaucracy and officialdom. In order to find a sponsor, you need to visit the region and talk to local people. This is obviously also necessary in order to check market conditions in the area that interests you. Sponsorship can be provided by a legally registered company or by an individual; for example, you might work in ship maintenance and repair, in which case you would approach a ship maintenance company as a self-employed person working as a sub-contractor. If you intend to work in one of the professions, you must show the proper qualifications in order to obtain your work visa: in the medical profession, for example, your qualifications would be inspected by the Ministry of Health. There aren't usually any tax liabilities but it varies according to the type of work and you should check. You might have to buy personal medical cover in some states.

Negotiating with the sponsor will require some hard bargaining. The fee you pay him is likely to be either a flat annual rate paid in regular instalments or a percentage of your revenue. Rates vary, but anything over 10 per cent of your revenue is high and you should try to negotiate on the basis of net rather than gross income. You're recommended to consult a local lawyer regarding the proposed deal with your sponsor.

STARTING A BUSINESS

There are three major considerations to be made by those thinking of starting a business in the Gulf:

- You must have a good knowledge of the region and the particular state in which you wish to start a business. Be prepared to undertake extensive research into the business sector you aim to operate within. You must have a viable business plan, which includes a study of the market conditions, the competition and your forecast results. You must be prepared to find the necessary investment from your own resources or through your bank and preferably by other means than applying locally, particularly if you're new to the region and without a track record. A credible plan might attract local support, possibly government support.

- The law requires that you have a local partner who holds the majority interest and can therefore control the business (as well as close it, if he feels like it...). The local partner, be it a company or an individual, doesn't need to contribute to the start-up investment or participate financially at all. As with self-employment (see above), there are various ways that a partner can be remunerated. The local partner requirement is currently under review in some states, however, in order to encourage foreign investment.

- When the business is registered, you must show the Ministry of Commerce that you have a substantial sum of money to invest. The required sum varies between the states (it's between $10,000/£6,500 and $50,000/£33,500 in most cases) and is reagrded as a guarantee against liabilities, although you may withdraw the money shortly afterwards!

The process is complex and financially risky, meaning that local knowledge is crucial. **You must also consult a good lawyer from the**

outset. An experienced lawyer will guide you through the registration complexities and his help will be vital in protecting your interests. This applies whether you're opening a modest shop or a major enterprise. As is the case all over the world, there are unofficial businesses operating in the region, but if anything goes wrong or you're ripped off, you have no legal recourse whatsoever.

Don't let these warnings put you off. All isn't doom and gloom, and many people have developed successful, highly profitable businesses in the Gulf. New operations are encouraged by the authorities and your local partner might be enthusiastically supportive (or he might be a severe liability). Export and manufacturing industries are especially strongly supported by government, particularly as regards the acquisition of land on which to construct a factory. If you set up such a business in a free trade zone, of which there are several in the region, it's granted exemptions from import and export duties, commercial taxes (see page 244), building and property licence fees, land tax and restrictions on the transfer of capital invested in the zone.

An alternative to starting a new business is to buy a going concern, which is a more straightforward process, as it doesn't involve lodging capital, obtaining sponsorship or registration; all you have to do is agree a price and transfer the ownership of the business.

Local Chambers of Commerce can advise about start-ups and are adept at cherry-picking potentially profitable newcomers to the region. Winning the confidence and support of a Chamber of Commerce will help your cause. Contact details are as follows:

- Bahrain Chamber of Commerce and Industry, PO Box 248, Bahrain (☎ 973-250 369);

- Kuwait Chamber of Commerce and Industry, PO Box 775, Safat 13008, Kuwait (☎ 965-243 3864);

- Oman Chamber of Commerce and Industry, PO Box 1400, Ruwi 112, Oman (☎ 968-707 674);

- Qatar Chamber of Commerce, PO Box 402, Doha, Qatar (☎ 974-423 677);

- Council of Saudi Chambers of Commerce and Industry, PO Box 16683, Riyadh 11474, Kingdom of Saudi Arabia (☎ 966-1-405 3200);

- Eastern Province Chamber of Commerce, PO Box 719, Dammam 31421, Kingdom of Saudi Arabia (☎ 966-3-857 1111);
- Federation of GCC Chambers, PO Box 2198, Dammam 3145, Kingdom of Saudi Arabia (☎ 966-3-826 5943);
- Jeddah Chamber of Commerce and Industry, PO Box 1264, Jeddah 21431, Kingdom of Saudi Arabia (☎ 966-2-651 5111);
- Riyadh Chamber of Commerce and Industry, PO Box 596, Riyadh 11421, Kingdom of Saudi Arabia (☎ 966-1-404 0044);
- Abu Dhabi Chamber of Commerce and Industry, PO Box 662, UAE (☎ 971-2-214 000);
- Federation of UAE Chambers of Commerce and Industry, PO Box 3014, Abu Dhabi, UAE (☎ 971-2-214 144);
- Ajman Chamber of Commerce and Industry, PO Box 662, UAE (☎ 971-6-422 177);
- Dubai Chamber of Commerce and Industry, PO Box 1457, UAE (☎ 971-4-221 181);
- Federation of UAE Chambers of Commerce and Industry, PO Box 8886, Dubai, UAE (☎ 971-4-212 977);
- Fujairah Chamber of Commerce, Industry and Agriculture, PO Box 738, UAE (☎ 971-9-222 400);
- Ras Al-Khaimah Chamber of Commerce, Industry and Agriculture, PO Box 87, UAE (☎ 971-7-333 511).

When doing business with Arabs, you will probably meet with hard but polite bargaining and find them expert at it. You need to be completely confident about the contents of your contractual agreement. If there are gaps, Arabs are brilliant at finding and exploiting them. Nevertheless, in the vast majority of cases, Arab businessmen meet their obligations fully. The experience of doing business with them is likely to be pleasant and friendly, and the trust built up on both sides will be long-lasting.

Incidentally, Arabs rarely say a direct 'no' to a proposition, so you must listen and observe carefully. If the response is 'Leave it with me' or 'I'll think about it', there's a good chance that the project will go nowhere.

The potential gains of starting and running your own business are great, but it isn't for the faint-hearted. You need to remember that you aren't a citizen of the country and when the time comes to leave and sell your interests, your partner has time on his side, while you might not.

Company Registration & Legal Obligations

Corporate law in the Gulf states is similar to that in western countries, in that businesses can be run as limited liability operations, private companies or other types of concern. As discussed, setting up a business or buying a going concern can be complex and you must obtain local legal advice and guidance about registration formalities. As a foreigner, you're likely to use a western/Arab joint venture law firm. When choosing, seek the advice of the Arab-British Chamber of Commerce, the DTI, Middle East Association and your Embassy's commercial sections.

WORKING ILLEGALLY

There are strict penalties for those living and working in the Gulf illegally, and these also apply to people staying beyond the term of a visitor visa (see page 73). Most illegals come from other Arab countries, Africa and the sub-continent of India; Saudi Arabia has a particular problem with illegals, who stay in the country following the annual pilgrimage to Mecca. To counteract this, frequent spot checks are carried out and there are widespread round-ups, but also occasional amnesties. Illegals aren't given a plethora of rights to appeal, as is sometimes the case in the west, but are simply deported.

LANGUAGE

The Arabic language has a very special meaning for Arabs, as does Arabic calligraphy, which was designed to be beautiful in order to convey the word of God (Allah), emanating from the Koran. Learning the language is a major step towards understanding the culture, as well as breaking down barriers. Arabs are impressively patient when speaking to those trying to learn the language and they humour expatriates who propose to learn Arabic, knowing that few manage it. English is the business language of the region and is widely spoken. Therefore it isn't necessary to learn Arabic, but it's appreciated if you learn at least some of the language, and this will also greatly enrich your time in the Gulf. Unfortunately, Arabic courses are few and far between and you may need to arrange your own private lessons. Your local embassy will have details of any courses that are available in your area, as will the British Council.

2.

WORKING CONDITIONS

Western expatriates are generally well qualified – they don't find work if they aren't – and these qualifications are carefully checked with the issuing bodies, irrespective of where they were obtained. Western expatriates therefore tend to occupy senior positions, with commensurate salaries and perks. Workers from south-east Asia and the Indian sub-continent (who are sometimes – politically incorrectly – referred to as 'Third Country Nationals' or 'TCNs') usually occupy menial, unskilled or semi-skilled jobs and are paid accordingly.

Even those with professional qualifications and experience as good as those of a westerner are unlikely to enjoy similar benefits, as the remuneration of foreign workers is related to what they would expect to earn in their home countries, which is invariably higher for westerners. However, this situation is beginning to change, especially in the field of technology.

A powerful sponsor or employer is a great weapon with officialdom, and observing his skilful negotiating can be an enlightening experience (see **Sponsorship** on page 37). The authorities, however, are usually helpful and don't tend to be difficult unless they have good reason. You will find your working life in the region easier if you're polite and patient. Smile and seek 'advice': requesting advice confers respect on the person asked and you will generally find that Arabs are friendly and helpful. Note that the recruitment of foreign staff is an expensive exercise for employers, including recruitment consultant fees, legal expenses and travel costs. As a result, few employers put their investment at risk by treating employees badly, and the great majority of expatriates prosper in the Gulf for many years.

TERMS OF EMPLOYMENT

Negotiating an appropriate salary is just one aspect of your working conditions. The checklist below is designed to act as a framework when entering into contract negotiations.

Salary

- Check the cost of living in the country against the salary offered. Most recruitment consultants have this information and the embassy's commercial section should also be able to supply details (see **Cost of Living** on page 246).

- The salary is usually paid in local currency and there are no restrictions on the export of funds to any other country. All banks handle this type of business.

- Note that the currency conversion rate is normally that which applies on the day you start work, which may or may not be to your benefit if the rate changes during your contract period. You're therefore recommended to do some research on conversion rate trends and the amount of fluctuation involved. If it's considerable, you should calculate the average and try to negotiate a good rate into the contract. This applies to all currencies except the US$, because Gulf currencies are pegged to the dollar and so the exchange rate is constant (barring major fluctuations in the dollar's value, which might cause temporary changes).

- If you work for a multi-national company, check where and in what currency you will be paid. Income tax is a factor if you're paid outside the region. You might also be eligible for overseas allowances and you need to investigate the effect of your move on your company pension plan.

- Salary reviews should be discussed at the interview. If it's a fixed-term contract, you might be eligible for a review, which is usually related to the company's or the individual's performance. The salary might be index-linked, although this is rare in the Gulf. Some employers are wary of taking on employees for more than a year, as they may put in one year of dedicated work and then spend the second year 'winding down'. If you're taking an open-ended contract, which is likely, you need to tie down the times of reviews and include these in writing.

- Salaries are usually paid at the end of each month, either in cash or directly into your local bank account. If you work for an international company, you might make other arrangements, but remember to check the income tax position in your home country (see page 243).

- Whether you receive overtime payments depends on the type of work you do. Most office and executive work doesn't pay overtime.

If it is paid, the relevant labour laws should provide scales and rules. It's wise to check.

Relocation Expenses

- Since your contract invariably involves your relocating from your home country to the Gulf, airfare(s) are usually paid by your employer, as are repatriation costs at the end of the contract. If you're married or contemplating marriage, check whether your contract includes the cost of flights and other expenses for your spouse and any children. Some companies employ only single people, or allow spouses to join employees at their own expense. are also covered. If the work contract doesn't stipulate the rules (if any) relating to this, you must clarify the position, particularly if you're married or contemplating marriage. Unmarried 'partners' in the current western sense are unlikely to enjoy married privileges in the region. In fact, living with a partner is culturally and legally unacceptable in some states; in Saudi Arabia, cohabiting is regarded as fornication.

- You might also be given tickets home for leave/holidays. If you're allowed to split your annual leave, for example into two holidays, check that tickets are provided for both trips.

- Expenses sometimes include an allowance for excess baggage for air travel. If major household effects are involved in the move (which is unlikely, except for multi-national company employees), you should negotiate an allowance and also clarify the situation concerning repatriation costs. If your company has agreed to all relocation expenses, it's likely to agree to all repatriation expenses too. This should include the goods you accumulate during your stay abroad, including, for example, a car.

- Air tickets are usually provided rather than cash advances or reimbursement at your destination. You might be asked to pay the shipping cost for your possessions, with reimbursement on arrival. As this can be a substantial cost, however, it's best to ask the company to organise and pay for it. Above all, you must ensure door-to-door delivery, or your effects might be carried only to the docks or airport, leaving you to find a local handling agent to clear customs and arrange delivery; you must pay extra for this.

- Few people send major household effects such as furniture to the Gulf, preferring to leave them in their home country, usually in the house that they rent out while away. (It can be unnerving at the start of your period of work overseas to have sold your home base and possessions). Most contracts include an allowance for personal effects with which to furnish your new home, or at least provide a cash advance for this on arrival.

- Relocation consultants are rarely used, except by multi-national companies.

- In the event of the cancellation of your contract by either your employer or you, he's legally responsible for your return to your country of residence, unless there's an agreement otherwise.

Accommodation

- On arrival, it's usual for hotel or short-term accommodation to be provided. This might be paid for by your employer or the cost might be deducted from your salary later, in agreed stages. You're usually helped to find accommodation.

- It's in your financial interest to find a permanent residence as soon as possible after arrival.

- If you're put in short-term accommodation, you will probably be expected to pay for the utilities.

Schooling

- You might be offered private education for your children, either in the Gulf or in your home country. Packages vary and you should negotiate strongly, as school fees can be high. You should also consider whether, as your children get older, it might be more beneficial to school them in your home country rather than in the Gulf. This move might not be covered in your remuneration package. It's advisable to check.

Working Hours

- Your contract will lay out the job's standard hours and practices. Working hours vary considerably in the region, although the basic hours are likely to be between 40 and 48 per week, depending on the organisation. Five, five and a half and six-day working weeks are common. The service sector tends to favour a five-day week with rest days on Fridays (the Muslim holy day or rest day) and either Thursdays or Saturdays. Companies with international connections favour Saturday as the other day, in order to match the working week outside the Muslim world as closely as possible. Working days are usually eight hours, with a one-hour lunch break.

● Some companies expect you to work hours longer than those stated in your contract and this can prove frustrating, particularly if there are no overtime payments. You might be unfortunate in having an Arab employer who only visits the workplace at the end of the day, and the employee culture is such that employees are expected to stay until the boss leaves, which may be long after your normal leaving time, although this is less common now. You might also find that you're working with people who come from a working culture that favours late nights and late starts, and you might be expected to follow suit, even if you're accustomed to early starts and finishes.

Leave

● Check the annual leave entitlement, which can vary but is usually a month. Ask if it increases with length of service.

● Public holidays are paid, but the number of such days can vary according to whether you work in the government sector or in private industry. It will come as little surprise that there are more days off for government employees.

● Note that you cannot be demoted to a lower position or have your contract terminated while you're out of the country on your official, contracted leave, unless you fail to return.

● Annual leave is sometimes postponed because of pressure of work, but this is certainly not unique to the Gulf. There's usually a sound reason for this, and few Arab employers these days treat expatriates as commodities to be exploited.

Insurance

● Private health insurance might be provided by your employer; if it isn't, you will have to use public health services or pay for private treatment or insurance yourself (see **Chapter 12**). Government hospitals in the region are, in the main, of a high standard (see page 202).

- You should also check the contract conditions regarding sick pay, which has traditionally been meagre in the Gulf, although contracts now tend to be more generous in this respect, especially for short-term sickness. For example, in Oman, many employees are entitled to full basic salary as sick pay after three months' employment, provided that sick leave doesn't exceed ten weeks in any year.

Company Pension

- Local companies are unlikely to have company pension schemes. The multi-nationals usually do.
- If there is a scheme, check what percentage of your salary you must pay.
- Are you able to pay a lump sum into the pension fund in order to receive a full or higher pension?
- Is the pension transferable to another employer or to another location with the same employer?

Employer

- Check the employer's background. If a recruitment consultant is involved, it should provide a clear picture of the employer's record. Ask to talk to a fellow countryman in his employ or talk to the Commercial Section of the British Embassy, which might know about the company or at least whether it has a poor reputation.
- Are its profitability and growth rate favourable?
- Is there a high staff turnover? If so, why?
- Are free or subsidised language lessons provided for you and your spouse?
- Is a transport allowance included in your financial package? Will you be supplied with a car (or a loan to purchase one), a driver or other transport to and from work? Is there free parking at your work place?
- Is there a staff canteen and, if so, is food provided free or at subsidised rates?

- Is professional training provided?
- Are there allowances for your children's education?
- Are you provided with servants?
- Are there any club memberships?
- Are there compensation allowances in the event of redundancy, severance payments or golden handshakes (in addition to the state indemnity)?
- Will the company provide employment for you at home on completion of your contract? This is an important matter. Consider also your repatriation plans and costs.

EMPLOYMENT CONTRACTS

On being offered a job, which in the vast majority of cases happens in the expatriate's own country, you will almost certainly sign a contract or at least a letter of agreement. This will contain the conditions of employment (see below) and perhaps include a detailed job description, indicating responsibilities and performance standards. On arrival in the Gulf, you can ask for this document to be formalised, with an official Ministry version in Arabic, or attested to by a notary, although there's little advantage in doing so. A verbal agreement is possible, but a written agreement is, of course, preferable.

In most Gulf states, your contract specifies your basic salary, job title, duties and responsibilities, the period of your contract, and possibly also details of the reporting structure and performance measures of the company. An employment contract should also contain termination conditions, including required notice of intent to terminate the contract on either side and liabilities to be incurred in respect of breaking the conditions of the contract. Your contract might include the phrase 'employment subject to obtaining the necessary permits'. This is unlikely to present problems, but make sure that you're able to obtain the required visas, etc. (see **Chapter 3**) before committing yourself to the move abroad.

Note that local labour laws apply whether you hold a contract or not. A company contract is likely to take precedence over basic labour laws where its stipulations are in excess of legal requirements, but you still have the protection of the laws as a minimum.

Traditionally, most expatriate contracts were for two years only, but it's becoming increasingly common for contracts to be open-ended. Employers have found that they can be held to a defined period if the employee proves unsatisfactory, and most contracts now have a termination notice period of between one and three months, or payment in lieu of notice. Contracts can be extended or renewed by mutual consent and frequently are if all parties are happy with things as they are. It's quite common for expatriates to stay in the Gulf for 20 years or more.

Most Gulf states have sophisticated, computerised control of their labour force and specify job categories that are open to foreign labour. Certain employment is reserved for nationals, particularly in the service industries. You might, therefore, find that your contract gives you the job title you would expect, but the official version on your work visa is something quite different. This might be because of full job quotas or other reasons. You're sometimes required to attend the Ministry on the completion of your contract to ensure that you have no complaints and to cancel your work visa.

EMPLOYMENT CONDITIONS

Employment conditions contain an employer's general rules and regulations regarding working conditions and benefits (unless otherwise stated in your contract). They're either explained in this chapter or reference is made to where in this book additional information can be found.

Validity & Applicability

Employment conditions usually contain an opening paragraph indicating the starting date and to whom the contract applies. Note that in many cases your employer retains your passport, as he is required to do by law, because you're his responsibility. Your work visa acts as an identification document in its absence.

Your status in the company has an effect on whether you're asked to surrender your passport: most senior executives don't comply and are rarely forced to, but workers at the middle and lower end of the scale almost always have to surrender their passports.

Salary & Benefits

The nature of remuneration packages has changed since the 1970s and 1980s, when they tended to be split into various elements: basic salary, housing allowance, transport, medical, education and travel. Now remuneration is usually one sum, including everything, giving people the freedom to dispose of it as they wish, although in some cases there's a bonus – based on either the company's or the individual's performance – and in almost all cases an 'indemnity'.

Indemnity: The indemnity has nothing to do with insurance but is an end-of-contract bonus which is required by law to be paid to expatriate workers as a sort of 'thank-you' for being of service to the state. (It's also known as 'end of service benefits'.) In most cases, your indemnity is calculated according to your basic salary, although in Saudi Arabia it's based on your total remuneration package including performance bonuses (where applicable). Indemnity scales are similar in all states and usually amount to 15 (in some cases 20) days of basic pay per year of employment for the first three years and thereafter a month's salary per year of employment.

Note that some Arab companies regularly delay the payment of salaries, cash flow problems being passed on to their staff. In this event, you have little alternative but to wait.

Working Hours & Overtime

The working week in the Gulf tends to vary between 40 and 48 hours, depending on the particular company's policy. Office hours are usually from 8.30 or 9.00 am to 5.30 or 6.00 pm. There are no differences in time keeping between summer and winter. In the month of Ramadan (see **Business Hours** on page 332, **National Holidays** on page 348 and **Religion** on page 352), the working day is reduced to six hours and legally this should apply to all staff, but many companies only apply it to Muslims, who fast during daylight hours.

Friday is the Muslim rest day and, if your company has a five-day working week, the other day off will probably be either Thursday or Saturday. Saturday is the more popular choice for international companies, as taking Thursday off would mean a reduction in the number of operational days in common with much of the rest of the world. Conversely, other companies insist on Thursday, as the school 'weekend' is Thursday and Friday.

Travel & Relocation Expenses

Your travel and relocation expenses depend on the agreement you make with your employer and are usually included in your employment contract. The employer might pay all or part of your relocation costs. An allowance is normally provided for personal effects and for air freight or excess baggage, and frequently a further allocation of funds is made as part of the remuneration package to cover furnishings in your new location.

Social Security Benefits

State social security applies to nationals only. Saudi Arabia experimented with a project to include expatriate workers (who made contributions from their salary, as did their employers), but it was abandoned and contributions reimbursed. The transient nature of the work force made the scheme too difficult to implement.

Medical Examination

All expatriates must undertake a government-controlled medical examination prior to the issue of a work residence visa. The examination includes a general health check to look for serious infectious diseases and infirmities, but especially for HIV and AIDS. The examination is likely to be more stringent for workers from the Indian sub-continent and south-east Asia, who may have greater exposure to disease and less access to advanced medical resources in their home countries than westerners. The AIDS test is mandatory, including for spouses and, if you're shown to be HIV positive, you will be expelled immediately. The test is also given when work visas are renewed, which is usually on a three-year cycle.

Health Insurance

Some but not all companies provide medical cover for their employees. Workers not covered must use public facilities or pay for private treatment or insurance themselves (see **Chapter 12**). The outlay might be covered in your contract. Some Gulf states are beginning to insist that companies provide health insurance for their employees.

Company Pension Fund

These are usually offered by multi-national companies, their affiliates and some major local organisations, but are uncommon in many local firms. It's important to continue your own national contributions if applicable while away. In the case of the UK, it's wise to continue with Class 3 national health contributions, as this maintains your eligibility for the national retirement pension.

Salary Insurance

Salary insurance is uncommon among expatriates. Each state allocates a quota of days' pay in the event of sickness or accident. A medical certificate must be submitted after three days of sickness.

Annual & Public Holidays

Your contract will stipulate your entitlement to annual leave, which is usually a month, although you should check whether this means 30 days or 22 (i.e. including or excluding weekends). You should also check whether you may split your leave into separate holidays (e.g. two breaks of two weeks each instead of one of four weeks) and consider the implications that this will have on the doubling of travel costs and the question of who pays.

National holidays are enjoyed by all, although these vary from state to state and there's usually a difference in their duration for workers in the private and public sectors (see page 348).

Compassionate & Special Leave

Compassionate leave is usually granted in the case of a close relative's serious illness or death. It might be allowed in addition to your holiday leave, with you still receiving full pay, or it might be deducted from your annual leave or be counted as unpaid leave. You will almost certainly have to pay your own travel costs.

Paid Expenses

Travel and hotel expenses relating to legitimate business trips are obviously paid by your employer and require the submission of relevant receipts. Entertaining expenses are determined by the company's policy on the matter; check what it is. Expenses aren't usually paid for normal travel between home and work. Lunch allowances aren't usually given, except for legitimate business entertaining.

Probationary & Notice Periods

Some contracts include a probationary period of around three months and it might be difficult to avoid this condition being included, particularly if you're in a middle or lower level position. Seniors with experience aren't always required to serve one. Probation periods are obviously a greater risk when you're working abroad than in your home country. For this reason, the majority of expatriates tend to come out to the Gulf on their own and bring their families out only when they've successfully negotiated the probation period.

Most employment contracts, particularly those that are open-ended, have a termination notice period of between one and three months, or payment in lieu of notice. Contracts can be extended or renewed by mutual consent and frequently are.

Education & Training

Most Gulf countries are devoting considerable resources to the development of their human resources, with extensive education and training programmes for young nationals and long-serving staff. Some expatriates can also benefit from these programmes, but most are excluded (many employers see training as a waste of time and money with transient expatriates) and need to work for an international company in order to be offered further training.

Part-time Work

In general, employers who have made the investment to bring you to the country take a dim view of your spreading your talents around by doing part-time work for others, and if you're discovered 'moonlighting' you could have problems.

Pregnancy Leave

Pregnancy leave is usually around three months and, when the woman returns to work, the law dictates that she must be offered her original position or a better one. Husbands are sometimes granted short periods of leave when their wives give birth, usually unpaid.

Changing Jobs

The Gulf states have different rules about changing jobs. The average expatriate is in the region because he has been given a job by a particular employer, who has had to meet the expenses of recruitment and relocation, perhaps for a family. Apart from any contractual arrangement, this also places a moral obligation on the employee to the employer, or it should do. In earlier years, workers were brought to the region on a fixed period contract, normally two years, after which the contract could be renewed by mutual consent. Arab employers learned by experience, however, that this didn't always work to their advantage, because the employee could then negotiate with a competitor for a new contract. A new employer then had the benefit of a seasoned expatriate, adjusted to the way of life and the business environment, with little to pay in the way of relocation and recruitment expenses. In some instances, there was one year's hard work followed by a year's wind-down as the contract approached completion.

Today, contracts tend to be open-ended and include clauses to protect the employer, such as a six-month period before the granting of a new work visa for a particular worker. This discontinuity means that, technically, the worker must leave the country for six months before reapplying for a visa. There are, however, ways around this. (There usually are in the region, if you know the right people.) A worker can transfer to a new employer if his original sponsor or employer provides him with a 'letter of no objection' or a 'no objection certificate' (NOC). If the sponsor is your employer (which is usually the case), he may be reluctant to allow you to go and work for another company, although he may be willing to issue and NOC in order to avoid the expense of returning you to your country of origin.

Nevertheless, don't assume that the change will be quick and simple; there will inevitably be numerous questions and checks. In order to have the full support of your new employer, it's usually best to leave the country for a period and return under a new agreement. Even then, if you return and take up employment with a firm that's in competition with your previous employer, you might find that matters become awkward; as a general rule, sponsors and employers are loath to fall out with each other, so the expatriate is likely be the loser.

Retirement

The retirement ages in the Gulf are usually 60 for women and 65 for men, but these aren't always strictly enforced. International companies tend to have stricter policies on age limits. There's respect for age in Arab culture, and older employees are likely to continue working until they feel it's time to leave. Occasionally, foreigners who have made significant contributions to their work in certain states have been granted citizenship. This has allowed them permanent residence as a naturalised citizen and in the odd instance they've been given a house and income.

Dismissal & Redundancy

The general rule is that you're given three written warnings detailing your failings or shortcomings before dismissal. If you break the law, you can be instantly dismissed if the situation warrants it and the employer is so inclined. If you become involved in an altercation serious enough to warrant police attention, for example, or if you're found guilty of drunken driving, your employer might dismiss you. You would be deemed to have defaulted on the terms of your contract and be ineligible for any indemnity payment due to you. However, an employee cannot be dismissed (or demoted) while on leave out of the country.

If you're made redundant, the termination clause in your contract (of one month or whatever is applicable) comes into effect. Your employer might enhance the offer if he feels that your work deserves it or if it will cause hardship for you to have to leave the Gulf.

Disputes

Arabs sometimes make far-reaching judgements based on the 'chemistry' between you and them. If they don't like you, they're likely to look for excuses to terminate the association. It's obviously in your interest to resolve any dispute amicably yourself, as you can never predict the outcome and, even if you 'win', it might be damaging or even disastrous to your career prospects. Expatriates should avoid legal tussles whenever possible, which are time consuming and can lead to untold difficulties. If a dispute arises that cannot be immediately resolved between your employer and yourself, take your case to the relevant Ministry of Labour (see page 38). If they agree with your interpretation of events, they will take the matter up with your employer on your behalf. Each state has its own labour laws, and an English-language version can be obtained from the Ministry. In general, the Ministries can be relied upon to make fair judgements in cases of dispute and don't tend to be biased in favour of local employers. Do be aware, however, that adjournments or delays in sorting out any disputes usually work to the detriment of the employee: delays mean time and money, and the expatriate will have a limited amount of both. Serious disputes, however, are rare.

The region has no tradition of organised trades unions, and their formation is illegal; strikes, therefore, are virtually unknown. It's possible to form an association within your company to make approaches on a collective basis to management, but this would have validity only within the individual company. Individual representation to the management *is* possible, but you will need to be understated, brave and have your return plane ticket handy!

3.

PERMITS & VISAS

The movement of foreigners is tightly controlled by the Gulf governments, and issuing of visas and other permits is subject to strict bureaucratic procedures. Those who are denied access therefore have little opportunity for appeal. Fortunately, the average expatriate doesn't need to deal with much of the bureaucracy. Most companies and institutions, large or small, have a 'fixer', whose job is to wade through the red tape generated by the various ministerial departments in order to obtain work and residence visas for foreign workers and their families. The fixer will also act as your guide whenever your presence is required.

The documents required to enter the Gulf states include the following:

- a passport valid for at least six months (it's useful to have at least three or four photocopies);
- at least six passport-size photographs;
- a marriage certificate (if applicable);
- birth certificates for all family members;
- a medical certificate in the case of workers (see note below).

Note that foreigners working in the Gulf must have a certificate to show that they're in good general health and free from HIV/AIDS and other sexually transmitted diseases, although tests are usually also carried out locally (see **Medical Examination** on page 63). Your sponsor (see page 37) will advise you what's required.

Note also that any visible connection with Israel, e.g. an Israeli passport or an Israeli entry stamp, will disqualify you from entry to all the Gulf states.

While you're in any of the Gulf states, you're required to carry identification documents, e.g. passport or national identity card and appropriate entry and residence visas (see below). Note that it's common for labour officials to carry out spot checks on businesses in search of workers employed illegally and to inspect passports in the possession of the employer.

This isn't to suggest that the region's countries are repressive regimes: expatriates have little to worry about if they conduct themselves in a reasonable way, obey the laws and observe the rules of the culture. Indeed, you will usually be treated with kindness and generosity. Saudi Arabia, however, is an exception, being the most conservative state in the region, with strict adherence to Sharia law, its city of Mecca (known in Saudi Arabia as Makkah) being the birthplace of Islam. The Saudis regard this as a particular honour, one that is reinforced by their wealth of natural resources. Ignoring the strict application of the laws and cultural rules can earn you serious retribution. Many foreigners, however, live and work happily in Saudi for many years.

VISAS

Vvisas are required by most visitors to the Gulf states, whether on holiday or business trips or intending to live and work there. In order to obtain a visa, you require a sponsor (see page 37), which is normally your employer if you're working. If you're visiting for a holiday or business, the hotel where you're staying can act as your sponsor. To request this service, you must send your travel itinerary and passport details by fax a few weeks in advance of your stay. Ensure that confirmation has been given and that your visa will be left at your point of entry **before** you depart. A small fee will be added to your hotel bill for this service. Additionally, your hotel might be able to obtain short extensions to your stay, provided they're sure of your itinerary during the stay. The hotel is responsible for you during your time in the country. If you're taking up work in the Gulf, your sponsor will normally arrange the necessary visas and permits for you.

In addition to entry and residence visas, exit visas are required by departing foreigners under certain circumstances in Qatar and Saudi Arabia, and transit passengers require transit visas in Saudi Arabia (see below).

Most visas and permits consist of passport stamps, so that immigration authorities can easily check that you have the necessary authorisation when you enter or leave the country. There are costs associated with the various visas and permits, but in the case of foreign workers these are normally met by your employer. Note that the prices quoted below should be taken as a guide only, as they're subject to change, as are the conditions and requirements; the relevant state's embassy or consulate can provide you with the current information.

Bahrain

All nationals of Gulf Cooperation Council (GCC) member states (i.e. the six Gulf states) and British citizens (by birth) may enter Bahrain without a visa and receive an entry stamp in their passport. British citizens can stay for a month and gain a short extension by applying to the Directorate of Immigration and Passports, Bahrain International Airport, PO Box 331, Manama (☎ 973-528 883).

All other visitors require one of the following visas. Note that, although certain visas are theoretically obtainable on arrival in Bahrain, young single women should be sure to arrange them in advance, as they will come under scrutiny at the point of entry owing to the recent increase in the number of prostitutes attempting to enter Bahrain.

Note also that the immigration authorities are very strict with those whose passport states their occupation as journalist, writer or editor, unless their visit has prior permission from the Ministry of Information (PO Box 253, Bahrain, ☎ 973-781 888). Even if your visit to Bahrain is unconnected with your work as a writer, you're likely to be refused entry or at best will be allowed to approach the Ministry of Information, under supervision, for permission to enter the country. Journalists on official visits are sponsored by the Ministry and are accompanied by an official during their visit, with transport supplied.

Tourist Visa: Bahrain has a burgeoning tourist industry and is keen to promote this further, as it's a valuable source of income. Tourist visas are issued for stays of two weeks to citizens of the European Union (EU), Australia, Canada, Hong Kong, Japan, New Zealand and the USA. Applicants must possess valid, up-to-date passports and a return or onward ticket. A small charge is made – around BD5 ($12) – and hotels can arrange visas if given advance notice (see above). Tourist visas don't allow you to engage in any employment.

Visitor Visa: These visas are for other foreign nationals and require the sponsorship of a Bahraini, who has to apply to the Directorate of Immigration and Passports on the visitor's behalf. They're valid for a month and cost BD22 (around $54). They don't allow employment.

72-hour & Seven-day Visas: These are obtainable at the point of entry for short stay business visitors and cost around BD10 ($24) and BD15 ($36) respectively. You need a return or onward ticket and a valid passport.

Business Visa: Those intending to stay longer than a week on business must obtain a business visa through the Bahrain embassy in their own country. Business visas are valid for up to four weeks. You must complete an application form and present your passport, photographs, an employer's letter indicating the purpose of the trip and a 'letter of no objection' or a 'no objection certificate' (NOC – see page 66) from your Bahraini sponsor, although this last is rarely asked for. There's a fee (e.g. £20 in the UK). The duration of the visa varies according to the nature of the trip.

Work Visa: If you're taking up employment in Bahrain, you require a work visa, which is normally valid for one or two years. This also entitles you to reside in the country. A medical examination is required and fees are applicable. Your sponsor normally arranges most of the necessary paperwork.

Family Visa: The immediate family of those working in Bahrain can obtain a family visa (sometimes also called a residence permit) for around BD22 ($54), which entitles them to residence status for the period of employment. Members of the family aren't allowed to work, unless separate arrangements are made and the appropriate work visas obtained.

Kuwait

You can enter Kuwait without a visa if you're a GCC national or an expatriate with authorised residence in another GCC state. All other visitors require visas, which must be organised in advance. The Kuwaiti government's insistence on this is understandable in view of the country's troubled recent history. There are just two types of visa:

Visitor Visa: Valid for three or six months, these are obtained from Kuwaiti embassies and consulates or via a Kuwaiti sponsor, who will apply to the Ministry of the Interior in Kuwait. Hotels also arrange visas for their guests (see above). A three-month visa costs around $45 (£30), a six-month visa around $72 (£48). Multiple entry visas may be issued upon application to Kuwaiti embassies and consulates; these are usually granted for the purpose of repeat business trips. They cost around $100 (£66) for six months, $110 (£75) for a year, $150 (£100) for two years and $120 (£180) for five years.

Residence Visa: If you're going to work in Kuwait, you need a residence visa. First, you must obtain an NOC (see page 66), which is provided by the Ministry of Social Affairs and Labour following application by your sponsor. If making arrangements prior to entry, your next step is to submit the NOC to the Ministry of the Interior. If you arrive on a visitor visa (see above), your sponsor will apply for an NOC and on receipt of this will apply directly to the Ministry of the Interior for your residence visa. When you receive approval for the visa, you must leave the country and return, with your NOC (although this requirement is sometimes waived); your residence visa will be issued shortly afterwards. A medical examination is required, including an HIV/AIDS test. Once you've obtained your a residence visa, you will be issued with a 'Civil ID' card, which must be carried at all times. As in the other Gulf states, your sponsor normally takes care of these administrative matters, leaving you simply to follow instructions.

Oman

Until recently, Oman was a fairly closed society, all non-nationals being required to obtain an entry visa. Visitor visas were issued only after careful consideration of the sponsor's application, which had to include an acceptable reason for the visit. The situation has changed and it's now easier to enter Oman, a country known for its varied, beautiful landscapes and charming people. GCC nationals can enter the Sultanate freely, while others require an NOC (see page 66) and a visa.

Tourist Visa: To obtain a tourist visa, you need a sponsorship letter from an Omani citizen, company or hotel. The visa is issued after presentation of a completed application form, passport with at least six months' validity remaining, photographs, travel plans, evidence of financial solvency and an onward or return ticket. The visa is valid for a month and employment is prohibited, although such visits are frequently used for interviews for future employment.

Business Visa: Business visas are obtained from the Sultanate's embassy or consulate in your country of residence. A completed application form, passport, photographs, an invitation letter or letter from your employer outlining the reason for the visit and type of business are needed. Visas are issued either for a short stay of two weeks or for three months.

Work Visa: The Ministry of Social Affairs and Labour issues the mandatory work visa (stamped 'authorised to work') to expatriates intending to take up employment in Oman. This must be renewed annually.

Residence Visa: If your family is living with you in the Gulf, they require residence visas, which must be renewed every two years.

Residence visas are stamped 'not authorised to work'. Family members must also have a medical examination.

Qatar

GCC nationals can enter Qatar freely, as can holders of full status British passports (with rights of abode). All other nationalities must obtain Qatari sponsorship through a hotel or an individual. It's necessary to check that the embassy or consulate you choose to approach has the facility to issue visas.

Tourist Visa: Only hotels are able to procure these, and the visa duration corresponds to your length of stay at the hotel. An onward or return ticket is required, along with the usual documents.

Visitor Visa: You can obtain a visitor visa either via a Qatari sponsor or by submitting your documents to the embassy or consulate in your home country. Single journey stays can be up to three months, but stays of over 30 days require a medical.

Business Visa: Business visas are valid for three months from their date of issue and are for a single visit for a period of one week, with possible extensions up to four weeks. The simplest and quickest route to secure a business visa is for your sponsor to organise one in Qatar.

Work & Residence Visas: The procedure for obtaining work and residence visas is lengthy and complex and is put into motion by your sponsor. A number of formalities must be observed, including a full medical examination (including an HIV test) and the submission of academic and professional qualifications. In many cases, these formalities are dealt with during a visit to Qatar on a visitor or business visa (see above). You might also need to supply original marriage and birth certificates if applying for family status. Residence visas are valid for between one and three years. Multi-entry visas are available in certain circumstances.

Exit Visa: The sponsored individual (i.e. the working member of a family) is required to obtain an exit visa if he has been in the country for 30 days or more. This can be obtained by your sponsor. Families are exempt from this requirement.

Saudi Arabia

Attempting to enter Saudi Arabia without authorisation isn't only pointless, but is also likely to prove costly. In fact, if you're hoping to fly into the country, you won't even get past the check-in desk. Similarly, if you arrive at one of the land borders, you will be quickly, and perhaps aggressively, turned back. Muslims find entry to the Kingdom much easier, the issue of visas for religious purposes (the *Haj* and *Umrah* visas) being a well-controlled, well-administered process. There are strict national quotas per country for these visas, which are issued annually, because the volume of people wishing to visit the holy places is enormous.

You must be particularly careful with dates shown on Saudi visas, which conform to the Islamic (*Hijra*) calendar (see **Calendar** on page 332). Overstaying your visa by even 24 hours can lead to fines and further delays.

Note also that there are no shortcuts that the individual himself can take with the immigration authorities and the rules applying to visas. Rejections and refusals can be permanent. Note also that Saudi Arabia is the only Gulf state where passengers in transit, by air or land, also require a visa, known as a transit visa.

Transit Visa: If you're changing planes at a Saudi airport and therefore have no option but to temporarily stop in the country, a 24 or 48-hour transit visa is required. You must surrender your passport to the immigration authorities, who will return it on your departure. If you're driving from Bahrain, Qatar or the United Arab Emirates (UAE) to Jordan, you might be granted a seven-day transit visa. Those driving between Jordan, Yemen or Kuwait via the Kingdom are usually allowed a three-day transit visa. When crossing Saudi borders, it's essential that your papers are in order and your transport plans are absolutely clear. Check the procedure with the Saudi embassy or consulate in your home country and seek permission from the destination country. Also be aware that, although transit regulations are written down, they're occasionally open to local interpretation, particularly at border points. Expect the unexpected.

Visitor Visa: At present, there's no substantial tourist industry in Saudi Arabia, so few tourist visas are issued, although things are changing gradually and the intention is to build a limited tourist trade. To obtain a tourist visa, you must be invited by a company or individual (the higher his standing and influence the better) who will act as your sponsor and undertake responsibility for you during you stay. The sponsor applies for the visa on your behalf and obtains a serial number. You must then approach a Saudi embassy and obtain a visa stamp in your passport, for which there's a small charge. Without the serial number, you cannot obtain a visa.

Although not officially sanctioned, it's sometimes possible to have a visitor visa converted to a residence visa (see below) while you're in the Kingdom. Strictly, you should return to your country of domicile to await the official process, but if your sponsor has sufficient clout, many things are possible.

Note that it's extremely difficult for young, single women to enter the country unless it's clear that they're closely related to expatriate workers. Business women will encounter serious obstacles to entry unless they're members of a Saudi family or have the sponsorship of a powerful Saudi national.

Residence Visa & Permit: Obtaining a residence visa is usually a lengthy procedure – around a couple of months – with a considerable amount of paperwork on the part of the employer and individual. Having been given a contract of employment, you must present your contract, academic and/or professional qualifications and the results of a full medical examination, including HIV test either to the Saudi embassy or consulate in your home country or to the authorities in Saudi Arabia via your sponsor. You will then be issued with a visa number, with which you can proceed to a Saudi embassy or consulate to obtain a stamped residence visa, which will be converted to a residence permit after your arrival in the Kingdom (where you might be asked to take the medical again!). Your residence permit (Iqama) includes your photograph and must be carried at all times, your passport having been retained by your sponsor.

Exit Visa: Should you go on leave or undertake a business trip outside the Kingdom, your sponsor will obtain an exit/re-entry visa, which is a stamp in your passport, and temporarily withdraw your residence permit. Having completed your stay or contract, you're issued with an exit-only stamp in your passport and are required to surrender the residence permit.

The requirement of an exit visa to leave Saudi Arabia while working there is a tedious restriction on your personal freedom and in an emergency can be problematic, if your sponsor isn't readily available to process papers. Fortunately, this rarely happens and the sponsor often has a deputy authorised to sign for him. In an emergency, your embassy might assist by intervening on your behalf.

If an expatriate holds a senior position in his company (e.g. Managing Director or General Manager), he might be able to obtain a multiple exit/re-entry visa, usually valid for six months. This visa allows easy passage in either direction but isn't automatically renewable.

United Arab Emirates

GCC nationals, expatriates residing in other GCC states and holders of British passports may enter the UAE without a visa. Other nationalities need a visa, obtained from a UAE embassy prior to travelling. Young, single female visitors should carefully check the entry requirements. An income minimum applies to family members visiting expatriate workers.

Transit Visa: Valid for 14 days, transit visas are intended for those travelling within the Emirates and for short-stay business trips. A sponsor or hotel can arrange one and they cost around AED120 ($33).

Visitor Visa: All visitors should obtain a visa before travelling, by applying to the UAE embassy in their own country. Hotels can act as sponsors for visas, provided they're given sufficient notice. Visitor visas cost around AED110 ($30) and are usually valid for 30 days, although 60-day visas are also available. Overstaying the period can result in a daily fine of around AED100 ($27).

Labour Card & Residence Visa: All foreign workers require a residence visa and 'labour card'. To obtain these, you must first undergo a medical examination. Non-westerners generally require a more extensive examination than westerners. In due course, a residence visa is issued and eventually a labour card, which is a kind of identity card to be carried at all times, your passport having been surrendered to your employer.

Residence visas are valid for three years and are easy to renew. There's an age limit of 50 years, but this can occasionally be overcome, if appropriate reasons are presented. New residents should remain in the Emirates for the first six months of their stay.

4.

ARRIVAL

The vast majority of foreign workers arrive in the Gulf by air. Most of the region's airports are clean, modern and free of crowds of tourists, although Dubai's new airport, with its famous duty-free shop (see page 327), is attracting an increasing number of tourists, and Sharjah airport is attempting to match its facilities. Oman airport, on the other hand, has relatively little traffic. The busiest is Saudi Arabia's airport, where expatriates can expect long queues, which can be confusing but tend to be friendly and non-hostile. As a working expatriate arriving for the first time, you will almost certainly be met and taken to your hotel or accommodation.

Arrivals by sea are virtually unheard of, except for pilgrims on their way to Mecca (known in Saudi Arabia as Makkah) for the annual pilgrimage (Haj), many of whom arrive at the port of Jeddah in Saudi Arabia.

IMMIGRATION

In general, the immigration services in the Gulf states are fairly well organised. If your papers aren't in order or your visa isn't at the immigration desk, however, you can expect long delays while your sponsor is located. Sponsors play a vital role in the immigration process and you should invest time to find yourself a good one (see page 37).

The authorities in Saudia Arabia and Kuwait are particularly security-conscious and you can encounter officious immigration officers and strict customs searches. (You will find many friendly people in Saudi Arabia, but very few of them are immigration officials.) Bahrain, by contrast, provides a good-natured welcome, with immigration and customs officers welcoming back returning expatriates. In general, officials are helpful and hospitable, and if you're good-natured and patient, you will be well treated. Rude or aggressive behaviour is always badly received.

In Saudi Arabia, men should avoid long hair, particularly if it's loose or untidy. Those favouring a bohemian or hippy look can be refused entry. Females are expected to dress very conservatively, with longish skirts, arms covered and preferably a head-scarf or hat. If your husband is a working expatriate he will probably bring an 'abbaya' (the black dress covering) to the airport if you're arriving for the first time.

CUSTOMS

All the Gulf states have rigorous customs inspections, involving x-raying baggage as you enter and leave. Saudi Arabian customs officers open most if not all bags, and you should give special attention to the contents of your luggage (see **Prohibited & Restricted Goods** on page 85). Personal consignments of freight are also closely scrutinised in all states, and you must provide a comprehensive list of contents. With shipments arriving by air, you're likely to be called to attend the clearance at customs. The airport authorities sometimes give a time limit in which to clear shipments and impose a daily storage if the limit is exceeded. When you leave the country, a full list of the personal effects being exported is required, but you don't need to attend in person.

Personal effects aren't subject to import or export duties. The import and export of cars, however, is a separate issue and involves de-registration in the case of export, as well as the provision of export plates and police clearance to ensure that there's no financial attachment to the car.

Visitors

The vast majority of visitors pass through the Gulf's airports without problems. However, visiting females, particularly those travelling without children, always invite close scrutiny, and an expatriate wife arriving in Saudi Arabia might be asked to find her husband (who is her 'sponsor' – see page 37) in the airport terminal and return with him to the immigration desk. If he isn't there, she might not be admitted.

Prohibited & Restricted Goods

The four major restrictions are on weapons, drugs, alcohol and what might be considered pornographic literature, either printed or recorded on video, DVD or CD. You should also avoid importing pig meat products (e.g. tinned ham), especially into Saudi Arabia (see page 314). Note, however, that the restrictions that apply to foreigners don't necessarily apply to nationals, especially those with influence.

Alcohol: The basic rule is not to bring alcohol into the region. As the consumption of alcohol is totally banned in Saudi Arabia, it's imperative that travellers don't attempt to carry alcohol of any description into the Kingdom. Until recently, even toiletries containing alcohol, such as aftershave, were confiscated by customs. The law isn't so strictly enforced now, but the penalties for carrying alcohol range from fines to delays and even imprisonment, at least while the case is being heard. Other Gulf states are more flexible on this issue. Bahrain and Dubai are likely to overlook the odd duty-free bottle, but you shouldn't take the risk of carrying one in Kuwait, Qatar, Abu Dhabi, Sharjah or Oman, where it would probably be confiscated. Alcohol is available in hotels in Bahrain, Oman, and Dubai, where it's reasonably priced (see **Alcohol** on page 287), and in all states except Kuwait and Saudi Arabia, most expatriates can obtain a liquor licence enabling them to purchase alcohol locally at special stores (see page 318).

Drugs: Most Gulf states carry a mandatory death penalty for those found in possession of 'recreational' drugs – both 'soft' and 'hard', including amphetamines, cannabis, cocaine, ecstasy, heroin, LSD and marijuana. Saudi Arabia is certainly the strictest, and the death penalty is likely to be imposed, the execution being carried out in public (if that's any consolation). Many of those who meet this fate are poorly-educated, manual workers from the sub-continent, who have been asked to carry a package for 'a relative', with terrible consequences. Other states tend to match the severity of the penalty with the quantity of drugs carried. If it's a small amount, obviously intended for personal use rather than trafficking, you might be let off with two or three years in prison. Westerners are sometimes released, especially if there's a sustained campaign to secure this through senior diplomatic channels, but don't count on it.

Although it shouldn't need repeating, you should never carry any packages into the region whose contents are unknown to you. Never deliver anything for anyone to the Gulf states unless you know exactly what it is.

It's also important to carry your doctor's prescription with you for any medicinal drugs that you're taking, as many are banned or allowed only in limited quantities in the Gulf. Even a seemingly innocuous medicine common in your own country can be prohibited; for example, tranquillisers and sleeping pills are illegal in much of the region. At best, these will be confiscated by customs officials; at worst, you could face fines and punishment. If in doubt, check in advance with the embassy or consulate of the country that you're planning to visit.

'Pornography': Magazines and newspapers found on most newsstands throughout the world won't necessarily be acceptable in the more restrictive atmosphere of the Gulf states. The interpretation of what constitutes salacious material varies widely. Once again, Saudi Arabia has the strictest rules, all luggage being opened for inspection at entry points: any images of uncovered parts of the female or male body, including arms and legs and certainly the bits in between, will be torn out by officials at the airport or the offending material confiscated. Even a seemingly innocuous publication such as **Time** or **Newsweek** might contain a photograph which is construed as being damaging to public morals. You should never attempt to import even soft pornography magazines.

As with magazines, any book whose content is deemed to be offensive, sexually explicit or politically sensitive (e.g. containing criticism of any of the Gulf states or of Islam) must not be imported. Similarly, religious material of faiths other than Islam is banned (as is public worship), so a copy of the Bible will be confiscated in Saudi Arabia.

No attempt should be made to conceal magazines, photographs and particularly videotapes, DVDs or CDs, as this might attract charges of attempted smuggling and could result in instant deportation. In Saudi Arabia the authorities often watch material immediatly at the airport. In most other states, they hold it for inspection, usually by the Ministry of Information. Having passed the inspection, it can be collected a day or two later. In order to avoid problems caused by such delays, business visitors are advised to send videotapes or similar materal (e.g. for presentations) by courier in advance of their visit, in addition to the copy they intend to take with them. The major courier companies have an arrangement with local customs allowing the courier services to inspect material prior to carriage and this system works quite well. (No courier will risk his licence being revoked by carrying illicit material.)

The import of literature needs to be considered very seriously, and taking risks is foolhardy to say the least. If caught, you will be dealt with by people unused to the leniency and flexibility common in other cultures, and you have little recourse to help.

Weapons & Ammunition: Firearms, swords and bomb-making equipment are banned and are confiscated, with penalties imposed. If you need to import a firearm, you must obtain an import licence and possession permit from the appropriate Ministry of the Interior, although it's unlikely that one will be granted.

EMBASSY REGISTRATION

Although there are mixed views as to how much assistance you're likely to receive from your embassy in times of difficulty, it's still wise to register with it on arrival if you're staying for more than a holiday. At the very least, embassies are a source of information; many have a commercial section, which can provide advice about doing business in the region, including details of commercial laws and taxes, as well as supplying useful contacts. In times of civil unrest, disorder or natural disaster, the embassy will be aware of your presence in the country and may help with evacuation. See also **Embassy, Consular & Legal Assistance** on page 338.

FINDING HELP

Help is readily available in Gulf communities. Newcomers are welcomed into the expatriate community, particularly in the more restrictive states, where foreigners tend to 'band together'. Thus you have access to a wealth of experience in dealing with schools, health services, clubs and associations, entertainment, etc.. Finance is a very common subject for discussion, and you most certainly will benefit from the investment advice and experience of those who have had long experience of tax-free salaries. You will also come across people keen to spend their money as quickly as possible, on boats, four-wheel drives, exotic holidays, etc..

CHECKLISTS

Before Arrival

The following checklist contains a summary of the tasks that should be completed before arrival in the region:

- Ensure that you have all necessary documents, including passports, visas, contract letter, marriage certificates and birth certificates (see page 72).

- Take certificates of your formal educational and professional qualifications.

- Check that your future employer has organised accommodation for you and who will pay for it (see **Chapter 5**). Also check whether you will be met on arrival.

- Arrange for shipment of your personal effects (see page 101) and find out who pays for this and for any excess baggage you will have on your flight.

- Check your existing contractual arrangements for medical and health insurance cover.

- Inform the tax office in your home country of your departure and review your home banking needs.

- Obtain an international driver's permit (IDP), as not all national licences are accepted in the region.

- Take some local currency for your immediate needs and also an international credit card, widely used in the region (see **Chapter 14**).

- Check whether your employer will provide an advance on your salary.

After Arrival

The following checklist contains a summary of tasks to be completed after arrival in the Gulf:

- Check the immigration date stamp in your passport to see how long you're permitted to stay. If the Islamic calendar is used, obtain a reliable conversion (see **Calendar** on page 332).

- Rent a car, if one isn't supplied by your firm (see page 192).

- Check that your sponsor/employer has started the paperwork necessary for your residence, as many matters depend on this (see **Chapter 3**).

- Open a local bank account (see page 232).

- Register at your embassy.

- Arrange schooling (see **Chapter 9**).
- Find a local doctor and dentist (**see Chapter 12**).
- Check the location of the nearest hospital.
- Arrange whatever insurance your employer doesn't take care of, e.g. health, home contents, car and third party liability (see **Chapter 13**).

5.

ACCOMMODATION

There's a wide range of apartments and villas available in the Gulf, both within and outside enclosed compounds (see below), but it should be noted from the outset that expatriates cannot own land or property in the Gulf states and therefore you will have no choice but to rent.

Most accommodation is in urban or suburban areas; the desert is for camels and the Bedouin. Most visitors are pleasantly surprised when they see the cities of the Gulf for the first time, their modern architecture co-existing with traditional houses and ancient wind-towers. New buildings are often spectacular, as oil has provided the money for the best architects, builders and materials. Indeed, there's competition between developers, who tend to be wealthy merchant families, to build the most impressive structure.

Many construction projects are under way and, when you're choosing accommodation, you should check whether further construction is planned on surrounding land, as the resulting noise, dust and general inconvenience can be intrusive, sometimes for 24 hours per day. Although programmes are continuing, however, fewer lower priced properties are being constructed, as the demand for unskilled workers in the region is declining.

TEMPORARY ACCOMMODATION

Your employer is likely to have organised temporary accommodation for you (and your family) while you settle into your new job and look for permanent housing. You will probably pay for this accommodation in the form of a deduction from your salary and it's in your interest to find permanent accommodation quickly, as fully furnished temporary accommodation can be expensive.

RELOCATION CONSULTANTS

Relocation consultants are most frequently used by multi-national companies and larger institutions moving into the region. Some consultants provide practical and cultural help to those new to the region. Culture shock is a real condition that affects many people unused to being outside their home country or culture. It can badly affect you in both your working and your family life.

Companies already operating in the Gulf don't usually require the services of consultants. (In a region whose workforce is largely foreign and transient, many companies and workers have long experience of moving and setting up in a new location.) However, employers are generally aware of the danger of culture shock and are ready to help when required.

The sensible newcomer spends the first few weeks of his contract settling in alone and doesn't commit his family to a move to the Gulf until he has obtained all the necessary permits (see **Chapter 3**), has completed his probationary period, if any (see page 65), and is able to judge whether he's going to enjoy the working and living conditions and whether his job is all that was promised. Note, however, that it can take three months or so to acclimatise to life in the Gulf, where it's normal to feel somewhat disorientated for the first few weeks. See also **Culture Shock** on page 338.

ARAB HOMES

The indigenous and expatriate populations tend not to live together. The Arab culture of extended families calls for large houses, and affluent families usually own detached villas. With up to three generations to accommodate, groups of two or more villas are common. The less well-off still prefer houses to apartments. A costly experiment was carried out in Saudi Arabia, in which groups of large apartment blocks were built to meet the needs of the local population in the vicinity of the major cities, but there were few takers. Local people were unused to this style of accommodation and didn't like being overlooked; there was also the problem of what to do with their animals. The indigenous population in most Gulf states is well provided with housing. Young newly-married couples are given low-cost loans and in some states these turn out to be gifts if the loans aren't repaid within a particular time limit.

Foreign workers tend to live in either compounds or apartments. The rapid development of the Gulf economies and the sudden influx of foreign workers meant that accommodation had to be constructed quickly, which meant that apartment blocks rather than individual houses were built. The term 'compound' refers to a group of houses or small, usually low-level, apartment blocks within a walled enclosure, rather like a private estate.

Some compounds are huge, and accommodation is usually available because of the continual movement of expatriates. Different compounds have different combinations of nationalities. Some have a cosmopolitan mix, others contain people from one nation only or perhaps from one social group or caste.

Depending on the size of the compound, the facilities may include a communal swimming pool, a restaurant and shop, tennis and squash courts and a gymnasium. Children might be catered for with a play area and there might be a form of community hall known as a *majlis* – the traditional Arab meeting area for visitors. Many compound houses are built in *majlis* style, with an area opening immediately from the front door where the men meet visitors and sit with them. The rest of the accommodation is to the sides or rear. (In Arab houses, women aren't seen unless the visitors are close relatives.)

Saudi Arabian expatriate life is invariably in compounds, and the choice of compound is very important, as you will spend most of your leisure time within its confines. In the United Arab Emirates (UAE), there are some compounds (mainly occupied by westerners) where the majority of accommodation consists of low-level apartment blocks. In Bahrain, Kuwait, Oman and Qatar there's a mixture of villas and compound dwellings, the latter comprising mainly villas and townhouses, with a few low-rise apartment blocks.

Separate apartment blocks, which tend to be higher than those within compounds, usually contain a high proportion of expatriates. A disadvantage of these is that they generally lack the extensive facilities found in most compounds and there may be fewer English-speaking people to 'show you the ropes' than in a compound. On the other hand, compounds can be rather ghetto-like, with a claustrophobic 'clubbiness', isolation from the local community and a lack of privacy.

The exterior and interior quality of buildings is high throughout the region, and improving as prospective landlords vie with each other to have the most attractive buildings. The average property is also more spacious than its equivalent in Europe or the USA. Rooms are generally large in all types of accommodation. Villas normally have generous patios and/or gardens, while apartment blocks have a swimming pool and gymnasium. Homes normally also have a better level and quality of maintenance than in western countries, due to the wide availability of low-paid labour.

A garage or covered carport for your vehicle is vital. With temperatures rising to 50°C (122°F) in the summer, a car left outside quickly becomes unbearably hot and the bodywork deteriorates if exposed to the sun for too long. Most new apartment blocks have underground car parking facilities and allocated spaces. Villas tend to have an attached or separate garage, or at least a carport.

BUYING PROPERTY

Buying your own property in the Gulf generally isn't an option, as only Gulf Co-operation Council (GCC) nationals can own land and property.

Therefore, all foreigners must rent their accommodation. Some long-term expatriates in the Gulf want to retire there, having become used to the excellent lifestyle and warm, sunny weather. Some of them manage to do this with the help of a long-standing sponsor who's prepared to continue the sponsorship as a gesture of friendship and reward for years of profitable association. A tiny minority circumvent the ownership law with a 'hidden' agreement with a friend who is a national, whereby the house is bought in the friend's name. This naturally requires a high degree of trust. There are calls for a revision of the property and land ownership restriction in the region, but as yet there are no signs of one.

RENTED ACCOMMODATION

The majority of property is rented unfurnished, whether it be a grand villa or a modest studio apartment. 'Unfurnished' might mean only the barest of essentials but is more likely to include a kitchen unit, curtain rails and lighting fixtures, or it might mean semi-furnished, with kitchen equipment, a cooker, refrigerator and washing machine. In most cases, it includes a television aerial socket with access to local stations and probably BBC and CNN via satellite; you might also have access to other networks and movie channels, although you might have to pay for them. There's also furnished property on the market, but it is harder to find and of course more expensive. Most people want a new property and there are plenty of them available.

Finding a Rental Property

Renting accommodation in the Gulf is a straightforward, well-established practice. Major international companies with trading links in the region often have housing arrangements in the form of long-term leases on properties for their staff. If you have to find your own accommodation, your sponsor and his staff will invariably help. There's considerable choice in all price bands and it's usually quite straightforward to find the type of property you want.

Having decided on a budget, you need to decide on the location of the property, weighing up the importance of access to your place of work, type and size of living space you want, whether villa or apartment, the number of bedrooms, etc.. Gulf cities are small by international standards and driving times between home and work are short, usually without substantial traffic jams.

There are a number of ways to find a rental property in the Gulf, including the following:

- Consult your company's human resources manager, work colleagues and friends. Word of mouth is usually the best recommendation in the region. Talk to members of any clubs and associations that you join.

- Check the notice boards outside accommodation blocks and look in the local English-language newspapers and magazines. Talk to porters or administration staff in the buildings that you like the look of. They will often know about the availability of accommodation.

- Consult estate agents. As well as having a wide knowledge of the market, area and costs, they generally provide transport and accompany you on viewings. Listen carefully to the proposed charges and in particular to the inclusions and exclusions, specifically the air-conditioning and utility charges. Ask for faxed confirmation before making a decision, and certainly before signing the contract.

- Estate agents are frequently the wives of sponsored expatriates, who have the time to get to know the area and the facilities on offer. This isn't the case in conservative Saudi Arabia, however, where you will depend more on pointers and recommendations from your firm and colleagues. If there's a local estate agent, it certainly won't be a female.

● Visit compounds, which frequently have an office of the company running it, and ask about availability and facilities.

Rental Costs

Rental costs vary enormously for villas of different sizes, some with swimming pools, others without, and between old and new apartment blocks, in good, bad and indifferent locations. However, rents don't vary a great deal between the different Gulf states. With plenty of new property being built, supply usually keeps pace with demand, and many Arabs are keen to rent property to expatriates, as it provides them with a regular, reliable income. Average monthly rents for good-quality unfurnished accommodation are shown below.

Type of Accommodation	Monthly Rent ($)
1-bedroom apartment	750–1,000
2-bedroom apartment	1,000–1,500
3-bedroom apartment	1,500–1,800
2/3-bedroom villa	1,800–2,250
4+-bedroom villa	2,250+

Furnished accommodation costs around 25 per cent more than the figures quoted above, and short-term lets are charged at a higher rate than longer ones. Serviced apartments are available in all states, although not widely, and cost between 30 and 50 per cent more than unserviced apartments; services normally include cleaning, laundry and linen-changing.

Air-conditioning might be included in the rent or be charged separately as part of your electricity bill. If there's a communal gas tank, gas is usually included in the rent. Otherwise, you can buy gas bottles (see page 105). Other utilities will be separate. (Water is usually charged as part of the electricity bill – see page 104). **You should check these items at the time of negotiation and on the contract.** You or your sponsor must also pay a deposit against damage to the property or to items of furnishing provided.

Note also that some states impose a local tax (*baladiya*) on property to cover expenses such as refuse collection and road maintenance. Whether the landlord or the tenant pays is one of the matters to sort out in the contract, although normally the property owner bears the cost.

Rental Contracts

It's usual for the rental contract to be drawn up with the owner of the property using your sponsor as the principal. There are a number reasons for this:

- Long-term contracts are usually for a one-year period, while short-term ones are from one month upwards. With a transient expatriate population, owners prefer to deal with a permanent citizen of their country, i.e. your sponsor, in case there are disputes to be resolved.

- Contracts usually call for advance payment, one or two cheques being issued, one of which is post-dated six months ahead. In the case of employees, the standard practice is for their employers to make the rental payments and then deduct monthly sums from the employee's wages.

- If the contract has to be terminated early, responsibility for doing so lies with the principal, which is, of course, in the interest of the expatriate. The owner might insist on his finding a replacement tenant, which can be difficult; your sponsor will be able to exert more influence with the owner than you would, particularly if the sponsor is a regular renter.

   Note that changing your accommodation mid-contract is always tricky, so you should choose your accommodation carefully in the first place to avoid the necessity to move.

In most rental contracts, there's a standard clause about returning the property in a reasonable condition, allowing for normal wear and tear. Any losses or damage must be made good. Anti-social behaviour such as noise or abuse of property will probably mean eviction. Expatriates are usually well-behaved, knowing that their hosts have little tolerance of bad or criminal behaviour.

Inventory

Furnished apartments are equipped with a wide range of goods, usually of reasonable quality. A copy of the inventory will be provided with the contract and items checked when you leave, with charges made for damage or losses. The return of your deposit depends on whether or not the property is left in good order.

HOME SECURITY

Security isn't a major issue in the Gulf, which is generally is a safe environment for everyone, including children. The entire region is well policed, serious crime is rare and attacks on people rarer still. Penalties for criminal offences are severe and discourage crime. Nevertheless, most homes have security doors with an intercom system, and apartment doors have a security 'peep-hole'. Apartment blocks also have front desk staff, security personnel and night watchmen.

MOVING HOUSE

Your initial move to the Gulf is unlikely to involve transporting much furniture. This is because people invariably come out initially for two or three months before deciding whether to move for a longer term. Even then, many expatriates don't sell their homes, but rent them furnished. If you do want to move furniture and other bulky items to the Gulf, shipments by sea are likely to take around a month from door to door.

There are plenty of freight, removal and shipping companies who transport goods to the Gulf. Note that your employer will probably insist on your obtaining at least three quotations, and make sure that your allowance for moving includes comprehensive insurance. Seek insurance quotes from independent brokers; freight carriers usually offer insurance, but the cover tends to be limited and expensive.

Even if you aren't moving all your possessions, however, you will need to take clothing, china and crockery, books, ornaments and familiar items with you in order to turn your new house in the Gulf into a home. Electrical goods are best purchased in the Gulf and are inexpensive because of import low taxes on these goods. Your TV set will probably not work in the region, so don't bother to take it.

It's important to make it clear that you require a door-to-door service and not just delivery to a seaport or airport. Some agents are vague on this issue and you should obtain an agreement in writing. Otherwise, you might have to handle the import formalities yourself, which can be a frustrating, time-consuming exercise. In fact, it will probably cost you money, as you might need to hire somebody to do it for you. You also need to keep an eye on the handling agent at the Gulf end to ensure that he doesn't try to wriggle out of taking the goods all the way to your home.

Some companies offer a 'turn-key' operation, which means that they provide the packing cases, pack the items to be carried in your home country, ship the goods, unpack them in the Gulf and set them up in your new home. All you do is turn up and open the front door. Check, however, that the company also handles all the formalities, customs declarations and payment of duties.

Moving house within a Gulf state is straightforward. The cheapest method is to pack your own possessions and hire one of the many operators with a small van to transport them. There are also plenty of local companies with the facilities to handle larger moves.

It goes without saying that none of the prohibited or restricted items such as drugs, alcohol, firearms or pornographic material (see page 85) should be brought into the region or moved within it. The contents of your packing cases and boxes will be searched at customs, and the penalties for being caught with any of these items are severe; in addition, you will probably lose your job. No sponsor will stand up for you if you break the law, as he risks losing face with his peers: his judgement will be questioned as to the type of person he has hired.

ELECTRICITY

The pressure on the electricity supply has been enormous in recent years because of the vast construction and industrial projects being undertaken throughout the region, as well as the demands of increasing numbers of people coming to live there. Until recently, the electricity supply in many Gulf states suffered from regular 'outages', particularly at the height of summer and in Kuwait. Not only would air-conditioning cut out, causing discomfort in the summer heat (people were sometimes reduced to getting in their cars to drive around with the air-conditioning on at full blast!), but there could be a costly loss of food in fridges and freezers. Recently, however, the electricity supply has improved considerably, and outages are rarer than they used to be, although they still occur when demand for air-conditioning is at its peak.

Registration

The electricity companies, which are usually also responsible for water, are efficiently run. When you move into a new home, you must register with them (usually requiring your passport, work or residence visa and accommodation rental contract) and ask for reconnection if the supply has been switched off. The addresses are as follows:

> **Bahrain:** Ministry of Electricity and Water, PO Box 2, Manama, ☎ 973-533 133.
> **Kuwait:** Ministry of Electricity, Water and Public Works, PO Box 12, Safat, 13001 Kuwait, ☎ 965-489 6000.
> **Oman:** Ministry of Electricity and Water (MEW), PO Box 1491, Ruwi 112, ☎ 968-603 800.
> **Qatar:** Ministry of Electricity and Water, PO Box 41, Doha, ☎ 974-410 613.
> **Saudi Arabia:** Ministry of Industry and Electricity, PO Box 5729, Riyadh 11127, ☎ 966-1-477 6666.
> **UAE:** Dubai Electricity and Water Authority, PO Box 564, Dubai, ☎ 971-4-348 888.

The meter must be read and the name on the account changed to yours. If the supply has been disconnected, you're liable for a reconnection charge. In some apartment blocks, the outgoing tenant is advised not to have the supply disconnected, so all you need to do is note the meter reading on your arrival. The owner will have ensured that the outgoing tenant has paid up to the time of his departure. Note that most large companies employ messenger boys who handle most dealings with the utility companies for you.

In some states you're required to pay a deposit, which is returned or credited to you after your final bill is settled. For example, in Kuwait, this is around KD100 ($330) and in Qatar around QR2,000 ($550). Non-payers who try to exit the country sometimes find that the authorities at the airport have been notified to look out for them.

Power Supply

The power supply throughout the region is 220v AC, although some buildings in Saudi Arabia have the American standard 110v AC supply to most (American-style) sockets and additional sockets supplying

220/240v by means of a step-up transformer. **Using a 110v appliance with a supply of 220v is obviously very dangerous.** Any appliance with a 240v AC standard will operate with the 220v supply. For computers, fax machines and similar sensitive equipment it's recommended that you use a voltage surge protector.

Wiring Standards

Almost all property in the Gulf is modern, having been built in the last two decades, much of it in the past five years. Therefore standards of installation are high and the work has been officially inspected and can be relied on.

Meters

Whether you live in an apartment block or a villa, you have your own meter. Generally these are sited in the basement or in a meter cabinet on each floor.

Plugs, Fuses & Bulbs

Throughout the Gulf, plug sockets are mainly three-pin and UK plugs will fit. In Saudi Arabia, there's a mixture of 220v and 110v AC supplies — many houses have both — and the 110v sockets accommodate American plugs. When purchasing electrical goods, you will find both voltages on offer because imports come from a variety of sources. Adaptors are available. Light bulbs are available with bayonet and screw fittings; you might have both types of fitting in your property. Appliances usually have fused plugs, and most properties have a circuit-breaker, which 'trips out' in the event of a short circuit. Large fuses are usually the earth trip type, and fuses of all sizes and amperages are easily obtainable.

Electricity Bills

Usually sent every month or every two months, bills are based on average consumption, with adjustments made for the actual amount of power used. They cover electricity and water, with an allowance for waste water (sewage — see page 106). The bills include the date of the reading, the previous metered consumption, the current metered consumption, the cost per unit and the charges for the period shown.

GAS

Electricity is the main source of power in most houses, with gas a backup for cooking. Many cookers have both electric hot-plates and a gas hob. (This duplicate system was adopted when electrical 'outages' were more frequent than they are now – see above.) There are no mains gas supplies in the region, but bottled gas is widely available with regular, countrywide deliveries. An initial deposit secures a contract and after an inspection of the proposed installation, a bottle exchange system operates. The gas supply business is very competitive in the region and there are plenty of companies vying for custom, but there's little to choose between them. Some apartment blocks have large butane gas tanks and the supply might be included in your rent.

WATER

Water from natural sources is in limited supply in this arid region and is totally inadequate for the Gulf's ever increasing demands. Large desalination plants along the coasts are the region's main source of water, and new plants are being built in most states.

Natural water supplies do exist, however, and there are many companies marketing bottled water, which has been checked for purity. The business is highly competitive, and each brand has its own distinctive taste – at least according to connoisseurs. Bottled water is used mainly for drinking and sometimes also for cooking. It usually comes in 500ml and 1.5 litre bottles, and there are regular deliveries of 5 and 20-litre containers to offices and homes. Tap water is used for cleaning, washing and some cooking; it's drinkable but can taste of chlorine. Note also that local tap water contains certain minerals which have been shown to cause kidney stones, of which there's a high incidence in the Gulf.

Water tanks are usually located on the roof of apartment blocks and villas, meaning that at the height of summer the water is hot. The water in the cold tap comes from this tank, but water from the hot tap, which passes through an internal boiler, is cool if the boiler is switched off – which means that if you want a cool shower in summer, you should use the cold tap until the hot water from the tank above enters the system, at which point you switch to the hot tap until it runs hot!

Advertising campaigns promote awareness of the need to use water sparingly, although Bahrainis consume more water per head of population than the inhabitants of any other country (they claim to be the world's cleanest people!). Nevertheless, the water supply is maintained continuously without much evidence of shortages. If shortages do occur, it's generally more to do with the pumping arrangements than a lack of water.

SEWAGE

Newer properties in urban areas are normally connected to mains sewage, whereas most older and rural properties have septic tanks, which must be emptied regularly. Charges for mains sewage disposal are usually small and are billed with those for electricity and water. In the case of tanker disposal, this should be included in your rent and payed by the owner.

RUBBISH DISPOSAL

Rubbish disposal is very efficient in the Gulf states. It needs to be, as the heat and high humidity would quickly create smells and attract vermin, leading to disease. Rubbish pick-ups are usually daily, very early in the morning. Apartment blocks tend to have chute systems: bagged rubbish is put in a chute to the basement. Villas have 'wheelie' bins or skips.

AIR-CONDITIONING

Air-conditioning is essential in the Gulf. With temperatures commonly reaching 40°C (104°F) and sometimes approaching 50°C (122°F) in summer, it would be impossible to live comfortably without it. Arabs are generally keen to resist major changes to their culture, but they are prepared to accept the benefits that technology has brought. Consequently air-conditioning is everywhere: in homes, workplaces, shopping centres and, of course, cars.

There are many types of air-conditioning, ranging from old fashioned, noisy, wall-mounted units, which vent hot air through a wall opening, to modern, whisper-quiet, central conditioning units. Split-level and floor units positioned in various rooms are efficient, but the most effective method is a central unit, usually temperature-controlled and probably almost silent as it's located away from your living space. The cost of central air-conditioning might be included in your rent, but this isn't always the case. If your home is metered separately, the electricity used is included in your standard bill.

Some expatriates make the mistake of leaving the air-conditioning on while they're out but this is both costly and unnecessary. If you switch your air-conditioner to high power for a few minutes when you return, it quickly cools the air to an acceptable temperature. Air-conditioning units are cleaned and serviced annually, in both homes and cars. This usually takes place around March, before the start of the long, hot summer.

Humidifiers are also widely available in the region and are useful for very young children and asthma sufferers.

HEATING

You're unlikely to need to heat your home very often. Freak conditions occasionally bring snow to the most northern parts of the region, but this is rare. Some air-conditioning units are dual-purpose and also act as heaters, but most people keep an electric fire for those rare occasions when heating is needed.

6.

POST OFFICE SERVICES

The efficiency of the postal service varies from state to state, although it's usually adequate but slow. Most post handled by the post office is personal, as international companies requiring a quick, efficient service usually use one of the major international courier companies instead (see **Courier Services** on page 116).

Post offices are found in most cities and major towns throughout the region. There tends to be a large central post office and a number of smaller sub-post offices in various parts of the town and its suburbs.

Note that there's no door-to-door postal delivery service in the Gulf, and you must collect personal post from the post office (see Post Delivery & Collection on page 113).

During Ramadan (see **National Holidays** on page 348), when working hours are reduced and workers become tired because of daytime fasting, the postal service experiences (even) more delays than usual and it can take up to a month to clear the backlog and return to normal.

Note also that financial services aren't available at the region's post offices and are offered only by the banks and some exchange bureaux (see **Chapter 14**).

CENSORSHIP

Incoming post is sometimes checked, the Gulf authorities being especially keen to intercept anything deemed to have pornographic content (see **'Pornography'** on page 87). At best, the offending article will be confiscated; at worst, you will be faced with a criminal charge, which is particularly likely in Saudi Arabia. Standard-size letters are usually unaffected, but any envelopes containing a magazine are examined – either through cuts made at the corners of the envelope or (increasingly) more thoroughly.

Make sure that post sent by known correspondents doesn't contain any material that might be considered offensive.

BUSINESS HOURS

Opening hours for post offices in most states are 7.30am to 12.30pm and 4.30 to 7pm, six days a week (excluding Fridays), although some main post offices don't close for lunch and offer a service between 4 and 6pm on Fridays.

DELIVERY & COLLECTION

There's no door-to-door postal delivery service in the Gulf, and you must normally collect your own post from your local post office. You should obtain a post office (PO) box number and instruct correspondents to use this rather than your street address. (If incoming post has a street address rather than a post office box number, the post office might eventually deliver it, but don't rely on this.) Note that collecting post from the post office can be a frustrating experience owing to often long queues, and it's preferable to have letters addressed to your employer's or sponsor's PO box number and ask administrative staff collect them for you, once or twice a day (there are usually two deliveries daily to PO boxes). Outgoing post can be handled in the same way through the company.

Note also that, although a post office is supposed to hold all your post until you collect it, if your box is full it's likely that some or all of it will be 'lost'. It's therefore advisable, if you're unable to use your employer's or sponsor's PO box, to have someone collect your post regularly when you're away for more than a few days. Post cannot be redirected in the Gulf.

Airmail delivery times from Europe to the Gulf vary between four or five days and a week. Post from the UK is usually the quickest owing to the greater frequency and volume of air traffic between the UK and the Gulf. US and Australian post takes around ten days. Parcels take longer, adding around a week to the average letter delivery time. Local post is usually quite quick, as there's no door-to-door delivery service. (Incidentally, those looking to promote their business via direct post can do so easily and cheaply thanks to the centralised box delivery system.)

Postage stamps are sold at post offices and some book shops. Hotels send letters for their guests and either supply stamps or make a charge for using their franking machines.

Note also the following general points regarding the collection and delivery of post:

● Make sure that regular correspondents address your post clearly.

● Put your address on all outgoing post.

- All outgoing post should be in a substantial envelope or wrapping. Note, however, that there are no official guidelines as to how packages should be wrapped, nor are wrapping materials available at post offices.

- Ensure that an airmail (*par avion*) label is affixed to all international post that you send.

PARCEL POST

To send or receive a parcel, you must go to a post office. Note, however, that parcel post should be used only for items that are neither urgent nor valuable. The Mumtaz service (see **Courier Services** on page 116) is quicker and more reliable.

You will receive notification by postcard when a parcel arrives and you must prove your identity in order to collect it. You should take your driving licence, work visa, passport or residence visa or permit. Officially, parcels addressed to individuals must be collected by the addressee personally, although you can sometimes send somebody on your behalf (but not always!). In this case, you should ensure that the person collecting the parcel has a collection slip signed by you, a letter of authorisation from you and one of the above documents (belonging to you), as well as identification of his own.

CHARGES

The following is a guide to postal charges in the Gulf, although these are subject to change:

Bahrain

The price for sending postcards is 155 fils ($0.40) to Europe and 205 ($0.55) fils to North America and Australasia. Letters cost 205 fils per 10g to Europe and 255 fils ($0.65) per 10g to North America and Australasia. Parcels cost a minimum of BD3 ($8) for the first 500g to all western destinations, BD1 ($2.65) for each extra 500g to Europe and BD1.5 ($4) for each extra 500g to North America and Australasia.

Kuwait

Letters and postcards weighing up to 20g cost 150 fils ($0.30) to all destinations outside the Arab world. Letters and cards weighing between 20g and 50g cost 280 fils ($0.55). Parcel rates vary considerably according to the destination.

Oman

Postcards to destinations outside the Arab world cost 150 baiza ($0.40). Letters weighing up to 10g cost 200 baiza ($0.50) and those between 10g and 20g 350 baiza ($0.90). Small packages sent outside the Arab world cost between OR2 ($5.20) and OR4 ($10.40), while packages of 1kg cost between OR4 and OR6 ($15.60).

Qatar

Postcards sent to most western destinations cost QR1 ($0.25). Letters up to 10g cost QR2 ($0.50), with an extra QR2 for each extra 10g. The first 1kg of parcels costs QR73 ($19.70) to Europe and North America and QR88 ($23.75) to Australasia. Each extra kg costs QR27 ($7.30) to Europe, QR50 ($13.50) to Australasia and QR57 ($15.40) to North America.

Saudi Arabia

Postcards cost 50 halalas ($0.15) within Saudi Arabia, SR1 ($0.30) internationally. Within Saudi Arabia and the Arab world, letters cost 75 halalas ($0.20) for the first 10g and 50 halalas ($0.15) for each extra 10g. Airmail letters to destinations outside the Arab world cost SR1.5 ($0.40) for the first 10g and SR.1 ($0.30) for each extra 10g.

UAE

Postcards cost Dh1 ($0.25) to Arab countries and Dh2 ($0.50) to most western countries. Letters up to 20g are Dh2.5 ($0.65) to the Indian subcontinent, Dh3 ($0.75) to Europe and Dh3.5 ($0.95) to Asia, Australia and the USA. A 1kg package costs Dh68 ($18.35) to the Indian subcontinent, Dh85 ($23) to Europe and Dh130 ($35) to Asia, Australasia and the USA.

REGISTERED POST

You can send and receive registered post in all the Gulf states, although in both cases it requires attendance at a post office. As with parcels, you're notified of receipt of a registered item and must provide proof of identity on collection. You must also sign to confirm receipt. It's advisable to send legal, contractual and other important documents by international courier (see **Courier Services** below).

The cost of registration varies but is around $1.75 in most states except Saudi Arabia, where a registered item costs just SR2 ($0.55) within the Kingdom/Arab world and SR3 ($0.80) to other destinations.

COURIER SERVICES

Virtually all important post in the Gulf, e.g. documents, legal and financial papers, and contracts, is sent via one of the international courier companies. This applies to local, regional and international post. The major courier companies operating in the region are Aramex, DHL, Fedex, TNT and UPS. In Saudi Arabia, DHL operates as SNAS in Saudi Arabia (these being the initials of the one of the Defence Minister's sons!) and has a virtual monopoly of courier services.

The various state postal services also offer their own courier service called Mumtaz (meaning 'super'), which is part of the international EMS service. This is around 30 per cent cheaper than the courier companies, but the service isn't as fast and doesn't have the same level of accountability: if an item goes astray, you're likely to be met with indifference, the post office being a government department.

7.

TELEPHONE

Telecommunication systems throughout the Gulf are excellent, both technologically and in the comprehensive range of services offered. At the time of the oil boom, it was realised that state-of-the-art telecommunications systems would be of major long-term importance in building the Gulf economies, and vast resources were made available to pay for them.

The Gulf states all operate their telephone systems as monopolies and are therefore free to charge what they want and offer whatever services they choose. Nevertheless, the systems are well run and maintained. Local calls are usually free and international calls are reasonably priced, although some observers claim that international call charges are an indirect taxation on expatriates. International call-back facilities are also available, through companies such as MCI and Switch/AT&T. Charges are made for satellite time even if contact with your international number isn't established, but these charges are quite low. Coin, card payphones and mobile services are available in all states.

EMERGENCY & SERVICE NUMBERS

The emergency services are usually combined under one contact number, the required service being contacted by the telephone operator (who will speak English as well as Arabic), although Saudi Arabia has separate numbers for police, ambulance and fire.

Current emergency numbers are as follows:

- **Bahrain:** 999.
- **Kuwait:** 777.
- **Oman:** 999.
- **Qatar:** 999.
- **Saudi Arabia:** Police 999, Fire 998, Ambulance 997.
- **UAE:** 999.

Emergency numbers can be found in the opening pages of all directories, as well as in tourist guides and daily newspapers, although it's advisable to keep a note of them close to your telephone for easy access in emergencies.

Telephone service numbers are published in the front of all directories and are also usually printed on the back of telephone bills. directory enquiries numbers are listed under **Using the Telephone** below.

INSTALLATION & REGISTRATION

You need work and residence visas in order to have a telephone installed in your home. Applications require a completed application form, a copy of your passport and residence visa or permit and, in some instances, a copy of your tenancy contract, together with the appropriate fee. If your tenancy agreement is in your employer's or sponsor's name (which is usually the case), you will also need a 'no objection certificate' (NOC) from him, as responsibility for non-payment or any other problems rests with him. The application form includes details about the number, type and colour of telephones required.

Installation is usually fairly quick in Bahrain and the UAE, where you can expect to be connected within a week. It takes longer in other states, however, and in Saudi Arabia installation usually takes around six months and can take up to a year; you have little option but to wait (and use a mobile phone in the interim – see page 127).

Installation charges in the different states and the companies to contact for further information are as follows:

- **Bahrain:** The charge for business and personal telephones is BD20 ($53). Full details of services and charges can be obtained from the Bahrain Telecommunications Company (BATELCO), PO Box 14, Manama (☎ 973-884 337, 💻 www.batelco.com);

- **Kuwait:** Installation charges include a refundable deposit of KD500 (£1,000). Details can be obtained from the Ministry of Communications, PO Box 318, Safat, 11111 (☎ 965-481 9033);

- **Oman:** Installation costs OR18 ($48) and requires a deposit of OR400 ($1,040) or, alternatively, an employer's letter of guarantee. Details can be obtained from the Oman Telecommunications Company (OMANTEL), Ministry of Posts, Telegraphs and Telephones, PO Box 789, Ruwi, PC 112 (☎ 968-696 844, 💻 www.oman tel.net.om);

- **Qatar:** The installation charge is QR200 ($54). Details can be obtained from the Qatar Public Telecommunications Corporation, PO Box 217, Doha (☎ 974-400 333, 💻 www.qtel.com.qa);

- **Saudi Arabia:** Installation charges are unpredictable. Details can be obtained from the Ministry of Communications, PO Box 3813, Riyadh 11178 (☎ 966-1-404 3000) or a local Saudi Telephone Company office, although you will need to be able to speak Arabic;

- **UAE:** Installation costs AED250 ($67.50). Details can be obtained from the Emirates Telecommunications Corporation (ETISALAT), PO Box 3838, Abu Dhabi (☎ 971-2-208 4753, 💻 www.etisalat.co.ae) or any ETISALAT office in the Emirates.

You must rent telephones from the national telephone company, which costs around $15 (£10) per quarter.

USING THE TELEPHONE

Country and area dialling codes, directory enquiries and other service numbers are listed below, by state.

Bahrain

- International dialling code: 973
- Being a small country, Bahrain has no area or city codes, although phone numbers usually indicate the district.
- Local directory enquiries: 181
- International directory enquiries: 191

Kuwait

- International dialling code: 965
- No area codes.
- All directory enquiries: 101
- General enquiries: 484

Oman

- International dialling code: 968
- No area codes.
- Local directory enquiries: 198
- International directory enquiries: 143

Qatar

- International dialling code: 974
- No area codes.
- All directory enquiries: 180

Saudi Arabia

- International dialling code: 966
- Area codes:
  - Riyadh 01
  - Mecca, Jeddah, Taif 02
  - Al Khobar, Dammam, Dhahran, Jubail, Hofuf 03
  - Madinah, Sakaka, Tabuk, Yanbu 04
  - Buraidah, Hail, Qassim 06
  - Abha, Al-Baha, Jizran, Najran 07
- Local directory enquiries: 905
- International directory enquiries: 900

United Arab Emirates

- International dialling code: 971
- Area codes:
  - Abu Dhabi 02
  - Al-Ain 03
  - Dubai, Jebel Ali 04

- Ajman, Sharjah, Umm Al-Quwain 06
- Ras Al-Khaimah 07
- Hatta 085
- Liwa Oasis 088
- Dibba, Fujairah, Khor Fakkan 09

● All directory enquiries: 180

INTERNATIONAL CALLS

All the region's states have the international direct dialling (IDD) facility, with immediate connection via satellite links. Occasionally there's congestion, mainly at weekends, when cheaper rates apply and many expatriates are trying to phone home. Call-back operations such as MCI and Switch/AT&T are also available, but with state monopolies in control of telecommunications, most services operate through them. Satellite phones are available in all states except Saudi Arabia, where they're illegal, but must be registered with the national telephone company (see under **Installation & Registration** on page 121).

CUSTOMISED & OPTIONAL SERVICES

Most of the standard customised and optional telephone services are available in all states, depending on the type of telephone that you choose. Services and charges in the UAE, which are typical of those throughout the region, are listed below.

Call Barring: You can bar either local or international calls (or both) from your telephone. There's no set-up charge but the service costs AED50 ($13.50) per quarter.

Call Forwarding: You can have all calls forwarded to another number or only calls received while your line is busy or when you don't answer within a certain time. Set-up is free and the service costs AED15 ($4) per quarter.

Call Waiting: When you're on the line, a signal tells you that another caller is trying to reach you. Charges are the same as for call forwarding.

CLIP: This service displays and stores the caller's number. Charges as for call forwarding.

Conference Calls: Allows you to conduct a three-way conversation. Charges as for call forwarding.

Do Not Disturb: All calls are diverted to a recorded announcement. Charges as for call forwarding.

The **Star** package offers call forwarding (on all calls), call waiting and conference calls for a quarterly charge of AED 30 ($8).

CALL CHARGES

● **Bahrain:** There's a quarterly rental charge of BD3.5 ($9.30) for homes and BD6.5 ($17.20) for businesses. Calls within Bahrain cost 100 fils ($0.25) for six minutes. International calls cost 510 fils ($1.35) per minute to most western destinations, reduced to 390 fils ($1) between 7pm and 7am from Saturdays to Thursdays, and all day on Fridays and public holidays.

● **Kuwait:** Local calls are free.

- **Oman:** Local calls of up to three minutes cost 25 baizas ($0.06), calls to other Gulf states 300 baizas ($0.80) per minute and calls to Europe and North America OR1 ($2.60) per minute.

- **Qatar:** Line rental costs QR100 ($27) quarterly. Local calls cost around 50 dirhams ($0.15). Direct-dial calls to Europe and North America cost around QR7 ($1.90) per minute and QR9 ($2.45) to Australasia. Rates are cheaper from 8pm to 7am on Saturdays to Thursdays and all day on Fridays and public holidays.

- **Saudi Arabia:** For details of call charges, contact from the Ministry of Communications, PO Box 3813, Riyadh 11178 (☎ 966-1-404 3000) or a local Saudi Telephone Company office.

- **UAE:** There's a quarterly line rental charge of AED45 ($12.15). Local calls are free.

BILLS

Across the region, billing is generally monthly, with payment made at the offices of the national telephone company. In some states, e.g. the UAE, payment can also be made through banks, although standing order facilities aren't yet available (there are plans for these) and you must arrange for someone else to pay your bills for you if you're away for an extended period. Grace periods for payment vary from 14 days to a month from the date of issue of the bill, after which disconnection takes place and there's a reconnection charge. Call charges are usually broken down by category – peak, off-peak and international.

DIRECTORIES

Each state issues a telephone directory, either as part of or separately from a commercial directory, such as yellow pages, which is published under licence from the appropriate Ministry of Communications. Directories are usually published every two years, which means that they aren't completely reliable as far as expatriate numbers are concerned (the foreign population being largely transient). However, the directory enquiries services provided by the various telephone companies are generally up-to-date. Directories are free and should be delivered, but the service is often erratic and it's better to collect a copy from the Ministry of Telecommunications.

PUBLIC TELEPHONES

Despite the continuing march of the mobile phone, public telephones are fairly widely available throughout the region, located on the street and in shopping malls, restaurants and shops. Calls can be paid for with coins, phone cards or, sometimes with credit cards. With many states offering free local calls, however, it's quite common to ask to use a private telephone in a shop or at a reception desk if you're calling a local number. For public telephones the procedure is standard:

- Check the dialling tone;
- Insert coins or card;
- Dial the number;
- In the case of a credit card payment, follow the instructions on the display.

MOBILE PHONES

Mobile phones are widely in use throughout the region (where it isn't unusual to see a conservatively dressed Arab woman, covered from head to foot in a black *abaya*, using the most up-to-date mobile phone), and all states offer mobile services through their national telephone companies. International mobile phone brands, including the latest models, are also available at competitive prices owing to the absence of tax. GSM chips are available for local use as well as 'roving' chips for calling overseas.

FAX, TELEGRAMS & TELEX

The national telephone companies of all the region's states provide telegram and telex services, although these are rapidly being superseded by the Internet and other forms of communication. These and fax services are available through hotels. Video conferencing facilities aren't widely available in the Gulf.

INTERNET

Internet services are available through the national telephone companies, which act as servers and are thus able to regulate the websites you may access. Not surprisingly, services in Saudi Arabia are the most restricted and you may not even be able to visit sites dealing with religion (other than Islam) or fashion. Users must have a fixed telephone line, and there are charges time spent on-line as well as the usual line installation and rental charges.

Charges are currently high in all states. In the UAE, for example, you might pay around AED200 ($55) to register with a service provider and AED85 ($23) for up to 14 hours' Internet access and thereafter AED6 ($1.65) per hour (there are no peak or off-peak times). However, as the Internet is a fairly recent introduction to the region, its administration and charges are in a fluid state. Further details can be obtained from the appropriate telecommunications authorities (see under **Installation & Registration** on page 121).

8.

TELEVISION & RADIO

Gulf Arabs are avid television (TV) viewers and are particularly keen on the many 'soaps' aired daily. The modest level of literacy in some states might contribute to this, as does the 'resistance' to work that some local people have. Women in certain states cannot go to work and have little option but to stay at home and watch TV, or visit relatives . . . who are probably watching TV.

Terrestrial and satellite TV channels are widely accessible throughout the region, and all viewers, both local and expatriate, have an impressive selection of channels to choose from. No independent television stations exist at present and it's unlikely that they will in the foreseeable future. The region's more conservative states, such as Saudi Arabia and Oman, initially tried to resist the onslaught of television (as they're now doing with the Internet). Oman wanted to avoid a consumer boom led by television advertising, while Saudi Arabia wished to control the effect of liberal foreign programmes on its culture. However, the advent of satellite television changed the situation dramatically, as state control became impossible. Although satellite dishes are officially banned in Saudi Arabia, Qatar and Bahrain, this isn't strictly enforced and the Saudi-backed MBC station is widely viewed throughout the Arab world (see **Satellite TV** on page 134).

All Gulf states have a national television company broadcasting in Arabic and English. Content is generally poor (even by western standards), many programmes being old and out-of-date. To make matters worse, programmes are often badly dubbed or subtitled. The situation is changing, however, as a greater number of modern international programmes as well as better quality, locally produced material is broadcast. State television avoids controversial subjects, and news bulletins invariably lead with stories about the ruling families and government business rather than international affairs. Throughout the region, state television cannot compete for audiences with satellite channels.

There are also plenty of radio stations in the region, although reception is mainly limited to urban areas (see **Radio** on page 136).

There are no TV or radio licence fees, and all funding comes from government or commercial sources.

TELEVISION

The Gulf states use the PAL standard, but the vast majority of TV sets and video casette recorders (VCRs) on the market in the region are of the multi-band variety, capable of receiving transmissions on PAL-1 (British), PAL-BG (European), Secam (French) and NTSC (American) systems.

It isn't worth importing TVs and VCRs into the region, as they're unlikely to work properly and are cheap to buy locally. The prices of TVs and VCRs vary to some extent between the states in the region but, as no tax is added, they're usually at least 10 per cent and up to 30 per cent cheaper than in western countries. The United Arab Emirates, with its large number of Asian expatriates, probably offers the best deals. However, if you intend to take home a TV or VCR purchased locally, it's important to check that it will work there. For example, you might find that you have a picture but no sound, although this can usually be rectified easily and cheaply with audio filters, available from the manufacturer's agents in your country. Note that your supplier might not be a reliable source of information on this subject.

Television sets come in all sizes and designs and are usually state-of-the-art, with integrated VCRs and flat or wide screens. Renting equipment isn't an option, owing to the low cost of buying equipment and the administrative difficulties of dealing with a transient market.

Terrestrial TV

There are two or three terrestrial stations in each state, except in Oman, which has only one, and the UAE, which has eight. All terrestrial stations are state-controlled and come under the remit of the Ministries of Information. Government control has a considerable influence on the content of programmes, particularly news bulletins. One exception is the local station covering the oilfields of the eastern province of Saudi Arabia (reception extends to nearby Bahrain), which is run by ARAMCO, the Arabian American Oil Company. However, its programmes are also rather bland, consisting, as might be expected, mainly of American re-runs. All stations in the region carry commercial advertising.

Bahrain: There are three channels: Channel 4 is the Arabic-language channel; Channel 55 is for English viewers (from late afternoon) and Channel 57 relays BBC Worldwide programmes during its 24-hour broadcasts. Depending on the weather conditions and the quality of your aerial, other English-language broadcasts from neighbouring Gulf stations can also be received.

Kuwait: There are three channels, two in Arabic and one in English.

Oman: There's only one channel, broadcasting mainly in Arabic, with an English-language news bulletin every evening and some English-language films.

Qatar: There are two channels, one in Arabic and one in English. The latter broadcasts from the late afternoon.

Saudi Arabia: There are two channels, one in Arabic and one in English. The English channel, Channel 2, has old-fashioned content and commercial breaks can last up to 20 minutes (in some cases they're more enjoyable than the programmes!). Viewers in the Eastern Province can also receive Channel 3, the ARAMCO TV station (see above).

UAE: There are television broadcasts from Abu Dhabi, Dubai and Sharjah. Channel 33, which broadcasts from Dubai in English, is the most popular station for English-speaking expatriates, with reasonably good programmes, most of them international but some local productions covering major news and sports events.

Satellite TV

There are 20 Arabic and 5 non-Arabic satellite stations available in the Gulf, broadcast from many locations, including Lebanon, Egypt, London and Rome. There are two types of satellite broadcast: commercial channels, available only via satellite, and government terrestrial stations which also broadcast on satellite, although with coverage limited to domestic boundaries. Digital TV is also available via satellite with a digital decoder.

Free-to-air satellite stations include BBC, CNN, MBC (London), LBC (Lebanon), ESC (Egypt), Future (Lebanon), Dubai, ART (Saudi Arabia and London), Bahrain and Syria, as well as certain terrestrial channels (see above). Most of these stations broadcast in Arabic, with some English news bulletins and the occasional bulletin in French. BBC and CNN are among the most popular free channels, although your property owner might not provide both.

Satellite dishes are officially banned in Saudi Arabia, Qatar and Bahrain, but despite this satellite television is widely received and the Saudi-backed station MBC provides an excellent service in Arabic, although avoiding subject matter deemed to be inappropriate for a Muslim audience.

There are also four pay-TV networks: Orbit, Showtime, 1st Net and Star Select, each offering ten channels with different programmes. In general, the pay-TV programmes are superior to the free-to-air satellite and terrestrial broadcasts, as they need to encourage people to subscribe. While English is by far the dominant language, Orbit and 1st Net offer Arabic channels too. Orbit's Showtime is probably the most popular network, and its movie and sports package includes extensive coverage of European football.

Costs vary, but Orbit equipment, for example, costs around $800 (£550), with a monthly fee of $30 to $50 (£20 to £35) depending on the number of channels required. There are many deals available on the pay channels, and it pays to shop around and ask friends and colleagues for recommendations. You should also haggle over the contract start date, so that you can try out a particular network before commiting to it. Note, however, that in apartment blocks the equipment and even the monthly charge might be included in the rent. (Some expatriates select their accommodation according to which satellite TV entertainment is offered as part of the package!)

Video & DVD

There's a tremendous demand for recorded films in the Gulf, and video rental shops are everywhere. The Saudis are the most avid viewers, some families seeing up to five videos every day, in addition to the television they watch. There's been a modest fall in demand since the introduction of satellite TV services, but the popularity of videos and DVDs looks set to continue for some time. The number of video films purchased is low compared to the number rented, as is the case in most countries. Films are available in Arabic, English, Hindi, Urdu and other languages and include the most recent, which sometimes arrive in the region before general international release (usually pirate copies from the Far East).

The quality of film production varies considerably, as many films are copies (in some cases copies of copies of copies), particularly in Saudi Arabia, where copying is a sizeable industry. The UAE and other states, however, have recently introduced strict laws against copyright infringement and misuse of intellectual property.

A deposit might be required when you join a video club, although an established company address might be accepted instead. Video rental charges are reasonable, around $1.50 to $2.25 (£1 to £1.50) per film, with monthly or volume deals available to regular customers. There's usually considerable flexibility regarding the time allowed to view and return films.

Note that pornographic videos, although widely circulated in the region, are strictly prohibited and punishment for those found in possession of such material includes fines in the more liberal states and prison sentences or deportation in Saudi Arabia.

RADIO

There's a wide range of radio programmes available in the region, with stations broadcasting in Arabic and English, offering music, news, soaps and educational programmes. Transmissions tend to be in FM and are consequently of good quality, although they tend to be limited to urban areas.

There are four types of radio broadcaster in the region: local stations in each state (see below), regional stations such as MBC FM, foreign stations such as Radio Switzerland and international stations such as BBC Worldwide and Radio Monte Carlo.

Most Gulf states have numerous music channels dedicated to rock and jazz, easy listening, classical, chart music, etc., some broadcasting 24 hours per day. Most music channels are commercial but there are also some non-commercial, government channels. One of the most popular channels among English-speaking expatriates is broadcast by the Arabian American Oil Company (ARAMCO), based in the oilfields of the eastern province of Saudi Arabia and known as 'The Voice of the Desert'.

Local Stations

Local radio stations in the Gulf are government-controlled by the Ministries of Information and include the following.

Bahrain: Bahrain has two radio stations, one in Arabic and one in English, the latter on 96.5FM and 101FM.

Kuwait: There are eight stations, in Arabic and English. The US military's Armed Forces Radio & TV Service (AFRTS) broadcasts on 107.9FM and the Voice of America is on 95.7FM.

Oman: Two stations, in Arabic and English, the latter on 90.4FM (94.3FM from Salalah).

Qatar: Two stations, in Arabic and English, the latter on 97.5FM and 102.6FM.

Saudi Arabia: Three stations, all in Arabic.

UAE: There are 12 stations in the UAE, broadcasting in Arabic, English, Urdu and Hindi. Two of the more popular, primarily English-language stations are Abu Dhabi's Capital Radio FM on 100.5FM and Channel 4 FM in Dubai on 104.8FM.

9.

EDUCATION

Education plays a pivotal role in the Gulf states' development programmes. All have been quick to realise the importance of improving their educational infrastructures, and oil has provided the money to do so. That isn't to say that education had previously been unavailable in the region, but limited resources, an insular attitude and the desire to retain the status quo meant that education had been basic and only the brightest pupils went on to higher education, and then only if their families could afford it.

The vast influx of foreigners into this formerly secluded region emphasisied the need to 'catch up'. Gulf governments realised that there was a need to provide a well-educated, resourceful local workforce for the future, displacing the continual need for expatriates to undertake even basic maintenance of state utilities. Major programmes for building schools and colleges of higher education were undertaken and continue to this day, and standards of education have been raised significantly. Arab students are now found in the world's most prestigious universities, particularly in the UK and USA, where their skills equal those of their counterparts from other countries. The old view of the backward, ill-educated Arab has largely vanished, and literacy rates range from 79 per cent in Kuwait to 85 per cent in Bahrain, although in Saudi Arabia only 63 per cent of men and 63 per cent of women are literate.

Oman in particular is currently undergoing something of an education revolution, as an increasing number of pupils are being taught English and prestigious American universities, including Cornell and Carnegie Mellon, are setting up campuses in the state.

There's a fairly wide choice of schools throughout the Gulf, although state (i.e. government-funded) schools aren't usually an option for foreign children. These are attended by local and expatriate Arabs, who share culture, language and religion. The private sector provides for the expatriate communities, and its schools are generally of a reasonable standard, especially for primary education. However, a child's secondary education is sometimes better provided for in their home country. The Ministries of Education control standards in the state schools and have some influence over the establishment, legitimacy and running of those in the private sector, in some instances stipulating that school hours and days match those of the state schools.

A key decision for expatriates with school-age children (particularly those at secondary school age) is whether to send them to boarding school in their home country and, if so, at what age? First, do you want to be separated from your child(ren) for months at a time? Do you feel it important that your children are brought up exposed to and aware of their national culture and environment by being educated at home? On the other hand, the Gulf is a wonderful environment for children, being safe and clean, with plenty of opportunities for exercise and sports, and with sunshine, sea and beautiful beaches; do you want to deprive them of all this by packing them off to boarding school in a country which may lack these advantages? You're advised to listen to advice from other expatriates who have made these difficult decisions.

When deciding on the type of education best suited to your child(ren)'s needs, you should also ask yourself the following questions:

- Are your Gulf state's educational system and examination qualifications recognised in your home country, the country in which your child will probably eventually have to make his way?
- When your child returns to your native country, will his education be ahead of or behind that of his peers?
- What is the academic record of the school you propose to select?
- How large are the classes? What is the teacher/pupil ratio?

STATE OR PRIVATE SCHOOL?

In order to help you decide whether to send your child(ren) to a private or state school, you should consider the points mentioned below. Note that in many cases state schools aren't an option, and that the vast majority of non-Arab expatriates send their children to private schools.

- If you're non-Muslim, you might not be allowed access to state schools. Even if you are, local Arab children and children of Arab expatriates are likely to have priority over other foreigners for places, which might be scarce.
- How long do you envisage staying in the region? If you don't know, assume it will be for two years, in which case you should opt for a private school. If you think that you will be in the region for many

years, you might consider a state school to teach your child the local culture, although very few expatriates send their children to state schools even in these circumstances.

- Will cultural differences cause problems? Sending your child(ren) to a state school will to a large extent remove them from the expatriate community.

- What about religion? Islam is the fundamental way of life in the Arab world and pressure might be exerted for your children to convert. Muslims believe that all of us are born Muslim, some people moving away from the 'truth' later.

- If your work prospects indicate a long-term future for your family in a Gulf country, you might see your child's integration into the local community as important. A later switch to private education, however, might prove difficult and stall your child's development.

- Note also that naturalisation and citizenship are very rarely granted to foreigners, even in the long-term, so your child(ren) are unlikely ever to be assimilated fully into the local culture.

- An obvious obstacle is the use of the Arabic language in state schools. The curriculum is entirely Arabic-based (English is taught only as a foreign language), although with very young children this isn't a problem, as they adapt so easily.

- Will you be able to help your children with their education, particularly in view of the language barrier?

- Is special or extra tutoring available in Arabic?

- What are the school days and hours? Are they similar to the hours you do at work? Will school holidays align easily with your periods of leave?

- Do you want your child to attend a co-educational or single sex school? In the Arab state system, schools are single sex, whereas most private schools are co-educational.

You should also consider the advantages and disadvantages of private schools in the Gulf (see below). If you decide to educate your child(ren) in the state system, you must visit the Ministry of Education offices for information about availability, qualifications and procedures.

PRIVATE SCHOOLS

Private schools are common throughout the Gulf, mainly to cater for the large expatriate communities. The majority are managed by and run for English-speaking western expatriates, although many local families choose to send their children to these schools, perhaps in the belief that the tuition will be better and also because of the international importance of the English language. There are schools for the children of Americans, British, French, Germans, Egyptians, Indians, Pakistanis, Filipinos, Japanese and many other nationalities, as well as international schools catering for a variety of nationalities. The vast majority of private schools teach in English, including the Indian and Pakistani schools. Minority expatriate groups such as the Japanese, French and Germans tend to send their children to international schools, at which the main teaching language is English.

Some private establishments restrict enrolment to pupils of the relevant nationality, e.g. a British government-aided school. Others might have rules concerning religion. International schools tend to have fewer restrictions.

Most private schools are co-educational and provide tuition to children from pre-school nursery groups through to university entrance examinations, preparing them for a variety of examinations – often British A levels or the International Baccalaureate, which can be taken in the Gulf. There are also plenty of private pre-schools, including play groups, nurseries, kindergartens and infant schools. These schools are voluntary, but widely attended, partly because they allow expatriate mothers to socialise. Restrictions on wives securing work visas mean that they can feel isolated at home.

In general, standards at private schools are high, with small class sizes and modern facilities, but some parents find that their children have some catching up to do when they return to their home country. Some schools catering for pupils from India and Pakistan face heavy demand for places, due to the large number of workers from those countries. There can be severe overcrowding, pupils sometimes being taught in shifts.

Private foreign and international schools tend to have more relaxed, flexible regimes and curricula and to be less formal in terms of dress, behaviour and pupil/teacher relationships than their equivalents in

Europe and North America. Some see this as a good thing, others as a negative. A drawback of private schools in the region is their high staff turnover. Like other expatriates, teachers tend to change jobs and locations quite frequently. This can lead to a lack of continuity in children's education and be a disruptive influence.

Structure: The school structure varies between different types of school in the Gulf, but those catering for American, British, Indian and Pakistani pupils tend to be either primary (for children aged 4 to 11) or secondary (11 to 18). Those catering for children of other nationalities are usually divided into four categories, as follows:

School Type	Pupil Ages
Pre-kindergarten & Kindergarten	3–6
Elementary	6–11
Secondary	12–14
High	15–18

Enrolment: Applications to private schools should be made as early as possible, particularly to international schools, which sometimes have waiting lists. You might need recent school reports or a previous headteacher's letter of appraisal. For UK and other western expatriates, the British Council is a useful source of information about educational establishments (see addresses and telephone numbers starting on page 147). Enrolment in private schools usually involves an interview with parent and child, and might also involve an examination (only for the child, you will be relieved to know!).

Hours & Holidays: There are many different types of school in the region, offering different curricula to children of various cultural backgrounds, and school hours and holidays vary accordingly, although a school day running from around 8am to 2.30pm is common, from Saturday to Wednesday inclusive. Some schools – particularly those catering for children of Asian workers – operate from early morning to evening, in two shifts.

Fees: The cost of private education can be high, but in some cases the fees are paid by your employer as part of your contract. It's vitally important to be aware of the cost of private schooling over the course of a child's education, particularly if this will include university. What might begin as a manageable expense can quickly become a major financial encumbrance if there are regular increases in fees, as there often are.

Choosing a Private School

The following checklist is designed to help you to choose a private school:

- Does the school have a good reputation and how long has it been established?

- Does the school have a good academic record? What percentage of its pupils obtain examination passes and go on to higher education?

- What does the curriculum include? Which country's curriculum is followed? Which examinations are set? Are the examinations recognised overseas, particularly in your country of origin? Do they fit in with your child's future educational plans? Ask to see a typical pupil's timetable to check the ratio of academic to non-academic subjects. Check the number of free study periods and the level of supervision.

- How large are the classes and what's the teacher/pupil ratio? Does the stated class size tally with the number of desks in the classrooms? Many schools provide a senior pupil to take prospective parents around the school and this can give a valuable insight into what the actual conditions are like.

- What standard of teaching equipment is in regular use, e.g. projection and visual aids, computer hardware and types of software?

- Is computer training available?

- Which countries do most of the pupils come from?

- Does religion play a part in the school?

- Are intensive English or Arabic lessons provided for children who don't reach the required standard. (Arabic is unlikely to be mandatory in foreign schools).

- What language lessons are available?

- What is the pupil turnover?
- What are the qualification requirements for teachers? What nationalities are the majority of the teachers? Ask for a list of the teaching staff and their qualifications.
- What is the teacher turnover? A high teacher turnover can be a bad sign and sometimes suggests poorly paid teachers and/or poor working conditions, although staff turnover in the region is rapid in many professions.
- What kind of discipline and punishment are applied and for which offences?
- What type of school reports are provided and how often?
- What sports instruction and facilities are provided? Where are the facilities located?
- What sort of school trips are organised? Are they always properly supervised?
- Is transport to and from school provided? Is there teacher supervision on the buses?
- What security arrangements are in place? What about the pickup of children at the end of school?
- What medical facilities are provided? Where are the nearest clinics and hospitals?
- What are the school terms and holidays?
- What are the fees and when are they payable?
- What extras must you pay for? These can include food, art supplies, sports equipment, excursions, uniforms and clothing, health and accident insurance, text books and stationery.
- What are the withdrawal conditions, should you wish or need to remove your child? A term's notice is usually required. You're likely to have paid some form of financial deposit when your child begins at the school and this will cover the school in the case of withdrawal.

Having made your choice of school, you should monitor your child's progress and listen to his views. Compare your findings with those of other parents. If something isn't right, see if there are grounds for complaint and take action if necessary. You or your employer are paying for your child's education and you should ensure that you're receiving value for money.

The following are the most highly regarded private schools in the region, listed by state. Note that the age ranges given are approximate and can change according to demand for places. Note also that few Saudi Arabian schools cater for children over 14, most of whom are sent to a boarding school either in another country — in some cases another Gulf state.

Bahrain

English-language Schools

- British School of Bahrain, Aldiya, PO Box 315775 (☎ 973-710 878). Ages 3–16.

- Dilmun School, Adilya, PO Box 26425 (☎ 973-713 483). Ages 3–11.

- Habara School, PO Box 26516 (☎ 973-712 868). Ages 2–11.

- The Infant School, Shaikh Salman Highway, PO Box 26625 (☎ 973-252 346). Ages 2–11.

- Sacred Heart School, Isa Town, PO Box 388 (☎ 973-684 367). Ages 4–16.

- St Christopher's Awali School, Awali, PO Box 25225 (☎ 973-753 632). Ages 3–7.

- St Christopher's School, Isa Town, PO Box 32052 (☎ 973-685 621). Ages 8–17.

International Schools

- Al-Hekma International School, PO Box 26489, Adilya (☎ 973-620 820). Ages 1–17.

- Al-Noor International School, Po Box 85 (☎ 973-736 773). Ages 3–17.

- Bahrain Bayan School, PO Box 32411, Isa Town (☎ 973-682 227). Ages 3–17.

- Bahrain School, PO Box 934, Juffair (☎ 973-727 828). Ages 3–17.

- Ibn Khuldoon International School, PO Box 20511, Isa Town (☎ 973-780 661). Ages 3–17.

● Naseem International School, PO Box 28503, Isa Town (☎ 973-689 684). Ages 3–17.

A useful source of additional information is The British Council, PO Box 452, Manama 356, Bahrain (☎ 973-261 555).

Kuwait

● American School of Kuwait, PO Box 6735, Hawalli 32042 (☎ 965-266 4341). Ages 4–18.

● The American International School of Kuwait, PO Box 17464, Khaldiya 72455 (☎ 965-564 5083). Ages 4–18.

● The British School of Kuwait, PO Box 26922, Safat 13030 (☎ 965-562 1701). Ages 3–18.

● The English Academy, PO Box 1081, Surra 45701 (☎ 965-534 0427/8). Ages 3–11.

● The English School (Fahaheel), PO Box 7209, Fahaheel 64003 (☎ 965-371 1070). Ages 4–18.

● The English School for Girls, PO Box 12592, Shamiya 71653 (☎ 965-561 9134). Ages 3–18.

● The English School (Salmiya), PO Box 379, Safat 13004 (☎ 965-563 7206). Ages 4–11.

● The Gulf English School, Po Box 6320, Hawalli 32038 (☎ 965-565 9361). Ages 4–18.

● The Kuwait English School (Salwa), PO Box 8640, Salmiya 22057 (☎ 965-565 5216). Ages 3–18.

● The Kuwait National English School, PO Box 44273, Hawalli 32057 (☎ 965-265 6904). Ages 2–13.

● The New English School (Jabriya), PO Box 6156, Hawalli 32036 (☎ 965-531 8060/1). Ages 4–18.

● The Universal American School, PO Box 17035, Khaldiya 72451 (☎ 965-562 0297). Ages 4–18.

A useful source of additional information is The British Council, PO Box 345, Safat 13004 (☎ 965-251 5512).

Oman

- American-British Academy, PO Box 372, Medinat Al-Sultan Qaboos, PC 115 (☎ 968-603 646). Ages 3–19.
- American International School of Muscat, PO Box 202, Muscat 115 (☎ 968-600 374). Ages 4–17.
- The British School – Muscat, PO Box 1907, Ruwi, PC 112 (☎ 968-600 842). Ages 3–18.
- Muscat Private School, PO Box 1031, Ruwi, PC 112 (☎ 968-565 550). Ages 3–18.
- The Sultan's School, PO Box 665, Seeb Code 121 (☎ 968-536 777). Ages 3–18.

A useful source of additional information is The British Council, PO Box 73, Postal Code 115, Madinat Al-Sultan Qaboos (☎ 968-600 548).

Qatar

- American International School, PO Box 22090, Doha (☎ 974-421 377). Ages 3–18.
- Central English-Speaking Kindergarten, On Ibn Al-Qasim, Doha (☎ 974-672 570). Ages 3–11.
- Doha English-Speaking School, PO Box 7660, Doha (☎ 974-870 170). Ages 3–11.
- Doha College, PO Box 7506, Doha (☎ 974-687 379). Ages 11–18.
- Doha Independent School, PO Box 5404, Doha (☎ 974-684 495). Ages 3–11.
- English Modern School, PO Box 875, Doha (☎ 974-672 406). Ages 3–18.
- Gulf English School, PO Box 2440, Doha (☎ 974-873 865). Ages 3–11.
- International School of Choueifat, PO Box 22085, Doha (☎ 974-650 053). Ages 3–11.
- Park House English School, PO Box 102, Doha (☎ 974-423 343). Ages 3–11.
- Qatar Academy, PO Box 1129, Doha (☎ 974-803 434). Ages 3–18.

- Qatar International School, PO Box 5697, Doha (☎ 974-690 552). Ages 3–18.

A useful source of additional information is The British Council, PO Box 2992, Doha (☎ 974-426 193).

Saudi Arabia

- Abqaiq Academy, PO Box 31677, Al-Khobar, 31952 (☎ 966-3-566 0410). Ages 3–14.
- Al Khobar British International School, PO Box 4359, Al-Khobar 31952 (☎ 966-3-895 1404). Ages 3–16.
- Asir Academy, Consulate General Box R, Unit 61901, APO, AE 09809-1901 (☎ 966-7-223 3961). Ages 4–14.
- Asir Preparatory School, PO Box 34, Khamis Mushayt (☎ 966-7-222 0545). Ages 3–11.
- British International School, PO Box 6453, Jeddah 21422 (☎ 966-2-699 0019). Ages 3–16.
- British School, PO Box 85769, Riyadh 11612 (☎ 966-1-248 2387). Ages 4–14.
- Dhahran British Grammar School, PO Box 677, Dhahran 31932 (☎ 966-3-891 9555). Ages 3–15.
- Hafr Al-Batin Academy, PO Box 10023, Hafr Al-Batin 31991 (☎ 966-3-787 4234). Ages 4–14.
- Jeddah Peparatory and Grammar School, c/o British Consulate General, PO Box 6316, Jeddah, 21442 (☎ 966-2-693 7380). Ages 3–14.
- Jubail British Academy, PO Box 10059, Madinat Al-Jubail, Al-Sinaiyah 31961 (☎ 966-3-341 7550). Ages 4–13.
- Jubail International, Jubail 31961 (☎ 966-3-341 7550). Ages 4–14.
- Medical City Primary School, King Khalid National Guard Hospital, PO Box 9515, Jeddah 21423 (☎ 966-2-665 3400). Ages 3–11.

- Taif Academy, Unit 61206, APO, AE 09802-1206 (☎ 966-2-725 4666). Ages 4–14.

Useful sources of additional information are the following British Council offices:

- The British Council Eastern Province (☎ 966-3-826 9036).
- The British Council Riyadh (☎ 966-1-462 1818).
- The British Council West Saudi Arabia (☎ 966-2-672 3336).

United Arab Emirates

- The American School of Dubai, PO Box 2222, Dubai (☎ 971-4-440 824). Ages 4–18.
- The British National Curriculum School, PO Box 5760, Dubai (☎ 971-4-441 614). Ages 2–14.
- Cambridge High School, PO Box 3004, Dubai (☎ 971-4-824 646). Ages 3–18.
- Dubai College, PO Box 837, Dubai (☎ 971-4-399 9111). Ages 11–18.
- The English College, PO Box 11812, Dubai (☎ 971-4-394 3465). Ages 11–18.
- Fujairah Private Academy, PO Box 797, Fujairah (☎ 971-9-224 001). Ages 3–18.
- Horizon English School, PO Box 6749, Dubai (☎ 971-4-491 442). Ages 2–14.
- International School of Choueifat, PO Box 1644, Ras Al-Khaimah (☎ 971-7-353 446). Ages 2–18.
- Jumeirah English Speaking School, PO Box 24942, Dubai (☎ 971-4-394 5515). Ages 2–14.
- Ras Al-Khaimah School, PO Box 975, Ras Al-Khaimah (☎ 971-7-352 441). Ages 2–14.
- Sharjah English School, PO Box 1600, Sharjah (☎ 971-6-552 2779). Ages 2–14.
- Sharjah International American School, PO Box 2501, Sharjah (☎ 971-6-380 000). Ages 2–18.

Useful sources of additional information are The British Council offices:

- The British Council Abu Dhabi, (☎ 971-2-659 300).
- The British Council Dubai, (☎ 971-4-337 0109).
- The British Council Sharjah, (☎ 971-6-572 2666).

HIGHER EDUCATION

The vast majority of expatriate students who go on to higher education attend colleges and universities in their home country, although universities in the Gulf are of a reasonable standard. Some, however, aren't open to expatriates, e.g. those in Oman and Qatar.

10.

PUBLIC TRANSPORT

Public transport in the cities and towns of the Gulf is confined to bus services, the one exception being a rail link in Saudi Arabia, but there are no rail networks or train services elsewhere in the region. The car is king in the Gulf – they're cheap to buy and run, and taxis are inexpensive – along with the aeroplane for long-distance travel within the region. Urban bus services in major cities are reasonably well run, although unpredictable, but are generally for the poorer sections of the community. Routes run between busy commercial and residential areas, rather than being comprehensive services covering all areas.

TRAINS

There's only one train service in the region and there are no plans for any more. The Gulf region is very large, populations are comparatively small and there's simply no demand for a rail network. International travel is easy and inexpensive by air and there are also inter-city bus services (see below). The region's one rail link is in Saudi Arabia, joining the central and eastern provinces. It runs from the the capital Riyadh to the city of Dammam via Dhahran, Abqaiq, Hofuf, Harad and Al-Yamamah. There's a twice daily service, with one departure in the morning and one in the afternoon. The service is run by the Saudi Railway Organisation, PO Box 36, Dammam 31241, Kingdom of Saudi Arabia (☎ 966-3-832 2042).

BUSES

Since buses are normally only used by poorer people, the provision of bus services isn't high on the agenda of the various Gulf administrations. Most services are run by city administrations, although businesses sometimes run their own operations, transporting their staff between home and the workplace. This is common with major construction companies employing hundreds of workers, some government ministries and hotel groups, but services are also provided by certain small companies. The United Arab Emirates (UAE) offers an international bus service run by a private concern, buses running between large cities, mainly capitals, of neighbouring Gulf states.

In view of the region's limited public transport, some of the major hotel chains run bus pick-up and return services for their arriving and departing guests, to and from the airports. Similarly, most hotels provide bus services to the nearest city centre. Guests wanting bus pick-up at the airport must request it when booking their room and provide details of their incoming flight. Hotel drivers hold up signs with passengers' names in order to identify themselves.

Bahrain: Bahrain has a sometimes erratic bus service, covering most of the towns and villages on the main island of Bahrain and also on Muharraq, the next largest neighbouring island, connected to Bahrain by a causeway. Fares are low, with a standard rate, whatever the route, of around 50 fils ($0.15). Some of the older buses don't have air-conditioning, and the drivers might not speak English. The main bus terminal is on Government Avenue in Manamar and there are others in Isa Town, Muharraq and Riffa.

The Saudi Bahraini Transport Company (SABTCO, ☎ 973-263 244) runs buses to other countries. Buses leave from the international bus station in Manama and you can take daily buses to Kuwait for BD14 ($37), the UAE (Abu Dhabi, Dubai and Sharjah) for BD17 ($45), Amman in Jordan for BD25 ($66) and Damascus in Syria for BD25 ($66). Six buses per day leave for Alkhobar and Dammam in Saudi Arabia, for BD4 ($11).

Kuwait: A fairly comprehensive service covers the city, but as is the case throughout the region, don't expect reliability. The main bus station is close to the junction of Al-Hilali and Abdullah Al-Mubarak Streets, known as Mircab bus station. Buses run from around 5am to 10pm, although during rush hour delays drivers are known to take short-cuts to make up for lost time, so you might miss your stop or the bus might not arrive at the stop where you're waiting for it!

Fares are inexpensive, usually between 100 and 200 fils ($0.35 to 0.70). If it's a driver-only bus, everybody boards at the front, but if there's a fare collector, men board at the back, women and young children at the front. A woman accompanied by a man can sit anywhere on the bus, but single women must sit in the front seats. Intercity bus services are limited, and all trips cost 250 fils ($85). Route 101 runs from the bus station to Al-Ahmadi and Fahaheel, while route 103 goes to Al-Jahra.

Oman: There are coach connections between the major cities of Oman (i.e. Muscat and Salalah), and small buses provide links with other towns and large villages throughout the country. Most intercity buses are operated by the Oman National Transport Company (ONTC) and all routes except Salalah cost OR4 ($10) or less each way.

Salalah costs OR8 ($20) one way, OR16 ($40) return. Abu Nawaf Road Transport has buses to Salalah for OR6 ($16) one way, OR11 ($29) return. Bin Qasim Transport and Al-Ghafri and Sons also offer services to Salalah, for OR7 ($18) one way, OR13 ($34) return. Muscat, the capital, has services between the various districts, ONTC's fares ranging from 100 to 300 baiza ($0.25 to 0.80), depending on the distance travelled. English timetables are available from the Ruwi bus station. International bus services are limited to Abu Dhabi and Dubai. Further information can be obtained from the Oman National Transport Company (ONTC), PO Box 620, Muscat, Oman (☎ 968-590 046).

Qatar: Commercial bus services in Qatar are confined to the capital Doha and outlying districts. In common with many similar services in the region, bus travellers are usually locals and the service is erratic.

Saudi Arabia: The Saudi Arabian Public Transport Company (SAPTCO), PO Box 10667, Riyadh 11443 (☎ 966-1-454 5000) operates a reasonable service using a modern, air-conditioned fleet of buses within and between the cities of the Kingdom. Male and female passengers are cordoned off from each other on Saudi buses, and unaccompanied women are rarely allowed to travel by bus. There are plenty of buses to Jeddah and they don't usually travel via Mecca (*Makkah* in Arabic), but you should check, as non-Muslims aren't allowed in the holy city. You can also travel to Dammam, Hofuf, Buraydah, Hail, Abha, Najran, Jizan,Tabuk and Sakaka. In addition, international services are available to Egypt, Jordan, Syria and Turkey.

SAPTCO buses offer services throughout Riyadh for SR2 ($0.55). The bus station is off Al-Bathaa Street. Jeddah's SAPTCO bus station is on Ba'ashan Street, and orange and white SAPTCO buses offer services around the city for SR2 ($0.55) and to the airport for SR3 ($0.80). There are plenty of services from Jeddah to Riyadh, Taif, Dammam, Abha, Khamis Mushayt, Bisha, Al-Baha, Jizan, Najran, Tabuk and Yanbu. As in Riyadh, check that intercity buses don't travel through Mecca.

UAE: There are bus services throughout the Emirates, run by a range of companies. The main routes are between Abu Dhabi, the federal capital, and Dubai. A complex network also operates between towns, villages and major conurbations. A commercial service operates between Dubai and Saudi Arabia, and superb road links ensure a quick, comfortable journey.

TAXIS

Taxis are widely available in the Gulf states and range from dilapidated bangers without air-conditioning (unless you count opening the windows, which usually makes things worse) to luxurious limousines. There are essentially three types of taxi in use in all the region's countries: at the bottom end are standard small cars, usually the Toyota Corolla (loved by all taxi drivers for its durability) or a similar Japanese import. These might or might not have a meter and, if they do have one, it might or might not work.

It's therefore important to establish the fare before engaging the taxi's services, preferably while you're still outside the car. If you don't agree with the suggested fare, look as if you're going to try another taxi and you will probably find that the driver quickly reduces his price. Don't accept the common response of 'as you wish' to your enquiry about the fare. It invariably leads to an argument at the end of your journey, because the driver's view of your wishes is likely to be different from yours — higher, of course. In the unusual event of a significant dispute, ask the driver to take you to the nearest police station; this usually ends the argument.

The second category of taxi is the clean, air-conditioned, modern car. Their services are normally well-regulated, and most states now insist on the use of meters. Finally, there are limousines operated on a booking system rather than picking up customers in the street. They tend to be used for airport travel, where passengers want to eliminate the risk of not being able to find a cab. This type of taxi service is also run by the top hotels.

Taxi drivers across the region might or might not speak English. You should therefore have the exact address of your destination (preferably written down in Arabic), particularly in the case of little-known businesses, shops and houses, and you might need to be able to identify nearby landmarks to help the driver, or your journey is likely to turn into a mystery tour. If you're unsure about whether the taxi driver has found the correct address, don't get out of the cab, despite his insistence that all is well, because you might find yourself stranded. Instead, ask him to check himself. Obvious newcomers to the region and tourists are prey to unscrupulous taxi drivers. Watch out for landmarks beginning to become familiar during a journey!

Locating addresses can be particularly difficult in Saudi Arabia, owing to the size of the main cities and the distances between them. Nevertheless, the vast majority of taxi drivers in the region are honest, well-intentioned people, who are helpful, humourous and non-aggressive.

Fares are generally low, particularly compared with European rates. With the introduction of modern fleets, however, some rates have been rising, e.g. in Dubai, where regulations to ensure high standards have been introduced by the authorities. As well as this, drivers have come under pressure to look for tips to reach targets set by their employers. If you're in a non-metered cab and have agreed the fare, a tip isn't necessary. In metered taxis, it's usual to round up the fare with a small tip. Some specific features of the region's taxis are as follows:

Bahrain: Taxis are identified by their orange wing fronts and backs, black-on-yellow number plates and a roof-mounted light showing the word 'TAXI', which is meant to be illuminated when the taxi is unoccupied. (It's usually better to look whether the taxi is carrying a passenger or not.) Taxis are usually metered and can be hailed in the street. You might need to insist that the driver uses the meter.

Fares are around 800 fils ($2) for 1.5km (1mi) and thereafter 100 fils ($0.25) per km. Metered taxis have a minimum fare, which increases from 10pm to 6am to around BD1.2 ($3). Taxis which have a yellow circle with the licence number in black on the driver's door and white and orange number plates carry up to five people, the fare shared. Whichever type of taxi you use, you should ask for at least an estimate of the fare before embarking on a journey.

Kuwait: Taxi markings are similar to those in Bahrain (see above), with distinctive orange wings. These are free-wheeling, go-anywhere, pick-up-anywhere taxis and you need to barter over the fare. The driver might stop to pick up other passengers and this should have some bearing on your agreed fare, but don't count on it; your driver's English is likely to deteriorate when it comes to discussing the subject and it won't be worth pursuing the point. There are also plenty of companies working on a call basis, where your call books the taxi and the fare is stipulated by the dispatcher. With these, the charge is straightforward and no tip is necessary. The drivers tend to speak more English than the drivers of free-wheeling taxis, being more used to foreign passengers.

Oman: Oman is served by orange and white taxis, whose fares are higher than in other states, and some orange mini-buses, which are considerably cheaper. Agree the fare in advance of your journey, as taxis are unlikely to be metered. Muscat's main taxi stands are in Ruwi, across from the main bus station, and at the Seeb clock tower roundabout. Taxi fares within the Greater Muscat area usually range between OR1 ($3) and OR4 ($10). Mini-buses cost between a third and a half of this.

Qatar: Qatar has orange and white taxis, and more luxurious, pre-booked cabs, the latter costing two or three times as much. Most taxis are metered, but ensure that the meter is in use. Fares are usually reasonable, although driving standards are anything but, a common problem throughout the region (see **Chapter 11**). The flagfall (minimum charge) is QR2 ($0.55) during the day, QR3 ($0.80) at night, and thereafter QR1 ($30) per 100 metres.

Saudi Arabia: Standard taxis in Saudi Arabia are painted yellow. They operate on a request stop basis, which means that they may pick up more than one passenger and are therefore potentially unsafe for women. Agree the fare in advance, as most taxis are unmetered. As mentioned above, make sure that you have a reasonable idea of the way to your destination, including landmarks with which to direct the driver. Drivers rarely speak much English. Remember that in Saudi Arabia, distances are greater, cities larger, districts more spread out and fares more expensive than in the rest of the region.

Riyadh also has white and orange taxis and Jeddah white and orange cabs. The flagfall for all taxis is SR3 ($0.80), thereafter SR1 ($0.25) per kilometre. Riyadh's white cab drivers are more likely to speak a little English. At some Saudi airports, notably Jeddah, you might be approached by unofficial taxi drivers when you exit the terminal. These are unlicensed drivers in private cars who claim to be cheaper than a standard cab, but are invariably more expensive. It's best to avoid them.

UAE: Old orange taxis — unmetered, usually uncomfortable, possibly smelly, but cheap — are on the way out in Dubai. Their numbers have declined dramatically, licences gradually being withdrawn by the authorities in an effort to upgrade the service. The old cabs are considered by some to be unsafe, although older vehicles have to pass an annual roadworthiness test, as do all cars.

Modern fleets, metered and painted cream, provide an excellent taxi service. Costs are a little higher than the old cabs but still excellent value and a lot less hassle. Operated by Dubai Transport Corporation, these taxis can be hailed in the street or booked by telephone, they maintain radio contact with their base, and their location and progress are monitored by radio link. The starting fare is Dh3 ($0.80).

Taxis in Abu Dhabi are painted white and gold and are metered. Travelling between Emirates can entail long journeys (e.g. between Dubai and Abu Dhabi) and requires agreed fares in advance of the journey. Roads are reasonable but can be dangerous because of the low standard of driving, particularly at night. Taxis are safe for women travelling on their own, as they don't pick up more than one passenger.

AIRLINE SERVICES & AIRPORTS

As well as having international commercial importance, the Gulf states occupy a prime location at the crossroads between east and west, so it's little wonder that many airlines have extensive services to the region. Most major international carriers (including Air France, British Airways, Cathay Pacific, KLM, Qantas and Singapore Airlines) have scheduled flights to the capitals and major cities of the Gulf, and a host of smaller national airlines also fly into the region, particularly from Africa, the countries of the former Soviet Union and the Far East. Royal Brunei and Turkish Airlines are among those that frequently offer excellent deals (but you should check their safety records!).

The Gulf states themselves operate world class airlines, with the latest aircraft and impeccably trained flight deck and cabin crews. Saudi Arabian Airlines (known as Saudia) has the largest fleet in the Middle East but isn't the favourite Middle East airline among foreign travellers and expatriates because of its prohibition of alcohol. It's nevertheless a major airline with a reasonably efficient service. When flying into Jeddah International Airport, seasoned travellers tend to use Saudia, which has its own section of the airport, allowing a much quicker passage through the airport formalities.

Gulf Air is co-owned by Bahrain, Qatar, Abu Dhabi and Oman, and was formed in 1973. It's currently the second-largest airline in the region and enjoys a strong reputation for it's service and safety. Gulf Air has faced competition since the 1985 inauguration of the national airline of Dubai, Emirates Airlines, which is growing rapidly. Emirates currently has 30 aircraft, including Boeing 777s and long-range Airbus 340–500s, which are used for non-stop flights to the USA and Australia.

Oman Air is another relative newcomer, as is Qatar Airways, flying out of Doha. Both strive hard to compete with the region's other carriers. Kuwait Airways operates services to more popular destinations and has been successful in staging a recovery after the conflict with Iraq. There are also a number of private charter companies operating out of Gulf airports. Find them in the yellow pages in each country. Costs are predictably high.

For those wanting to travel within the region, there are frequent and reasonably priced flights between the Gulf states. The use of internal flights in the larger states (i.e. Oman, Saudi Arabia and the UAE) is also common.

The airports in the Gulf vary from the luxurious to the dreary and the primitive. Dubai International Airport is the most modern, an impressively sleek building, rivalled in modernity only by the new airport at Hong Kong. Riyadh Airport is modern, clean, quiet and efficient. Seeb International at Muscat in Oman is excellent, and Bahrain's airport is up to international standard. Other airports are in need of modernisation.

Security checks at all the region's airports are efficient, as are the immigration and customs services. As a rule, air travel to and from the Gulf is comfortable, even pleasurable, without the crowd stress sometimes encountered at busy western airports.

Bahrain: Bahrain's international airport (PO Box 586, ☎ 973-321 151) is 6.5km (4mi) north-east of Manama.

Kuwait: Kuwait's international airport (PO Box 17, Safat 13001, ☎ 965-433 5599) is 16km (10mi) south of Kuwait City.

Oman: Seeb International Airport (☎ 968-519 809), is 40km (25mi) west of Muscat.

Qatar: Doha International Airport (☎ 974-462 1681), is 8km (5mi) south-east of Doha centre.

Saudi Arabia: There are three international airports, King Khalid International Airport (PO Box 12531, Riyadh 11483, ☎ 966-1-221 1000), 35km (22mi) north of Riyadh, King Abdul Aziz International Airport (PO Box 6326, Jeddah 21442, ☎ 966-2-684 2227), 18km (11mi) north of Jeddah and King Fahd International Airport (PO Box 3477, Dammam 3147), 13km (8mi) south-east of Dhahran.

UAE: There are six international airports: Abu Dhabi International Airport, 37km (23mi) from the city; Al-Ain International Airport, 20km (12mi) west of Al-Ain; Dubai International Airport, 4km (2.5mi) from the city; Fujairah International Airport, 5km (3mi) from the city; Ras Al-Khaimah International Airport, 15km (9mi) from the city; Sharjah International Airport, 10km (6mi) from Sharjah.

11.

MOTORING

Motoring is the primary means of transport in the region, both for local journeys and also for trips between cities and states. Public transport provides only a limited service (see **Chapter 10**) and a car is a necessity for many journeys. In addition to this, many Arabs are in love with their cars, the four-wheel drive reigning supreme as the most desirable vehicle. Although stories of Arabs having so much money that they dump a car when the ashtrays are full are apocryphal, it's common for cars to be abandoned (literally) when they break down or need expensive repairs or even when the owner decides to buy a new one!

At the start of the oil boom in the 1970s, the amount of road traffic in the region was limited, as car ownership was restricted to affluent businessmen. Even the number of trucks and vans was limited. When increased oil revenues poured into the Gulf states, this changed dramatically. Economies mushroomed, as did the number of motor vehicles in the region, both commercial and private.

Road links were among the first priorities when the Gulf economies expanded, with huge amounts of money and labour devoted to them, and the region's road systems are now among the best in the world. Further improvements are being made, and the road link between the eastern province of Saudi Arabia and Bahrain is the largest project of its kind in the world. Roads provide access to just about everywhere in the Gulf, apart from extremely remote areas and the empty deserts. There are no toll charges and motorway traffic generally moves freely.

As the volume of cars increases annually, urban and suburban streets are becoming busier, although traffic jams are rare. There are three main 'rush hours': from 8 to 9am, from 12.30 to 2.30pm and from 5.30 to 7.30pm. Traffic densities vary between Thursdays and Saturdays, some companies taking Thursday off (in addition to Friday) and some Saturday.

In the month of Ramadan (see **National Holidays** on page 348), working hours change and this can have a considerable effect on traffic flow, particularly in Saudi Arabia, where working hours in some local companies changing to night time. Driving standards in the Gulf states are generally poor (see page 185) and accidents common (see page 186), especially in Saudi Arabia. As fatigue sets in towards the end of Ramadan (as a result of fasting during daylight hours) driving can be even more dangerous than usual, and wise expatriates avoid driving late at night at these times, especially in Saudi Arabia. The United Arab Emirates (UAE), the most 'relaxed' state, with some of the cheapest petrol and lowest car prices in the Gulf, has one of the world's highest road accident death rates! (Is there a connection?) The roads between Sharjah and Dubai are especially dangerous, particularly at night.

Note also that it isn't uncommon to encounter camels on the road in the Gulf states, particularly at night, which can be fatal for all concerned.

VEHICLE IMPORT & EXPORT

The private import of cars into the Gulf is rare, as vehicles are inexpensive throughout the region (although large used American cars with low mileage, are much prized by Arabs, with their large families). Import taxes are very low compared with countries outside the region, but it's more common for foreign workers to export cars to their home country.

When moving residence between Gulf states, there are a few formalities to observe if you decide to take your car. Any outstanding hire purchase payments on the vehicle must be made, together with any traffic fines. Proof of ownership must be established with the traffic police, who will issue a clearance certificate for customs; this incurs some small charges. The vehicle must also be de-registered and export plates issued before it may be exported to another GCC country.

BUYING A CAR

Buying a car in the Gulf is relatively straightforward. All popular makes are available, as well as every luxury vehicle you might want. Prices are low in comparison to western countries, as no import tax is added. As a result, the turnover of new cars is high. Although diesel fuel is around 12 per cent cheaper than petrol, this isn't a major consideration in choosing between petrol and diesel engines, as all fuel is cheap in the Gulf (see **Fuel** on page 190).

New Cars

When buying a car in the Gulf, take into account the servicing facilities offered by the main dealer of the make that you choose (see **Garages**

& Servicing on page 191). Japanese and Korean cars are widely available, and German cars (especially Mercedes and BMWs) are popular for their reliability. Most British cars are virtually non-existent, although the Jaguar has recently made something of a comeback. Notable exceptions are the prestigious Range Rover, Land Rover and Rolls Royce. A top of the range Range Rover can be bought for little more than $70,000 (£46,500) and a 'roller' can be yours for a mere $170,000 (£115,000).

As with most purchases in the region, bargaining is expected. And with a purchase of this size, you should polish your skills before approaching a dealer. As a general rule, avoid any finance plans offered by the dealer, as you will pay more than you need to in order to cover his commission. This is also the case with any insurance he might offer. A deposit of around 10 per cent of the purchase price is usually required by loan companies, the balance being paid in monthly instalments. The usual procedure is that the lender (e.g. bank) issues the dealer with the required number of monthly, dated cheques and you make regular payments into your account to meet the debits (see **Registration** on page 171). Unhonoured or defaulted ('bounced') cheques are serious criminal offences in the region (see page 234).

Used Cars

Second-hand car sales have been growing in the region but aren't a major part of the car business in the Gulf, where cars are regarded as a more or less disposal item and it's common for old cars to be simply dumped rather than re-sold. The UAE has the most buoyant market for used cars, probably because of the large number of lower-paid workers, from the Indian sub-continent and the Far East. The used car market is geared to lower paid people, who cannot afford new cars. It isn't particularly well-organised or regulated, so a prospective purchaser is very much on his own. There are few second-hand showrooms of the kind found outside the region, and used cars are generally sold in back streets and on waste ground. If you want to buy a second-hand car, you're recommended to take someone who speaks Arabic – preferably a local – with you.

If you intend to buy a used car in the region, there are a number of points to bear in mind:

- Check that the car has an up-to-date registration certificate. If it has no certificate at all, don't buy it; you might be liable for outstanding registration payments if the certificate is out of date.
- Check that it has a current test certificate.
- Check that the chassis and engine numbers tally with the registration certificate.
- Check the ownership of the vehicle.
- Check the vehicle for signs of serious damage. If you're ignorant about cars, take somebody with you who can spot these.

You have some protection when buying second-hand, as the traffic administrations in the region require the seller and buyer to contract the transfer of ownership at the department's offices, where any false or invalid documentation is likely to be exposed. The sale is completed by the new certificate of registration being issued in the new owner's name. Don't take any short cuts to hasten the deal – they're illegal.

SELLING A CAR

Western expatriates have little difficulty selling their cars. Potential purchasers know that expatriates are conditioned to look after their cars, have them regularly serviced and keep them in excellent condition. The cars of other nationals aren't viewed as positively. As outlined above, selling a car is essentially a matter of producing the correct paperwork, and the transfer of ownership takes place at the police traffic department's offices.

At the inspection and price negotiation stage, accompany the prospective purchaser on a test drive (if you feel brave enough). Take payment in cash and don't accept cheques. Give the buyer a receipt and keep a copy. Tell your insurance company and claim a refund if applicable.

VEHICLE REGISTRATION

When importing or buying a new or used car in the Gulf states, you must register it with the police traffic department. (In some states, vehicles must be registered annually.) The department issues a certificate, which must be kept in the car at all times; you should keep a photocopy in case it's lost or stolen. The original will be called for in any incident which involves the police – and even minor accidents require police attendance. You risk a fine if you cannot produce it.

When you buy a new car, the dealer might arrange the registration for you with the traffic department of the local police administration. In some cases, particularly at large dealerships, a police representative might call at the dealer's office and complete the formalities there, including the issuing of registration plates. In most Gulf states, the certification process is computerised, which makes it efficient. Buying a second-hand car involves the transfer of ownership, which requires that both the selling and buying parties visit the traffic department.

The following documents are necessary for the registration of new cars, with some minor variations between the Gulf states:

- A completed application form, obtained from the police traffic department;
- A letter from your sponsor stating that he has 'no objection' to your purchase and registration of a car (also known as a 'no objection certificate' or NOC);
- A copy of your passport;
- A copy of your residence visa (see below);
- Several passport-size photographs;
- Details of any hire purchase agreement (see below);
- Proof of insurance (in some states).

In the case of purchase on credit, the registration document might show the lender (e.g. bank) as the official owner until the loan has been repaid. In order to have ownership registered in your name, you must provide a letter from the lender confirming that the loan has been repaid; the traffic police administration will amend the document accordingly. Photocopy and file everything relating to evidence of ownership of your car.

The registration fee is usually around $110 (£75) and is payable annually, with the certification updated accordingly. A technical inspection is required for all cars over two years old at the time of registration or re-registration (see below). Note that you cannot buy a new car without showing proof of residence in the country.

Although the design of registration plates varies between GCC states, all are numerically based, with colour differences indicating the type of car, e.g. private or commercial. Geographic indicators aren't part of the registration scheme. Some countries carry the numbers in both Arabic and English, others only in Arabic.

When a car is exported, it must be de-registered, which involves the surrender of the registration certificate, payment of any outstanding fines for traffic offences, payment of a de-registration fee (around $130 (£85), presentation of proof of ownership (indicated by evidence of the discharge of any loans), purchase of export plates and the issue of a 'no objection certificate' (NOC) by the police. A customs certificate is then displayed on the car. If the car is to be scrapped, de-regulation is also necessary.

TECHNICAL INSPECTION

Annual inspections are required for cars over two years old (and commercial vehicles over a year old) and are carried out by the traffic police at their test stations. In some Gulf countries, e.g. the UAE, certain long-standing car dealers are allowed to carry out these inspections and issue test certificates, which are required for the renewal of annual registration. The test checks the standard features, including the lights, brakes, steering, tyres and exhaust emissions. You're recommended to check your car for obvious faults before you have it tested, or the whole process must be repeated. Arrive at the test centre as soon as it opens, or better still, have somebody take it for you, as queues are common. A test costs around £130 (GB£85), although a re-test is free.

ROAD TAX

There are no road taxes in the Gulf states, although small administrative fees are imposed for vehicle registration and annual re-registration (see **Registration** above).

DRIVING LICENCE

Western visitors are allowed to drive in the region using their national driving licence for a limited period. In Bahrain, Kuwait and the UAE, you must also have an International Driving Permit (IDP), obtainable from your home country for a small fee (e.g. £4 in the UK), and an IDP is also recommended for the other states. In Qatar, the period is seven days; in Saudi Arabia, it's three months, although you must have written approval (in Arabic) from the traffic police for any period over a month; in all other states, the period is a month. The application of the law is flexible, however, particularly if you're a tourist and unlikely to be in the country for much more than a month or if you're a foreign worker and are in the process of applying for a residence visa.

After this period, you must obtain a local licence, for which you must have a residence visa. The nationality of the person applying for a local licence has a bearing on the application process. For example, a UK licence holder only has to provide his licence, fill out an application form, take an eyesight test and sometimes a blood test to determine his blood group (this is put on the licence, in case of emergencies) in order to be automatically issued with a local licence. Many other nationalities have to take the particular state's driving test and some must take (expensive) driving lessons. The official driving age is 18 (although many local youngsters ignore this rule!).

If you're applying for a local driving licence, you must produce the following documents:

- a residence visa and photocopies;
- an NOC from your employer or sponsor, which might need to include a statement of your salary;
- a photocopy of your passport;
- a copy of your accommodation rental contract;
- passport-size photographs;
- a valid foreign driving licence with, in some cases, an Arabic translation;
- in some cases, an IDP (see above);
- in some cases, confirmation of your blood type from a recognised official source;
- a completed application form, with the relevant fee.

As indicated above, there are small variations in these requirements between the Gulf countries. In the UAE, for example, the traffic authorities take your photograph at their offices for inclusion on your licence. Saudi Arabia insists on the blood test details and the Arabic translation of your foreign licence. Many countries issue a licence for the period of your residence, but some limit the period (e.g. to three or ten years). In the latter case, renewal is usually straightforward, with payment of a fee the only formality, although some countries require a fresh eye test.

In Saudi Arabia, your local licence application is invariably dealt with by your employer at the same time as your residence and work visas. Note that driving licence offences in Saudi Arabia incur fines of between $75 (£50) and $225 (£150), as well as short jail terms (usually one day). Note also that in all states, if you're involved in even a minor traffic accident, you must be able to demonstrate that you've observed the licence application procedure. You must carry your licence at all times when driving.

CAR INSURANCE

Car insurance can be expensive and the traffic authorities usually insist on evidence of it as part of the registration process. At one time, car insurance wasn't mandatory in the Gulf states. In fact, a number of them frowned on insurance in general, which was regarded as contrary to the will of God. In Saudi Arabia, it still isn't compulsory to have car insurance; yet this strict and conservative country is where a foreigner is in most need of cover in the event of an accident. In all states, workers using company vehicles should check the extent of their personal liability in the event of an accident.

Third party, fire and theft is the most basic type of cover, but in view of the large number of minor traffic incidents that occur in the region – both while driving and when cars are parked – you're strongly recommended to take out fully comprehensive insurance. The ancient law relating to the payment of 'blood money' in the case of injury or death (see page 342) makes it all the more important, particularly in Kuwait, Saudi Arabia and the UAE.

If you're travelling between GCC countries, your cover is likely to remain valid, but it's vital to check if this is unclear on your policy. Taking a car beyond GCC borders or sending it home requires separate insurance. In the latter case, cover might be provided under the freight agreement. It's advisable to check.

It should also be borne in mind that driving while under the influence of alcohol or drugs (see page 188) renders your insurance invalid, which means that you're liable for the payment of damages and will probably spend time in jail while this payment is being organised. Your work contract might also be cancelled, depending on your employer's attitude and the length of time that you're going to be absent from work. An Arab employer might try to help you, but bad behaviour on your part adversely affects his standing in the community, so you shouldn't count on it.

Premiums: Premiums obviously depend on the type of cover required, the age and type of vehicle to be insured, its value and any no-claims benefits involved. High-performance cars are expensive to insure, and younger drivers also pay higher rates. A mature driver in an average car should expect to pay around $300 (£200) per year (without no-claims bonus – see below). You can usually negotiate a lower premium if you accept an excess (deductible). As in many countries, you're recommended to shop around to find the best quotation and, as with most transactions in the region, you should barter to obtain the best deal.

No-claims Bonus: No-claims records are recognised throughout the region, although you're usually required to produce written verification of your insurance record. The discount is usually a premium reduction of 10 per cent for each year of no-claims, often up to a maximum percentage (e.g. 50 per cent), but it tends to be counteracted to some extent by increasing annual premium rates!

Claims: It's imperative – and a legal requirement – to obtain an accident report (see **Accidents** on page 186) for even a minor knock, as garages won't carry out repairs without one. When you receive a report, make a claim to your insurance company without delay. In most cases, either you will be asked to obtain three quotations for the repair work or the insurance company will require you to use an approved garage. If the accident was minor, you can proceed immediately to have the work done. (You might wish to avoid making a claim altogether, pay the repair bill yourself and retain your no-claims bonus – see below). In the case of a serious accident, your insurer will usually advise you how to proceed with your defence and ultimately deal with resulting claims and repair issues.

Try to have your main dealer carry out the repairs. A main dealer has more incentive to carry out a professional job, whereas the insurance company's garage is likely to work to a pre-agreed scale of costs, which is unlikely to be to your benefit. It will also be easier to make a complaint to a main dealer if the repairs are inadequate. If there's a discrepancy between quotes, try to persuade your main dealer to match the cheaper one.

If you're the guilty party in an accident and are found to have been under the influence of alcohol or drugs at the time, your insurance company is within its rights to withdraw the policy or not accept any liability. Some companies might downgrade your policy to third party costs instead of comprehensive cover, but this is highly unlikely. Liability for all costs, including medical charges and loss of earnings, will fall on you.

Breakdown Insurance: You can sometimes negotiate insurance protection against breakdown costs by paying an additional premium.

RULES OF THE ROAD

The following points will help you to adjust to the driving conditions in the Gulf, although you might sometimes feel that you're the only one abiding by them!

- Driving is on the right of the road in all states. If you aren't used to driving on the right, take the time to practise on quiet streets. Particular care should be taken at junctions and when leaving lay-bys, T-junctions, one-way streets and petrol stations.

- The wearing of seat belts by drivers and front-seat passengers is compulsory in the region but isn't strictly enforced. However, traffic police sometimes run programmes to encourage people to 'buckle up'; these can take the form of random cash awards. Fines are sometimes imposed on those not wearing seat belts, e.g. BD10 ($27) in Bahrain and OR10 ($26) in Oman.

- There are no general regulations across the region about the equipment to be carried in cars, but a spare wheel and the tools to fit it are necessary in all countries. A first-aid kit and fire extinguisher are required in some Gulf states, and a set of jump leads is useful, as car batteries wear out quickly in the heat.

- There's also no general rule regarding traffic priority, although in Oman you're supposed to give way to the traffic coming from you left. Even this 'rule', however, is rarely adhered to by local drivers, who often don't bother to look when joining another road, and you should therefore drive defensively at all times. If you're in doubt about who has priority, give way. Police, ambulance, fire and all emergency vehicles have right of way irrespective of signs or markings to the contrary. Reversing into main roads is forbidden.

- At roundabouts, traffic already on the roundabout has the right of way – in theory. In practice, the situation is more 'competitive' than that. Many large roundabouts have traffic lights on the approach roads and on the roundabouts themselves, making them easier to negotiate.

- Most traffic lights are positioned on posts at the side of the road, sometimes with a smaller set at driver eye level. The sequence of lights is usually red, amber, green, amber, red, but in some cases red changes straight to green in the first phase of the sequence. (Note that the sequence can vary even within a state, e.g. in Saudi Arabia!) Amber, which officially means 'get ready to start or stop', has a very loose interpretation on Gulf roads, i.e. it's largely ignored and many accidents result, although police have become strict with those ignoring red lights.

- At busy junctions, there might be left-filter lights and lanes, sometimes with U-turns permitted, sometimes with restrictions on U-turns. Watch for pedestrians, who often ignore the pedestrian signals.

- Road signs are of a reasonable standard in most of the region, and internationally recognised signs are used. Priority is indicated at most junctions; for example, all secondary roads have either a stop sign or a give-way sign, supported by the usual triangular road marking. Nevertheless, you should drive defensively when on a main road joined by side roads, as many drivers ignore give-way signs. Distances on most road signs are given in kilometres, although there are still some old signs with distances in miles!

- Pedestrians generally have right of way and, if you're involved in an accident involving a pedestrian, you're deemed to be responsible. You must take particular care when local women are crossing the road: they invariably believe that they have right of way, whatever the traffic signals say, and their vision might be obscured by their head coverings. In villages where people are unused to traffic, they can also misjudge the speed of vehicles.

- White lines are intended to delineate traffic lanes, although some drivers seem to believe they're for alignment with the middle of their car's bonnet. A solid single line or solid double lines means 'no overtaking in either direction'. A solid line to the right of the centre line, i.e. on your side of the road, means that overtaking is prohibited in your direction. You can overtake only when there's a single broken line in the middle of the road or double lines with the broken line on your side of the road. No overtaking is also shown by the international sign of a red and a black car side by side. Overtaking can take place on either side, although 'undertaking' in the inside lane is illegal in some states. Rapid lane-changing without signalling is an offence, although you're unlikely to be pulled up for doing so (the police indulge in the practice as much as anyone else) unless an accident results.

- There are no bus, taxi or cycle lanes in the Gulf states.

- Headlamps must be used when driving at night, preferably dipped when facing oncoming traffic. Be wary of drivers flashing headlights, which might seem to signal 'after you'; it invariably actually means 'I'm coming through'. On motorways, flashing headlights behind you means 'Get out of my way!'. Hazard lights are used for the purpose for which they were designed and frequently also for slowing down for a traffic jam.

- The use of horns isn't restricted, as it is in other countries.

- Cyclists and motorcyclists are a fairly rare sight on the region's roads, but you should give any you do come across a very wide berth, because the car driver has to provide a strong defence in the event of an accident. Note also that cyclists, particularly those from India and Asia, sometimes ride in the opposite direction to the traffic flow and are occasionally penalised for this, i.e. knocked down. However, there's no law against this, which makes the driver liable in the event of an accident. You have been warned!

- Tinted windows are illegal (unless you're a well-placed local).

- The use of hand-held mobile phones while driving is illegal, although it's a common occurrence. Note that it's possible to be 'caught' for breaking this rule without being stopped; a policeman may note your registration number, in which case you must pay the appropriate penalty when re-registering your car (see page 171).

Saudi Arabia: As mentioned elsewhere, Saudi Arabia is a much more insular and state-controlled society than the other Gulf countries. This also applies to driving. The long list of traffic offences that carry punishment and the severity of some of the penalties will make you extra careful when driving here. Most obviously, it's strictly forbidden for women to drive, although it's possible that this law will be relaxed. Traffic fines are high and often accompanied by a jail term and/or lashes. For example, jumping a red light can incur a fine of around $225 (£150) plus three days in jail, while reckless driving will cost you $375 (£250) plus 20 days in jail and/or 20 lashes. Note that passengers in a car as well as the driver can be penalised for reckless driving.

Note that there are service roads for shops, petrol stations and parking parallel to the main roads in cities and towns in Saudi Arabia. Extra care should be taken at junctions where there are service roads, as it isn't always clear whether traffic signals apply to the service road as well as to the main road, except when the traffic is crossing at right angles. Note also that Saudi Arabia uses the American system of right-lane filtering while traffic signals are red, provided that the way is clear.

SPEED LIMITS

Speed limits, which are given in kilometres per hour, vary from state to state, but 100 to 120kph (62 to 75mph) is standard on inter-state highways and between 45 and 60kph (28 and 37mph) in towns and built-up areas. Limits are clearly indicated on roadside signs. Although speeding is often ignored by police (who are as likely to exceed the limit as anyone), fines are imposed as a result of radar monitoring, with both fixed and mobile units in operation: fixed cameras flash as you pass, if you're over the limit. Mobile units are usually operated by two police officers a certain distance apart and speeders are pulled in by a third officer around 150m further along the road. The more you exceed the limit by, the higher the fine. Your licence, which you must carry at all times, is temporarily confiscated and is returned only on payment of the fine at the police station indicated on the ticket. Note, however, that you can be 'caught' speeding without actually being stopped; in this case, you will be notified when you come to re-register your car (see page 171) and must pay the fine before being allowed to do so.

TRAFFIC POLICE

Traffic police tend to operate as a semi-autonomous department within the police force. They're usually efficient, helpful, friendly and not at all confrontational, unless a serious offence has taken place. In fact, in view of the carnage that they sometimes have to deal with, they're impressively calm and restrained. Traffic police patrol in cars, motorcycles and helicopters, and police ambulances provide emergency cover as required. The latter also patrol the region's numerous beaches.

The police are often uninterested in minor traffic offences (in fact, in any traffic offences, as the police often drive as recklessly as any other motorists) and see their primary function as dealing with accidents (see page 186) – a case of the cure taking precedence over prevention. Some Gulf countries operate a scale of fines and issue penalty points for traffic infringements. Twelve points can mean a driving ban or even confiscation of the car. The law, however, is generally more lenient than it is in European countries: penalty points are usually deleted annually. In the UAE, the police operate a telephone line on which you can check how many, if any, penalty points you've amassed. It's wise to check before the re-registering your car each year, as you won't be allowed to do so if you have unpaid fines. There are no on-the-spot fines, payments being made at police offices or designated banks.

Checkpoints are frequently set up in the region, mainly to check that drivers' papers are in order and that you're carrying your driving licence and a valid vehicle registration document. If not, you're fined. Some Gulf states also use these checkpoints to search for illegal immigrants or those who have overstayed their visa. This is particularly common in Saudi Arabia, where many people attempt to stay in the country after gaining legitimate entry for the pilgrimage to Mecca (the Haj). See also **Police** on page 351.

GULF ROADS

Roads in the Gulf are invariably excellent. Most have been built in the last 25 years, and they don't have to handle high volumes of traffic. The most significant road development has been in Saudi Arabia, where the main cities are now connected (sometimes across vast expanses of desert) by excellent motorways. International routes were also built between the Kingdom and Jordan to the north, Kuwait, Qatar, Bahrain and the UAE to the east, and Oman and Yemen to the south. A major enterprise was the King Fahad causeway, a 25km (15mi) road bridge linking Al-Khobar in the eastern province of Saudi Arabia with Bahrain. A small toll (BD2/$5) is charged for vehicles coming from Bahrain. (The link is used extensively by eastern province Saudis and expatriate workers travelling to Manama, the capital of Bahrain, for rest and relaxation in the less conservative environment.)

There are two principal road routes into Kuwait: from Beirut following the trans-Arabian pipeline through Syria and Jordan, and from the road connecting Lebanon and Iraq. These roads are for the adventurous only and in the current political climate you're advised to seek official guidance and permission before using them.

All foreign residents entering or leaving Oman by road must obtain permission in advance from the relevant authorities, although nationals and expatriates with residence in the neighbouring UAE should have no difficulty in obtaining permission to drive between the two states. There are excellent inter-Emirate roads, which are usually dual-carriageways. Distances are modest, the journey from Dubai to Abu Dhabi taking around one and a half hours and from Dubai to Fujairah or Khor Fakkan on the east coast, through spectacular landscape, around two hours.

Petrol stations are common throughout the region, both on major roads and in towns and villages. Some have service centres and there are garages throughout the area where emergency work is carried out. Road signs, usually in both Arabic and English, are generally clear.

OFF-ROAD DRIVING

Driving off-road into the desert is one of the favourite pastimes for expatriates and nationals in the Gulf (see **Wadi Bashing** on page 304). But desert driving is a special skill, calling for four-wheel drive vehicles, planning and comprehensive equipment (see below). The golden rule is never to travel alone, because breaking down or losing your way can be fatal. In fact, you should travel in a convoy of at least two vehicles, with enough room to accommodate all passengers in one of them in case the other breaks down.

There are a number of things that you should do before setting off:

- Make sure that your car is capable of undertaking the type of journey you're planning. This invariably means using a four-wheel drive vehicle.

- Leave a description of your vehicle, the names of the people travelling, your route, time of departure and estimated time of return with a responsible person, who can raise the alarm if necessary.

- Ensure that you have a full fuel tank and the correct radiator coolant level.

- Tyres must be in good condition and at the correct pressures, including the spare. You might need to deflate the tyres to achieve greater traction on soft sand.

- Check that your tool kit includes a jack, wheel spanner, wood block (to provide a solid, flat surface), tyre pressure gauge and small, 12-volt compressor that works off your car's cigarette lighter or other battery connection.

- Ensure that you take some matting (to put under the tyres if you get stuck in soft sand) and a rope or towing strap.

- Carry a food supply and at least ten litres of drinking water per head. Supplement this supply with soft drinks and avoid alcohol, which is dehydrating.

- Be clear on your chosen route and carry a compass or global positioning system (which are no longer expensive), preferably both. Carry a GSM mobile phone to call for help in the case of emergencies and make sure that it's fully charged before you travel.

When driving off-road, you should observe the following rules:

- Use established tracks, which are usually the safest routes.

- Never travel at night unless forced to by extreme circumstances. You won't be able to judge the terrain ahead and might encounter a sudden drop or difficult ground.

- At the height of summer, avoid travelling in the middle of the day when the sun is at its hottest and the sand at its softest.

- When driving on sand, maintain a steady, moderate speed and avoid sudden braking or acceleration, both make the tyres sink into the sand.

- Leave a substantial gap between vehicles so that a number of vehicles don't fall into the same trap.

- If a vehicle in your party becomes stuck, stop and approach it on foot to assess the problem. Don't drive to it or you might experience the same difficulty.

- Keep in low gear when approaching a high dune and go straight up and down, never sideways at an angle. The latter approach might be tempting, but it's easy to roll. Best of all, go around not over dunes.

If you become stuck or lost, keep calm so that you can think clearly and positively, and do the following:

- When stuck, try to drive out smoothly in a straight line, with straight wheels. Use low gear, four-wheel drive and drive as slowly as possible. Don't spin or over-rev because this will dig you deeper. If the vehicle isn't too badly bogged down, try to dig sand away from in front of all the tyres, leaving a slight incline upwards.

- If the vehicle remains stuck and there are enough people, try 'bouncing' the vehicle out.

- Deflate the tyres, remove excess weight and try again.

- Look for material in the surrounding area to provide grip for the wheels: wood, branches, desert scrub, etc..

- Stay with or near the vehicle; if you're on a frequently-used track, there's a good chance that someone will come along to help.

- If you see a Bedouin camp, approach it carefully, call out while still a considerable distance away and wait for permission to approach. Bedouins are helpful to any traveller, provided that their etiquette is observed.

- Keep in the shade of your vehicle, covering the windows if possible.

- Check your supplies, particularly water, and try to drink early in the morning and during the evening. If there's condensation at night, you can collect it on glass or kitchen foil shaped into a container.

- Start a fire because the smoke might attract attention. If you're carrying a reserve of petrol, use it to burn extra clothing.

- Lay out a large sign with clothing in the form of a cross or SOS. Flash a mirror at any search patrol.

ARAB DRIVERS

The standard of driving in the Gulf is generally poor and features a cavalier approach similar to that encountered in Mediterranean countries such as Italy, Spain and Portugal. To make matters worse, it isn't unusual to experience arrogance on the part of nationals and inexperience on the part of Indian and Asian drivers. There's a regional attitude that 'these are our roads, you're the visitor, we have priority'. Lane discipline is virtually non-existent, and local drivers tend to make use of all available space on the road and to suddenly change their minds and direction, which is seen as versatile, imaginative driving rather than as nerve-jangling and potentially fatal. (There's also a curious regional habit of lowering the driver's window and sticking a foot out of it – presumably a kind of 'air-conditioning'.)

The only time when locals drive defensively is when heavy rain falls. On these rare occasions, expatriates come into their own, being accustomed to such conditions. But be very careful, as many locals and Indians, for example, are unused to driving in rain. Another common Gulf problem is people driving while using a mobile phone, which has led to some spectacular crashes. It's now illegal in all states to drive while using a hand-held mobile.

As a foreigner in the Gulf, you should drive defensively at all times.

Losing your temper should be avoided if possible. If you're the innocent party in an accident, your defence might be compromised if you become aggressive. And never use physical force.

Note that, if you drive a sports car, you might be invited to race on the motorway by young locals looking for excitement. Needless to say, this isn't recommended.

MOTORCYCLES

Motorbikes and motor scooters are generally absent from the region's roads. This is partly because of the high temperatures in the Gulf, which aren't conducive to wearing the protective clothing needed by motorcyclists. There are a few high performance bikes, however, usually driven by western expatriates. Similarly, a few traffic police patrols use motorcycles, and outriders sometimes accompany the ruling families and visiting dignitaries. Normal traffic 'rules' (see page 177) apply to motorcycles.

ACCIDENTS

Road accidents in the Gulf are common, and in Saudi Arabia — with its high-speed roads and extreme temperatures, which put an addditional burden on tyres — accidents are often fatal. The UAE has one of the world's highest road accident death rates. On the other hand, minor accidents are invariably accepted in the fatalistic way of the Middle East and dealt with in a reasonable way by the drivers concerned.

In the case of an accident, whether the car was stationary or moving, you should generally leave it where it is, notify the police and wait for them to arrive at the scene. In the UAE, however, the rules now allow cars involved in minor accidents to be moved to the side of the road to avoid causing traffic disruption. In fact, failure to do this can result in a fine. Traffic police telephone numbers are published in newspapers, and you're advised to keep a note of them in your car. The police decide who is the offending driver and issue an accident report, which is a statutory requirement. If it's a clear-cut situation, such as a 'shunt', there's unlikely to be a prolonged discussion about liability. If the other party is a local Arab and the policeman has a limited knowledge of your language (and vice versa) then you might be at some disadvantage — in small communities, locals tend to know each other or recognise tribal identities.

If you're clearly at fault and are asked to sign the report form, you might think it reasonable to do so. You're recommended, however, to decline politely, claiming lack of understanding of the language. Insurance companies everywhere advise you not to make any statement that could be construed as accepting responsibility at the scene of an accident or indeed afterwards, and this is also the case in the Gulf. However, the colour of the copy of the report form you're given can be an indicator of where the policeman believes the blame lies: so if it's pink or red, you might want to make your case a little more convincingly!

The police's sympathy tends to be for the party who appears to be the most aggrieved. Therefore, don't adopt a reticent, 'stiff upper lip' attitude: if you're innocent, indulge in a little drama. Do so politely, of course, and with firm, good-natured resolve. It's difficult to over-emphasise the value of approaching officialdom in a polite manner. Arabs are generally warm-hearted and respond to a friendly approach. Conversely, they can be very tough if you become aggressive. (In Saudi Arabia, the police have their own way of settling such disputes: by putting both parties in jail until one admits liability!) When it comes to making a judgement over a minor incident which involves the imposition of a small fine, don't be surprised if the police favour the financially disadvantaged party.

A police ruling about the guilty party can be challenged, but you should be confident that you can prove your case before embarking on this course. This course of action should only be taken if the case is considered serious. The procedure is to contact a senior duty officer at the traffic police headquarters, make your case and take his direction as to whether the case should be judged in court. Incidentally, going to meet the official, as opposed to telephoning him, is perceived as a sign of respect.

If you're unfortunate enough to be involved in an accident, proceed as follows:

● Stop immediately. If a vehicle is blocking the road in either direction, switch on your hazard lights or, if you have one, place a warning triangle some distance away to alert oncoming traffic. Some cars, e.g. Mercedes, have a triangular warning sign on the inside of the boot: open the boot to display it.

● If anyone has been injured, call the emergency services, both ambulance and police. Don't move an injured person unless it's absolutely necessary to save him from further injury, and don't leave him alone except to summon the emergency services. Cover him with a coat or blanket, unless the weather is hot. Note that motorists are required to stop and offer help at the scene of a serious accident.

● Call the police (see above).

● Don't leave the scene of an accident.

● Don't move any vehicles involved in the accident (see above).

● It's helpful to take a picture of the accident scene if you have a camera or make a sketch, to show the position of the vehicles involved.

- If there are witnesses to the accident, take their names where possible, particularly those who support your version of events. Write down the registration numbers of all vehicles involved, their drivers' names, addresses and insurance details. Give any other drivers involved your name, address and insurance details, if requested.

- If you've caused material damage, including damage to stationary vehicles when parking or manoeuvring, you must tell the owner of the damaged car as soon as possible. The police will assist.

- Remember that no repairs can be carried out by a garage without an accident report, no matter how small or insignificant. And you cannot buy touch-up paint to do the work yourself.

- If you're detained by the police, ask someone to contact your family, friends, employer or lawyer. It's important to pre-establish a line of communication. Your sponsor will be very important in the case of a serious incident, since he has responsibility for you. However, it can be useful to have an intermediary between you and your sponsor, as your sponsor might not want to leap into action directly on your behalf. Don't sign a statement, particularly if it's written in Arabic, unless you're certain what it contains and agree with every word.

- In the case of an accident that will lead to an insurance claim, you must inform your insurance company as soon as possible. You will be asked to collect and fill out a claim report, to be attached to the police accident report (see page 175).

DRINKING & DRIVING

Drinking and driving is a particularly serious issue in the Arab world.

There's no allowance for any alcohol in your bloodstream, even in Gulf countries where alcohol is permitted.

If you're found guilty of drinking and driving after being stopped for erratic driving or a minor accident in one of the more liberal Gulf countries, you will probably incur a fine of around $1,500 (£1,000), a night or two in jail and the suspension of your licence for a period. **This is a minimum penalty!** A similar offence in Kuwait or Saudi Arabia or a serious accident resulting from drunken driving in any state can lead to extended jail sentences, heavy fines, the loss of your job and deportation. Note also that all instances of drunken driving result in court cases, and your embassy, sponsor and friends can do little to help you if you're found guilty. If you're prosecuted, your insurance company won't meet claims; this can be very expensive if you have to pay medical and repair bills and compensation. You will also find it difficult or very expensive to buy insurance in the future.

Taxis are plentiful and cheap throughout the region; so when drinking (and even the morning after a drinking session), it's sensible to take one.

CAR THEFT

Car theft is reassuringly rare in the region. There are number of reasons for this, the primary one being lack of motivation. The Gulf countries have excellent 'safety nets' and welfare programmes for their citizens, and many free services are also available to the foreign workforce, so there isn't the deprivation found in many other countries. In addition to this, most of the Gulf states are small and well-policed. Theft is a particularly serious crime in Saudi Arabia, bringing severe punishment, including amputations, particularly for repeat offenders. Border regulations are also generally strictly observed. It's possible for some stolen cars to find their way abroad on boats, usually to Africa and the sub-continent, but rarely does this invlove new or expensive models.

New cars invariably have alarms, immobilisers or other anti-theft devices that are a further deterrent, while theft of items from cars is also rare. Joy-riding occasionally happens, but again isn't a significant threat. If your car is stolen or anything is stolen from it, report this to the police in the area where it was stolen. You can do this by telephone but should go to the police station to fill in the necessary report. Then tell your insurance company.

PARKING

Parking is becoming a problem in Gulf cities, free spaces rapidly disappearing and parking meters being introduced. Construction in cities seems to be continuous, putting further pressure on available parking spaces. To try to ease the situation, all buildings, whether business premises or private accommodation, must now be constructed with underground car parks, and both your residence and place of work will probably have parking facilities. It's important to clarify this issue when renting your accommodation. Parking without cover in the extreme summer temperatures is most unpleasant. And if your place of work doesn't provide parking or provides only open-air parking, you can expect to start and finish every working day covered in sweat. The ubiquitous shopping malls usually provide covered parking spaces, either above or below ground, to protect their customers from overheating.

Parking areas are usually well sign-posted and rules about on-street parking clearly indicated on roadside signs. If you park illegally, you may receive a ticket — or you may not; parking tickets have a habit of 'disappearing' from windscreens in the Gulf. In the latter case, you will be advised of your indiscretion (and have to pay the appropriate fine) when you come to re-register your car (see page 171).

Parking standards in Saudi Arabia can be jaw-droppingly low, as Saudis believe that they may park anywhere — and usually do, e.g. on the pavement, two or three abreast at the side of the road, even in the middle of the road! And they usually get away with it. Traffic police in Saudi are often too busy to worry about such minor infringements (although the Bahraini police discovered a new source of revenue when Saudis began to come over the new causeway and brought their parking skills with them). The pursuit of parking offenders in the region is rare, however, and the penalties imposed are weak.

FUEL

Leaded and unleaded petrol and diesel fuel are widely available throughout the region, with well-appointed petrol stations plentiful in towns and along major roads. Fuel is cheap, which is helpful in a region where the car is almost a necessity. Fuel prices, which are similar throughout the region, are fixed, making shopping around unnecessary. Premium petrol currently costs around $0.26 (£0.17) per litre, low grade petrol around $0.21 (£0.14) and diesel around $0.17 (£0.11).

Both self-service and service-assisted petrol stations are in operation, and it's common to have your windscreen washed when you fill up. All stations provide free air and water, and staff check and pump up your tyres if requested. It's usual to leave a small tip for this. Many petrol stations also have the facilities to change engine oil. This service is well used by locals, who know the value of clean oil in the extreme heat and dust. Pump signs are in Arabic and English, and pumps are colour-coded according to international norms, e.g. green for unleaded.

Elaborate car-wash units are standard and much-used to counteract the dust and sand that can accumulate on cars. Police patrols have been known to stop drivers of very dirty cars and tell them to have the cars cleaned. Gangs of car cleaners used to be a feature of car parks in the region's towns and cities, but most have been disbanded because the cleaners were invariably working illegally.

GARAGES & SERVICING

Not all cars are easily serviced in the region, and it can be difficult to find parts for some of the more exotic and unusual models (which makes it important to check before buying a new car). All Japanese-made cars have widespread service facilities, and this applies increasingly to Korean cars. Maintenance for American cars made by General Motors or Ford is also widely available. The availability of after-sales support for European cars varies. Cars made by Mercedes and BMW, which are popular for their reliability, have extensive (and expensive) service back-up. Less popular European makes, such as Peugeot and Fiat, lack an after-sales service network, as do most British cars. Notable exceptions are the prestigious Range Rover and Land Rover, which have widespread service facilities. There are also numerous Rolls Royce engineers resident in the Gulf.

The quality of dealer service varies widely and you're recommended to seek advice about which dealers and service centres to do business with. Book work in advance, as it takes longer than in most western countries. (It isn't unusual for locals to jump the queue!) It's generally best to have your car maintained at the main dealer where you purchased it. It's more likely to be serviced by a qualified mechanic, and you will also have some recourse in the event of a botched job. Small garages should generally be avoided, not just because of their potential lack of experience but also because they sometimes use counterfeit spare parts from the Far East.

ROAD MAPS

There's a lack of good road maps covering the Middle East. Most maps are fairly basic and show only national borders, major roads and significant landmarks. Maps showing roads in urban centres are usually out of date, the mass of new construction outpacing the mapmakers. Satellite mapping is becoming more widely used in the region, however, and in the near future accurate maps should be widely available.

Maps are on sale at book shops in most towns and sometimes in hotel shops and supermarkets. The Ministries of Information can usually supply a basic map of their state in the form of the natural topography, urban areas and main road systems. Most centres of the expanding tourist industry, however, are in urban areas near beaches and are therefore easy to find without a map, so you may have no use for one.

CAR RENTAL

Car rental is widely available, and all the major rental companies have desks at the international airports and offices in the main cities. Avis, Europcar, Hertz and the other international firms (including Budget, who still operate in the Gulf) compete for business with regional and local companies. Rental company telephone numbers can be found in the yellow pages and the numerous tourist publications available in every hotel and book shop. When travelling to the Gulf for the first time, you're recommended to book a car before departure, although you should have little difficulty in hiring a car on arrival, except perhaps in the peak 'tourist' season (November to March). Fly-drive deals to the region are widely available. Note, however, that the roads surrounding the airports tend to be busy and you might prefer to take a taxi from the airport to your hotel and rent a car from there.

The major international companies are most likely to provide the newest and most reliable cars, and are usually the quickest to respond in the case of problems with your car. Rental rates are reasonable throughout the region. A small car can costs around $25 to 30 (£17 to 20) per day or $165 (£110) per week in high season (i.e. November to March). Local operations provide cars at the lowest rates, but they're likely to be older and might not have been serviced properly. Similarly, in the event of problems, you're less likely to receive as much help.

To rent a car, you can usually present your national licence and passport (or residence permit), although it's wise to have an International Driving Permit (see page 173), which is compulsory for car hire in Bahrain, unless you're from another GCC state. A copy of your passport or residence visa is required (the rental company can usually copy them for you), and the name of your hotel or accommodation will also be noted.

It's wise to pay by credit card for the additional protection this offers; if you're paying in cash, a substantial deposit is likely to be required. If more than one person will be driving, all names should be entered on the agreement and the insurance extended to cover them. When paying your bill, check the amount carefully and recheck the amount on your statement later. Also check carefully that you aren't charged for a speeding or parking fine that might have been imposed on a previous driver.

Below is a list of major car hire companies in the Gulf:

Bahrain

- Avis Car Hire, ☎ 973-531 144.
- Budget, ☎ 973-534 100.
- Europcar, ☎ 973-321 249.
- Express Rent-A-Car, ☎ 973-234 111.
- Hertz, ☎ 973-321 358.
- Oscar Rent-a-Car, ☎ 973-291 591.

Kuwait

- Al-Mulla, ☎ 965-245 8600.
- Avis, ☎ 965-245 3827.
- Budget, ☎ 965-481 0844.
- Europcar, ☎ 965-484 2988.
- Hertz, ☎ 965-484 8034.
- Thrifty, ☎ 965-246 0339.

Oman

- Avis, ☎ 968-601 224.
- Budget, ☎ 968-794 721.
- Europcar, ☎ 968-700 190.

- Hertz, ☎ 968-566 208.
- Thrifty, ☎ 968-604 248.

Qatar

- Avis, ☎ 974-622 180.
- Budget, ☎ 974-419 500.
- Europcar, ☎ 974-438 404.
- Hertz, ☎ 974-621 291.

Saudi Arabia

- Avis, ☎ 966-1-222 639.
- Hertz, ☎ 966-1-220 2678.

United Arab Emirates

- Avis: Abu Dhabi, ☎ 971-2-323 760; Dubai, ☎ 971-4-282 121.
- Budget: Abu Dhabi, ☎ 971-2-334 200; Dubai, ☎ 971-4-823 030.

MOTORING ORGANISATIONS

There's a number of motoring organisations in each Gulf country, but they aren't regionally organised. Semi-official bodies such as motoring clubs issue International Driving Permits for their members. Small organisations providing breakdown and recovery services for fees operate in most countries and are advertised in the local press and the yellow pages directories.

PEDESTRIAN ROAD RULES

Pedestrian crossings are indicated by diagonal white and black stripes, but aren't usually illuminated. In towns, at main roads and at junctions, pedestrian crossings are linked with the traffic lights. **Never assume that traffic is going to stop for you on a pedestrian crossing**. It's best only to cross when you're sure that the road is clear.

At a pedestrian crossing with traffic lights, the signal to cross or stop will be displayed by a green or a red silhouette of a man. When the green light starts to flash, this indicates that the traffic lights will shortly change to green, when the traffic will quickly move off. There are no rules restricting where you can cross the road, but not using a crossing is extremely dangerous. In the event of an accident, a driver will always be judged at fault and the penalties for injuring or killing a pedestrian are severe — which is little consolation if you're the victim.

12.

HEALTH

The quality of health care in the Gulf states is generally high and equal to that in western Europe and the USA, except for highly specialised treatment. Owing to the region's small populations and the numerous medical facilities in the private and public sectors, long waiting lists are almost unheard of. For specialised treatment, however, it's sometimes necessary to seek medical assistance outside the Gulf, and locals who can afford it often do so. Members of the ruling families and wealthy Arabs invariably have all major operations outside their own territory, particularly in London and American cities. Although some of the region's doctors and medical staff are local, the vast majority are foreign and were trained in their home countries. The attraction of the Gulf for them is the same as for most other expatriates: financial reward.

American Mission Hospitals, which used to operate on a part-private (for those who could afford treatment), part-free (for those who couldn't) basis, played an important part in the development of medical services throughout the region and can still be found there today, although they no longer offer free treatment. All Gulf states now have public health services providing free or very low cost health care for their nationals and it's important to note that these services are also available to expatriates. For some time, however, many Gulf States, e.g. the United Arab Emirates (UAE) and Bahrain, have been encouraging businesses to provide medical insurance for their employees, to lighten the burden on the national purse. Tourists visiting the Gulf countries should have travel insurance that includes cover for private medical treatment, but they also have access to state medical facilities in the case of emergencies.

Gulf Arabs tend to be healthy, and life expectancy is between 69 (Oman) and 75 (Kuwait) years of age for men and between 73 (Oman) and 79 (Kuwait) for women. The infant mortality rate has dropped significantly in recent years, although it varies considerably between the states. A developing problem is the increasing incidence of heart disease and related complaints, attributed to recent changes in the diet of the local people, notably the availability and popularity of fast food, and an increased intake of fat. The traditional, plain diet of rice, yoghurt and goat meat is a thing of the past.

Among expatriates, common health problems include alcoholism (particularly among bachelors, owing to loneliness and depression) and respiratory problems caused by sand and dust in the air – a situation exacerbated by continuous building work in most states. Hard work and long hours in often extreme heat can also affect the immune system and compromise the body's ability to counter illness. Expatriates – particularly manual workers – can suffer sunstroke and sunburn. You should be excused work outdoors if the temperature reaches 50°C (122°F), which isn't uncommon at the height of summer (particularly in the upper Gulf), although it's unusual for work to be stopped under these conditions. In the summer, humidity causes added discomfort, with eye infections common. Dehydration is also a threat and is a potentially fatal condition that shouldn't be underestimated – not only by those working outdoors but also by anyone playing outdoor sports, including 'leisurely' pursuits such as golf.

The 'winter' months of October to March, however, bring some of the best weather anywhere in the world, with continuous warm sunshine generating a feeling of well-being and providing the opportunity for a wholesome, outdoor lifestyle. Good weather is also beneficial to mental health, and people in the Gulf tend to be happier and livelier than those who have to cope with cold, wet, depressing climates.

EMERGENCIES

If you're a western expatriate, don't expect the region's emergency services and ambulances to be as efficient or widespread as in your home country. Ambulance services exist in some states, but these are usually controlled by the police (and used primarily for road accidents) or by the state hospitals. If you need to get to hospital quickly, the most reliable method is to use your own transport or go by taxi. This is common in the region. Even the victims of road accidents, if their injuries aren't too severe, are often bundled into a car or taxi and taken to hospital. Police and emergency services are sometimes equipped with helicopter services, but these are only used for road accidents, beach accidents involving drowning and evacuations from difficult terrain.

On arrival in any of the Gulf states, you should immediately take note of the emergency telephone numbers, the location of the major hospitals and their facilities, and the quickest route to the nearest hospital with an accident and emergency department. Your work colleagues can advise you about the best places to go. Keep the telephone number of a taxi service by the telephone in case your own transport is unavailable. Your private doctor will usually make house calls if requested in non-emergency cases.

In the case of a medical emergency, observe the following procedure:

1. If you're able to, go directly to the nearest hospital with an accident and emergency department.

2. If you don't have your own transport and an ambulance service exists, call the ambulance number. The operator will be able to speak both Arabic and English and will respond in the language that you use. (Although English is widely spoken by the emergency services, telephone operators, etc., it's useful to know a few appropriate words of Arabic to use if the need arises.) You will be asked to identify yourself and give your address; remember that you might have to give directions, using nearby landmarks rather than the street number. You will also be asked about the type of medical problem. If it's life-threatening, such as a heart attack or a serious accident, make this clear.

3. Ask for an expected time of arrival of an ambulance and whether trained medical personnel will be in attendance. The answer might persuade you to call a taxi.

4. If calling a taxi, make sure that the driver or taxi company understands the urgency of the situation.

STATE HEALTH BENEFITS

Note that there's no social security system for foreign workers in the Gulf and there are no reciprocal health arrangements between Gulf states and other countries. A contributory health scheme (GOSI), also involving retirement pensions, was experimented with in Saudi Arabia some years ago but was eventually abandoned as unworkable because of the transient nature of the expatriate workforce. Nevertheless, foreigners (including residents, visiting businessmen and tourists) are entitled to use public hospitals in all states except Oman (see below), without needing to be referred by a doctor (although in Qatar and the UAE you must register for a health card – see below). Patients are sometimes required to register at the hospital and will need to take their passport and visa.

The following is a summary of state health care services in each of the Gulf states. For lists of hospitals and main clinics in each state, see **Hospitals & Clinics** on page 202. For information on private medical insurance, see page 217.

Bahrain

Nationals and foreign residents have access to emergency and regular health care at public hospitals. However, foreign residents are recommended to obtain private medical insurance to cover all eventualities. Further information is available from the Ministry of Health, PO Box 12, Manama, Bahrain (☎ 973-289 810).

Kuwait

Emergency and out-patient treatment is free for everybody, but you're required to pay for treatment if you're admitted to hospital. In cases of financial hardship – rare in Kuwait, where the social services are particularly generous – nationals are helped, as are foreign workers. You're recommended to register with a doctor soon after arriving in Kuwait. Further information can be obtained from the Ministry of Public Health, PO Box 5, Safat, 13001 Kuwait (☎ 965-246 2900).

Oman

Nationals receive free treatment in public hospitals, but foreigners must pay. It's therefore essential that you have private medical insurance, whether provided by your employer or paid for yourself. There's no national ambulance service, so you must arrange your own transport in emergencies. For further information, contact the Ministry of Health, PO Box 393, Muscat, Oman, (☎ 968-602 177).

Qatar

Qatari nationals and visitors are provided with free or subsided treatment at state hospitals but are required to register for a health card, which must be produced to gain treatment. To register, you must take your passport and visa to the Ministry of Health. Private treatment is readily available in the country, but expensive, so foreign residents should have medical insurance.

Saudi Arabia

The standard of health services in Saudi Arabia is high, as health care is given priority and plenty of investment, and there's a wide range of facilities in clinics and hospitals across the nation. Public and private health care are available to all residents, although you're less likely to need to wait for private treatment. Private care is, however, expensive and it's therefore important to be covered by a health insurance plan.

United Arab Emirates

Nationals and foreign residents have access to state medical care, but need a health card. Application forms for health cards are obtainable from clinics and from the Ministry of Health (PO Box 848, Abu Dhabi, ☎ 971-2-330 000). Completed forms should be returned to the Ministry, with two passport photographs, two photocopies of you passport, a letter of employment and the appropriate fee – currently AED275 ($75). Expatriate workers tend to choose private treatment if they're covered by the necessary medical insurance – private care can be very expensive. In a country where the majority of the population comes from the Indian sub-continent, many private clinics are run by doctors from that region. Costs at these clinics are reasonable, but westerners are usually required to pay more than non-westerners, who generally earn less.

HOSPITALS & CLINICS

All Gulf cities and major towns have at least one modern hospital and usually several others with highly trained staff and state-of-the-art equipment. Poorer sections of the cities have older facilities, which nevertheless offer acceptable services. Hospitals are listed in telephone directories and the yellow pages, and addresses can be found in tourist publications. When choosing a hospital, your best bet is to seek recommendations from colleagues and friends.

There are several different types of hospital, including public and private hospitals and military establishments. Some hospitals in the private sector are luxuriously appointed and could easily pass as five-star hotel accommodation. Their prices are at a similar level.

Most of the region's private hospitals have an out-patients' department and an accident and emergency unit, although casualties are likely to be directed towards public hospitals by the emergency services, e.g. in the case of road accidents.

The term 'clinic' is used in the region to denote a general practitioner's surgery.

There's little overcrowding in hospitals and clinics in the region, where hospitals and major clinics are open 24 hours a day and usually operate on a first come, first served basis. Arabic and English are widely spoken, English being frequently used in private hospitals, where many staff and most patients are foreign. Accommodation in private hospitals is generally in single rooms rather than wards, and parents can stay with their children. Facilities usually include such 'luxuries' as a television and radio in every room, a cafeteria, a mosque or prayer room and a library. Costs for accommodation vary considerably, according to whether a hospital is super-luxurious (i.e. with a large mosque and library) or more modest (i.e. with small ones). Treatment costs usually vary according to the standard of accommodation.

The following is a summary of the main hospital facilities in each state.

Bahrain

Salmaniya Hospital (☎ 973-255 555) is the primary public hospital, while the American Mission Hospital (☎ 973-253 447) and Bahrain International Hospital (☎ 973-591 666) offer private treatment. State doctors sometimes refer patients to the Bahrain Defence Force Hospital (☎ 973-663 366) for specialist treatment, particularly orthopaedic. Awali Hospital (☎ 973-753 366) is mainly used by employees of the Bahrain Oil Company.

Kuwait

Public hospitals include the Al-Adan Hospital (☎ 965-394 0600), Amiri Hospital (☎ 965-245 0005), Farwaniya Hospital (☎ 965-488 8000), Mubarak Al-Kabir Hospital (☎ 965-531 1437) and the Sabah Hospital (☎ 965-481 2000). Private hospitals include the Al-Salem Hospital (☎ 965-253 3177), Hadi Private Clinic (☎ 965-531 2555), International Clinic (☎ 965-574 5111), Kuwait Clinic (☎ 965-573 5111) and the Mowasat Private Clinic (☎ 965-571 1533).

Oman

Hospitals include the Adam Hospital (☎ 968-434 055), Al-Buraimi Hospital (☎ 968-650 033), Al-Nahda Hospital (☎ 968-707 800), Ibra Hospital (☎ 968-470 535), Khoula Hospital (☎ 968-563 625),

Quriat Hospital (☎ 968-645 003), Royal Hospital (☎ 968-592 888), Rustaq Hospital (☎ 968-875 055), Sohar Hospital (☎ 968-840 299), Sultan Qaboos Hospital (☎ 968-211 151).

Qatar

Hospitals include the American Hospital (☎ 974-442 1888), Doha Hospital (☎ 974-432 7300), Hamad Hospital (☎ 974-439 2222) and the Qatar Medical Centre (☎ 974-444 0606).

Saudi Arabia

Some of the country's hospitals aren't only regionally renowned, but internationally recognised for their quality, particularly the King Faisal Specialist Hospital and Research Centre (☎ 966-1-464 7272) and the King Khaled Eye Specialist Hospital (☎ 966-1-482 1234). Other hospitals include the Maternity and Children's Hospital (☎ 966-2-665 2600) and King Fahad Hospital in Jeddah (☎ 966-2-665 6436) and the King Fahad National Guard Hospital (☎ 966-1-252 0088), King Khaled University Hospital (☎ 966-1-467 0011), Riyadh Royal Armed Forces Hospital (☎ 966-1-477 7714) and Security Forces Hospital (☎ 966-1-477 4480) in Riyadh.

United Arab Emirates

There are plenty of state and private hospitals in the country, offering excellent facilities and treatment, and the government has embarked on an ambitious project to build more by 2005, as well as additional health centres. Current facilities include The American Hospital in Dubai, Dubai London Clinic (☎ 971-4-446 663), The Gulf Diagnostic Centre in Abu Dhabi (☎ 971-2-658 090), New Medical Centre Hospital Sharjah (☎ 971-6-536 936) and the Tawam Hospital in Abu Dhabi (☎ 971-3-677 410). Note that The American Hospital is a new and luxurious hospital, but treatment is expensive and it experienced an unexpectedly high level of staff turnover shortly after opening.

DOCTORS

The region is served by excellent doctors, and there's a high ratio of doctors to patients in all states. Doctors are administered either by the various Ministries of Health or, if attached to military establishments, by the Ministries of the Interior. Doctors in the latter category are also available to the general public under certain circumstances. Many of the Gulf's doctors come from Europe, the USA, Egypt, India and Pakistan, and their qualifications are verified by the Ministries before they're allowed to practise in the region. Most embassies keep details of their nationals who practise medicine in the region. Alternative medicine practitioners aren't as common as they are in Europe and the USA, and you should check that they've been given state registration before using them. On the other hand, there are excellent antenatal and obstetrics services throughout the region, in both the public and private sectors; if you don't have private cover, the public services have a first class reputation.

Doctors are allowed to advertise and commonly do in the yellow pages. but it's best to choose a doctor according to word-of-mouth recommendation. If you have private health cover, you can change your doctor as you feel necessary, make appointments easily and in some instances simply walk in and see a doctor. Doctor's appointments in the public sector are normally given within 24 to 72 hours of the request. If making use of public health facilities, however, you're recommended to attend in person to ensure that you obtain help quickly, rather than relying on the telephone appointment system. Surgery hours vary but there are always two periods, usually between 9am and 1pm, and from 5 to 8.30pm. A same-day appointment can usually be arranged, and in an emergency you will be seen very quickly.

A routine first diagnostic visit to a private doctor costs from $60 (£40), with additional costs for any tests required. Many private doctors are able to process simple blood and urine tests on their premises and usually have electro-cardiogram equipment. A call-out fee for a home visit increases costs and in some cases a night-time visit incurs a surcharge. If you're referred to a specialist, costs can run to hundreds of dollars. When you pay, you receive a receipt to claim from your insurers.

MEDICINES

Medicines are dispensed from pharmacies, which are denoted by a green cross. Many medicines are available from pharmacies without prescription, including some that require a prescription in most western countries (although antibiotics can no longer be bought over the counter). On the other hand, some medicines that can be bought without prescription in other countries require one in the Gulf and you should check with a doctor. Most pharmacies also carry non-medical items, such as cosmetics and perfumes, but costs are likely to be higher than at other shops. General medicines, such as painkillers, cough medicine and eye drops, are widely available in supermarkets and larger stores.

Note, however, that Health Ministries in the Gulf have banned the use of tranquillisers, anti-depressants and in some instances sleeping pills, except for extreme cases associated with certain types of mental illness. (Ministers have seen the problems caused by their overuse in the west.) If you're dependent on any of these medicines and carry them with you, you must ensure that you're also carrying the doctor's prescription and preferably a letter from your doctor confirming that you need them. You're most unlikely to be able to obtain new supplies when in the region, so have enough for your requirements, but not so many that you could be suspected of carrying drugs for sale. For import restrictions, see **Drugs** on page 85.

If you take a medicine on a regular basis, make sure that you know the content name and formula, not just the brand name, as many brand names vary from country to country and between manufacturers. You might have to renew your prescription from a local doctor, as many pharmacists aren't authorised to accept foreign prescriptions.

Most pharmacies are open from 9.30am to 1pm and from 4.30 to 8.30pm or later, Saturdays to Thursdays. A notice in the local press indicates the duty pharmacy open outside these times. Many hospitals have a 24-hour pharmacy, where you can obtain prescription and non-prescription medicines.

It's important to obtain a receipt if you want to claim from your insurance. Medicines are quite expensive and there have been cases of over-prescribing in the private health sector, perhaps because of a link between the prescriber and the pharmacy.

DENTISTS

As is the case with doctors, there are excellent dentists throughout the region, the vast majority of them foreign, particularly from Scandinavia, Britain and Russia. Most embassies keep details of their nationals who practise dentistry in the region. Dentists and orthodontists advertise in telephone directories, expatriate magazines and tourist guides. Most dentists in the region are private, although local nationals are sometimes treated at public hospitals. As with doctors and hospitals, ask for recommendations from friends and colleagues before choosing a dentist.

Surgery hours are generally 9am to 1pm and 4 to 8pm, Saturdays to Thursdays, with some emergency provision. Treatment costs vary but not by much because of the competition that exists. Many dentists have their own work rooms and technicians producing crowns, bridges and prosthetics, and this speeds up treatment. If you need extensive treatment, discuss a payment plan with your dentist to spread the cost over a period. If you're insured, the insurers will require the dentist to fill out the appropriate paperwork; check that he does so properly.

OPTICIANS

Arabs have a tendency to develop eye problems, particularly as they get older, possibly because of the dry, dusty environment that they live in. There are numerous opticians in the Gulf, many of them Syrian, as well as possibly the widest collection of designer glasses on offer anywhere, with all the top names available. Most prescription glasses are supplied within 48 hours, and opticians, not wishing to lose a sale, can sometimes be cajoled into supplying glasses while you wait.

Eye tests are always free, and you will be given a written copy of the results to take with you. Contact lenses, including disposable, soft and extended-wear lenses, are widely available.

You must buy good quality sunglasses because of the region's bright sunlight and glare. Poor eye protection can lead to cataracts.

COUNSELLING & SOCIAL SERVICES

Public social services are available only for the local population. If expatriates show signs that they need counselling, they will almost certainly be repatriated. This might seem harsh, but foreign labour is brought to the region to work; if you're unable to do so, you're sent home. You're therefore recommended to consult one of the many confidential private organisations offering help to those suffering from depression or alcoholism or experiencing problems with their marriage, for example. Drug-related problems can result in immediate deportation and even the death sentence (see page 85).

SMOKING

The region is generally far more tolerant of smoking than most western countries, although the anti-smoking lobby is gaining ground. The offices of some international companies have designated smoking areas or are entirely non-smoking. Otherwise, there are few smoke-free buildings, although some restaurants (particularly in hotels) have no-smoking areas and most taxis and other forms of public transport forbid smoking.

SEXUALLY TRANSMITTED DISEASES

The problem of AIDS/HIV is taken extremely seriously throughout the region, where there are reports of an increasing number of cases among the local population, usually attributed to contact while abroad or with foreigners locally. (The authorities are particularly tight-lipped about the possible number of sufferers, and there's a tremendous social stigma attached to sufferers that does little to further the education process.) Unfortunately, there has been a recent influx of prostitutes from the former eastern bloc countries into some Gulf states, who enter for short periods pretending to be tourists and are therefore not required to take the HIV/AIDS test. In earlier times, unmarried Arab men were inhibited sexually by social and religious strictures, but when their world was opened up by the influx of foreigners and worldwide travel, sexual promiscuity became commonplace. Apparently, Arab males object to the use of condoms, so HIV/AIDS looks set to spread quickly.

For the expatriate workforce, an AIDS/HIV test is mandatory in order to secure a residence and work visa, and no one suffering from HIV or AIDS is allowed to live or work in the Gulf. There are no exceptions. Re-tests must be taken at the renewal of work and residence visas, which is usually every two or three years. If a test is positive – and doctors must report this – you will be deported immediately. In some cases, you will be escorted to your home, guarded while you pack and taken to the airport within hours.

Less serious sexually transmitted diseases are dealt with less harshly than AIDS/HIV, but as a foreigner your future in the country is at risk if you contract one. Promiscuous and adulterous behaviour can incur penalties in their own right (see page 342).

BIRTHS & DEATHS

It's recommended that you fully acquaint yourself with the implications of giving birth in one of the Gulf states.

In many cases, the child isn't affected, but any children that he has might not enjoy the same rights of nationality, citizenship, abode, etc. as his parents and grandparents (see **Citizenship** on page 334). Medical facilities in the Gulf are excellent, but many expectant mothers opt for delivery in their home country in order to establish the child's rights of nationality (as well as to be able to show him off to family and freinds).

If you decide to have a baby in the Gulf, the birth should be registered at your consulate or embassy, where a passport will be issued for the new-born, as well as at the local Ministry of Health (see below).

Abortion is illegal in the region, although it's undoubtedly carried out. (Arab women becoming pregnant as a result of 'promiscuity' or even rape can be killed by their family to purge the disgrace.) Foreign women requiring abortions are therefore obliged to leave the country.

If a foreign worker dies in the region, it might be necessary to notify the immigration authorities and cancel his passport and visas. A death certificate must be prepared by the attending doctor, either in a hospital or elsewhere, before the body can be released for burial, cremation or repatriation. The death certificate, passport and other papers must be presented at the appropriate embassy or consulate for validation and to cover matters such as insurance and the execution of wills.

Foreigners who die in the Gulf are normally returned home for burial or cremation. The arrangements are usually carried out by the deceased's relatives or friends, but sometimes by his employer or, if necessary, the embassy. Health or life insurance might cover the expense of this. It's possible for foreigners to be buried in the Gulf: Some states have cemeteries for non-Muslims and in some cases cremations can be arranged. However, Saudi Arabia doesn't allow the burial of non-Muslims on its soil.

All births and deaths must be registered at the Civil Registry section of the Ministry of Health in the area of the country where they take place. Everyone, irrespective of nationality and status (i.e. whether they're resident or just visiting), is subject to this requirement. A birth must be registered within a week at the local registry office or the hospital where the birth took place (if it has a registration facility). The responsibility for this rests with the parents, who must obtain the appropriate certificate. A death must be registered within 24 hours at the registry office in the district where it took place.

13.

INSURANCE

Many strict Muslims look with displeasure on the idea of protection against what they see as God's (Allah's) will, and it's only relatively recently that the insurance industry has developed and grown in the Gulf. Nevertheless, it's essential for foreigners to have comprehensive insurance, as in any other country.

As a foreign worker you might be assisted in obtaining insurance by your employer, who's responsible for bringing you to the country, returning you home after the completion of your contract and also for your welfare while there. In some cases, however, employers don't provide workers with medical insurance, sickness pay, maternity leave, etc. beyond the national legal requirement. Check this when considering who to work for (see **Chapter 2**).

If a company car is provided, you should ensure that you, as driver, have comprehensive insurance and that, in the event of a serious injury or death, you're fully covered for any 'blood money' payments (see page 342). If you buy a car on hire purchase, the lender (usually a bank) will demand comprehensive insurance as a condition of the loan (see **Car Insurance** on page 175).

SOCIAL SECURITY

The Gulf states don't have obligatory state or employer-contribution insurance schemes. Small populations and high gross domestic products allow the Gulf states to fund the welfare of their people without needing to impose many financial obligations upon them. (This also means that the governments avoid the high costs of administering such schemes.) Nationals are automatically provided with extensive state help, including medical care, sickness and maternity cover, child care, pensions, unemployment benefit and in some instances housing and disability benefits. Foreign workers have access to medical facilities in some of the region's countries (see **Chapter 12**), but to little else. In fact, Gulf governments are beginning to pressurise companies to provide medical insurance for their employees to ease expatriate pressure on state healthcare programmes, and private medical insurance is recommended for most foreigners (see page 217).

Saudi Arabia experimented with a social security system some years ago, designed to include foreign workers and retirees. The plan was abandoned a few years later, however, one of the problems being the transient nature of the working population, largely made up of expatriates. (To their credit, the Saudi Arabian authorities arranged refunds to people who had made contributions.)

PENSIONS

There are no state pension schemes in the region for foreign expatriates, although certain state institutions and some international companies have corporate pension schemes. If you were paying into a state pension scheme while working in your home country, you should continue to do so, even if in a reduced form, such as Class 3 contributions in the UK. These are usually one of the best investments you can make, for the continuous return they provide upon retirement. (You might also be eligible for certain benefits, e.g. the payment of medical costs, while in the Gulf.) Nevertheless, expatriates should take advantage of their high disposable income in the Gulf to set up a personal pension plan. There are many companies offering a variety of schemes, either based on lump sums or supported by regular savings.

INSURANCE COMPANIES & AGENTS

There are plenty of foreign and local insurance companies in the region, and you should take advice and recommendations from your work colleagues and friends about who to use. The foreign companies are often geared towards the expatriate communities, although locals also use them. Companies range from those catering for modest, personal needs up to major reinsurance businesses such as the Arab Reinsurance Group (ARIG), specialising in marine, aircraft and major projects insurance. Most companies have representative offices throughout the region, advertise regularly in local press and are listed in the telephone book and yellow pages. Visits, rather than phone calls, to companies and brokers are recommended when discussing rates.

There's a limited number of insurance brokers in the Gulf because the market isn't very large and there are fewer insurance companies than in Europe and North America. It can also be difficult to obtain unbiased insurance advice, as brokers are sometimes influenced by the commission offered by particular insurance companies.

Note also that, although there have been few instances of insurance companies going broke in the region, companies are sometimes reluctant to meet claims or protract the handling of claims. Like insurance companies everywhere, some in the region use any available legal loophole and delaying tactic (e.g. adjournments, delays, etc.) to avoid paying claims, and these practices are by no means confined to local companies. In general, it pays to deal only with a reputable company.

There may also be an advantage in using a company that has offices in your home country, as, in the event of a disputed claim, you might be able to pursue the matter there. In the event of a dispute, you should obtain legal advice for anything other than a small amount. If you believe that you have a valid claim, you should pursue it, despite any obstacles placed in your way. One problem with this is that you rarely have time on your side, because you might have a short-term work contract or a contract drawing to a close. Nevertheless, if the claim is significant, you should persevere.

INSURANCE CONTRACTS

Read all insurance contracts before signing them, having first insisted that an English copy is attached.

The Arabic contract will be used as the basis in law, since any disputes will be subject to the laws of the Gulf country. Make sure that you fully understand the agreement that you're being asked to sign, no matter how tedious this might be – as it almost certainly will be. Policies often contain legal loopholes in the small print and, if you don't understand everything, you should obtain independent legal advice before entering into an agreement.

HEALTH INSURANCE

There's a large number of international companies specialising in private health insurance in the Gulf and elsewhere. Comprehensive health insurance costs from around $50 ($35) per month for regional coverage. However, price shouldn't be your only consideration when comparing policies, and you should also consider the benefits of different policies.

As with all insurance, when taking out a health insurance policy do some homework and check the small print, particularly regarding what is and isn't covered.

All policies include limitations and restrictions; for example, 'pre-existing' medical conditions are unlikely to be covered, certain occupations are often excluded or attract surcharges, and high-risk sports aren't usually covered, although the definition of 'high risk' does vary from one insurer to another. Many companies also limit costs for a particular treatment within a calendar year, in addition to having an overall annual limit for all treatment. Be suspicious of policies that restrict the number of days that you're allowed to spend in hospital.

There might be an upper age limit on acceptance for a scheme and, if you're offered a private health policy that terminates at retirement, it would be wise to avoid it; if you're forced to obtain a new policy at the age limit, it will be very difficult to find one at a reasonable premium – perhaps at all. Note that some companies terminate your policy at the end of the stipulated period if they believe that the costs they've incurred have become too high. If you're purchasing an international policy, note also that some policies exclude cover in the USA, owing to high medical charges there. You can often pay to have different areas or types of cover added, but it might be expensive to do so.

Bear in mind that insurance companies can be very particular about their claim forms and are strict about them being filled out fully by the relevant doctor or dentist. Many medical professionals understandably find this tedious, but you must insist that it's done to order.

DENTAL INSURANCE

Full dental insurance can be very expensive and if, you want extensive cover, you must purchase a 'gold standard' health plan. Emergency fillings and extractions are normally included in standard health plans, but when it comes to more specialised treatment involving crowns, bridges and other prosthetics, the costs escalate substantially. Even 'gold standard' policies have exclusions, sometimes with regard to the content of fillings, the number of visits to a dentist and the volume of work carried out in any year. Policyholders also need to check that cover includes x-rays and simple cleaning. Cosmetic procedures and children's orthodontics aren't included in most plans (if they are, the premiums are usually high).

HOLIDAY & TRAVEL INSURANCE

Expatriates in the Gulf have a wide choice of nearby holiday destinations, being enticingly close to many attractive places. But, unless you want to risk having your holiday or trip ruined by the myriad of difficulties that can beset travellers, you should take out holiday and travel insurance. This is sold by several types of company in the region, including travel agents, insurance companies and transport firms. Package holiday companies and tour operators also offer insurance policies, some of which are compulsory if you wish to book a holiday with them, but these can be very expensive and offer only limited cover.

Before taking out travel insurance, carefully consider the range and level of cover you require and compare policies. Short-term holiday and travel insurance policies might include cover for holiday cancellation or interruption, missed flights, departure delay at both the start and end of a holiday, delayed, lost or damaged baggage, personal effects and money, medical expenses and accidents (including evacuation home), personal liability and legal expenses, and default or bankruptcy on the part of a tour operator or airline (although the chances of falling victim to the last are reassuringly low, as all Gulf airlines are state-owned and tour operators are usually run by wealthy Arab families).

Health Cover

Medical expenses are an important part of travel insurance, and you shouldn't rely on the cover provided by charge and credit card companies, household policies or even private medical insurance (unless it's an international policy stipulating the territorial coverage), none of which usually provide adequate cover. **Many Gulf companies require you to travel both inter-Gulf and internationally on business but don't always provide insurance cover. If you find yourself in this position, insist on adequate protection.** Your insurance company can advise you as to the extent of cover you're likely to need and what it will cost.

Always check any exclusions in contracts by obtaining a copy of the full policy document, as not all relevant information is included in insurance leaflets and cover notes. For example, pregnancy-related claims might be excluded, and there might be specific policy conditions for those over a certain age – usually retirement age, when medical premiums can become expensive. 'Dangerous' sports are usually excluded from most standard policies (although, as mentioned before, the definition of 'dangerous' varies), and high-risk sports and pursuits should be specifically covered and listed in a policy (there's usually an additional premium). Special winter sports policies are available, which are more expensive than normal holiday insurance.

Annual Policies

For people who travel abroad frequently, whether on business or for pleasure, an annual travel policy usually provides the best value, but carefully check what it includes.

Claims

If you need to make a claim, you should provide as much documentary evidence as possible to support it. Travel insurance companies gladly take your money, but they aren't always so keen to pay claims and you might have to persevere before they pay up. Always be persistent and make a claim irrespective of any small print, as this might be unreasonable and therefore invalid in law. Insurance companies usually require you to report a loss (or any incident for which you intend to make a claim) to the local police or the insurance carrier within 24 hours and to obtain a written report. Failure to do so can mean that a claim won't be considered.

HOUSEHOLD INSURANCE

Buildings insurance is unnecessary for expatriates, as foreigners aren't allowed to own property in the region, and costs such as emergency assistance and plumbing and electrical repairs are likely to be covered by the owner's insurance, although you're advised to check. However, you should be sure to take out insurance for your belongings, which can include expensive items such as furniture. Your effects should be covered at least against fire, theft and damage, although theft is rare. Most policies insure them against the standard risks of fire, smoke, lightning, water damage, explosion, storm, theft, vandalism, malicious damage, impact and natural catastrophes. The insurance is based on replacement value (new for old), with a reduction for wear and tear on clothes and linen, and most policies include automatic indexation of the sum insured in line with inflation. It's important to shop around to find the best rates, as you would in your own country, and bartering won't do any harm.

Contents insurance might also cover loss or theft of money (e.g. up to £375/£250), replacement of locks following damage to or loss of keys, frozen food and garaged cars. Items of high value must be catalogued and photographs and documentation (e.g. a valuation) provided. The security of the building will be scrutinised and premiums adjusted according to the ease of entry for a burglar. All-risk policies might include a worldwide extension covering jewellery, cameras, etc..

Check whether you're covered for damage or theft while you're away from your property and are therefore unable to inform your insurance company immediately. Also take care that you don't under-insure and that you periodically reassess the policy's value and adjust the sums insured (and therefore the premium) accordingly. You can arrange to have your insurance automatically increased annually, by a fixed percentage or amount, usually in line with inflation. If you make a claim and the assessor discovers that you're under-insured, the amount due to you will be reduced by the percentage by which you're under-insured. For example, if you're insured for $300,000 (£200,000) and you're found to be under-insured by 50 per cent, you will receive only $150,000 (£100,000) in compensation.

Claims

When claiming for contents, you should produce the original bills if possible (always keep bills for expensive items) and bear in mind that replacing imported items locally might be more expensive than buying them overseas. Note also that most contents policies contain security clauses and, if you don't adhere to them, a claim won't be considered. Policies usually only apply when there are visible signs of forced entry, although you might also be covered for theft by a domestic servant.

If you wish to make a claim, you must usually inform your insurance company in writing within 48 hours of the incident, rarely more than a week. If the incident is of a 'serious' nature (the definition of 'serious' varies from policy to policy but usually includes theft, criminal damage and injury), notification should be within 24 hours and you may also be required to inform the police. It's preferable to call at your insurance office to explain the details of your claim and perhaps fill out the required paperwork on the spot rather than merely to advise them by telephone.

Notification by phone in the first instance is fine, but a visit is necessary to ensure that you receive proper attention. It's important that the insurance company understands the full circumstances of your claim, and this is more easily achieved face-to-face. Where circumstances require police attention, the police report must accompany any claim you make to your insurer.

Insuring Abroad

You might be able to insure the contents of your rented accommodation in the Gulf with an insurance company in your home country, but it's hard to see any advantage in doing so. Gulf insurers offer competitive rates, meet claims as well as their overseas counterparts and provide an English translation of the policy, although perhaps in somewhat fractured English.

THIRD PARTY LIABILITY INSURANCE

In many countries, it's common to take out insurance against claims for damage, etc. brought against you or your family as a result of your negligence. This form of protection hasn't yet become common in the Gulf, although the 'compensation culture' prevalent in the USA and spreading to Europe might soon infect the Gulf.

14.

FINANCE

For many westerners, working in the Gulf presents the opportunity of a lifetime to build a financial cushion for the future. With attractive financial packages, no personal taxation (although Saudi Arabia is currently considering the introduction of a 5 per cent personal tax), low living expenses and perhaps a home property to let in order to provide extra income, many expatriates are able to save significant amounts of money for the first time in their lives.

When arriving in the Gulf to take up work and residence, you should ensure that you have sufficient cash, travellers' cheques, internationally-recognised credit cards and other forms of finance to sustain you until your first pay day. Credit or charge cards are useful, and Visa, Mastercard and American Express are widely accepted, although some restrictions might be applied to the last, particularly if you're bargaining for a discount. However, cash is king throughout the region, particularly with small traders and for low-cost items.

Note that you cannot set up an account at a local or locally-registered international bank or other financial institution until you have a work and residence visa. There's therefore no possibility of arranging a loan until the paperwork legalising your presence in the country has been completed. Even then, a loan will almost certainly require underwriting by your sponsor or employer. Your employer might give you an advance on your salary to tide you over (although you may be reluctant to ask for one before you've even joined the company!).

GULF CURRENCIES

The six Gulf currencies are linked to the US$ and are therefore susceptible to the ups and downs of that currency. Otherwise, they're quite separate, although the Bahraini dinar, Kuwaiti dinar and Omani riyal have similar values (between $2 and $2.65), as do the Qatari riyal, Saudi riyal and UAE dirham (around $0.27). All six currencies are decimalised, as explained below. Note that, in this book, local currency values are given where appropriate (with US$ equivalents); costs and prices that apply throughout the region are given in US$ (with GB£ equivalents). All prices should be taken as guides only, although they were correct at the time of publication.

Bahrain: The Bahraini dinar (BD) is divided into 1,000 fils. Coins are of 5, 10, 25, 50 and 100 fils. Bank notes are in denominations of 500 fils, BD1, 5, 10 and 20. The exchange rate is $1 = BD0.3770 and currently £1 = BD0.6259.

Kuwait: The Kuwaiti dinar (KD) is divided into 1,000 fils. Coins are of 10, 20, 50 and 100 fils, notes in denominations of KD0.25, 0.5, 1, 5, 10 and 20. $1 = KD0.3058 and currently £1 = KD0.4950.

Oman: The Omani riyal (OR) is divided into 1,000 baiza (or baisa). Coins are 5, 10, 25, 50 and 100 baiza, notes are 100 and 200 baiza, and OR0.5, 1, 5, 10, 20 and 50. $1 = OR0.3850 and currently £1 = OR0.6233.

Qatar: The Qatari riyal (QR) is divided into 100 dirhams. Notes come in QR1, 5, 10, 50, 100 and 500 denominations. Dirham coins are no longer used, although curiously prices are sometimes quoted in riyal and dirhams and then rounded up or down to the nearest riyal. For example, QR1.3 is rounded down to QR1, while QR1.7 is rounded up to QR2! (In the former case, it's preferable to buy items singly, while in the latter case you save money by buying in bulk.) $1 = QR3.6393 and currently £1 = QR5.8924.

Saudi Arabia: The Saudi riyal (SR) is divided into 100 halalas. Coins come in 5, 10, 25 and 50 halala and SR1 denominations. Notes are in SR1, 5, 10, 50, 100 and 500 denominations. $1 = SR3.7505 and currently £1 = SR6.0724.

UAE: The UAE dirham (abbreviated to AED, as in this book, or Dhs) is divided into 100 fils. Coins are in 5, 10, 25 and 50 fils and AED1. Notes are in denominations of AED5, 10, 20, 50, 100, 200, 500 and 1,000. $1 = AED3.6727 and currently £1 = AED5.9465.

It's wise to have some local currency when you arrive at your Gulf destination to cover small purchases and taxi fares, although you might well be met at the airport by your sponsor's staff or your new colleagues.

Currency exchanges and banking facilities are available at most major airports and many are open 24 hours a day. Exchange rates, however, are unlikely to be favourable at these outlets. More competitive rates can be obtained from city-centre financial establishments. You should avoid changing money at your hotel, as hotel rates are probably the worst on offer.

IMPORTING & EXPORTING MONEY

There are no restrictions on the import and export of funds into and out of the Gulf states. Everyone holding a residence visa in any of the Gulf states is allowed to open a bank account and to import and export funds, although it's unusual for people to bring funds into the region. Accounts held overseas are of no interest to the fiscal administrations in any of the states. No declarations of currency are required when entering any of the territories, so travellers can move currencies in and out without restriction and in any form that they choose.

International bank transfers are an area of local expertise, as handling the outflow of money has been a lucrative industry in the Gulf for some years. The volume involved reflects the large number of expatriates who move to the region and who export the majority of their earnings to their home country. Many open offshore bank accounts to avoid income tax in their own countries.

All the retail banks will transfer money to any destination and in any currency. Many people find it convenient to use their own bank to transfer money overseas, but there are plenty of institutions offering this service, so shop around to obtain the best deal. The main variables involved in transferring funds overseas are the exchange rate offered by the different institutions and any commission charges. The rate quoted might look attractive, but if the combined charges are high, you might be better off elsewhere. At the receiving end, your own bank will undoubtedly make a charge too, depending on the amount involved. Some banks are greedier than others, and loyalty to long-standing customers seems to be a thing of the past.

Apart from banks, there are plenty of exchange companies operating in the region, usually owned by the major trading families, who have long experience in the business and frequently give better rates than the banks. Different transfer systems are available, and the speed of transfer is the main determinant of the charge levied. The methods are postal, bank-to-bank, telex, telegraphic and SWIFT (or similar titles). Banks and exchange houses in the Gulf are generally competitive, speedy, accurate and reliable, but the efficiency of the transaction also depends on the institution involved at the receiving end. Electronic transfer is usually the quickest method, although long delays can occur if you're sending funds in, for example, US$ to a GB£ account, and delays can also occur between different banking systems (e.g. if the banks have no reciprocal arrangement). It's therefore simpler and quicker to send money between branches of the same bank or banks with close affiliations. You should monitor the charges being made at the various stages until the money arrives in your account and query any that you feel are unwarranted or excessive.

If you intend to send significant amounts of money abroad for business transactions, such as buying a property, ensure that you're given the commercial rate of exchange. The tourist rate or standard rate that you see quoted in your newspaper or posted on the bank's currency exchange board can be considerably bettered for large exchanges and transfers.

Another way to transfer money is to use a bank cheque or draft, which you can send yourself by registered mail or courier or which can be sent by bank-to-bank mail at a small additional cost. If, however, the cheque or draft is lost, stolen or goes astray for any reason, this can cause you a lot of administrative 'hassle'. Personal cheques can be sent, although these are subject to delays in clearing. For example, a US$ personal cheque made out to a GB£ account will go from your UK bank to a New York clearing system before the funds finally return to your account, and this can take some time. It's obviously essential to check that all the details shown on a cheque or draft are absolutely accurate.

CASH & TRAVELLERS' CHEQUES

Cash is widely used in the Gulf, although credit and charge cards are also popular. As in many countries, the quickest way to draw cash is to use an automated teller machine (ATM), found at banks and shopping malls. Withdrawals of cash from an overseas account can be made using an international network such as Visa or Mastercard. It's also possible to withdraw cash using a credit card, although this incurs high charges. Foreign currency can be changed at many outlets in the Gulf, although, as mentioned above, it's inadvisable to change currency at your hotel, where the rate will invariably be much less favourable than at a bank or bureau de change. The region's bureaux de change usually offer competitive exchange rates, but you should check to see if commission applies, and it's worthwhile shopping around. Most airport exchanges handle major foreign currencies, but for obscure currencies you may need to make special arrangements.

Carrying travellers' cheques is more convenient and generally safer than carrying a lot of cash. However, at certain times and in some places it can be difficult to cash travellers' cheques. Shops and restaurants, for example, don't readily accept travellers' cheques. As well as banks and bureaux de change, most hotels change travellers' cheques, but at much poorer rates of exchange. Banks charge a small commission for exchanging travellers' cheques and the exchange rate is invariably better than that offered for the conversion of banknotes. Proof of identity (e.g. passport) is required. Always keep a separate record of travellers' cheque numbers when you cash them, noting when and where this takes place. Most cheque issuers offer a replacement service for lost or stolen cheques (although there's little danger of theft in the Gulf, where the crime rate is low), but the time taken to replace them varies significantly. American Express claims to have a free, three-hour replacement service at any of their offices worldwide, provided that you can supply the serial numbers of the cheques in question. Without the serial numbers, replacement can take some days.

It's unlikely that you will be able to purchase travellers' cheques in Gulf state currencies, and, as local currencies are tied to the US$, you should use US$ cheques (or cash) in preference to any other in order to avoid possible exchange fluctuations.

Don't change travellers' cheques to any currency other than that of the country you're in. For example, if you're travelling between different Gulf states, resist the temptation to change your money in one place to meet your needs in all the different states that you're visiting. If you do, you're likely to find that the exchange process takes two steps: if you're buying Saudi riyals in Bahrain, for example, your dollars will be converted to Bahraini dinars and then from Bahraini dinars to Saudi riyals. Although the currencies are linked, there will be a commission charge on each transaction.

BANKS

There's no shortage of banks in the cities, towns and villages of the Arabian peninsula. There are international, regional and local banks, all well financed, well regulated and well run. Although there have been one or two notorious banking scandals in the region, notably the closure of BICC bank, banks are generally solid and well supported, and both the regulation and finance exist to forestall major incidents in the future.

Banks fall into a number of categories. Some central banks operate as clearing banks as well as being the regulatory institution. There are also corporate or merchant banks, providing venture and investment capital for institutional investors. Investment banks extend their services to individual investors, notably 'high net worth individuals' interested in portfolio management. Finally, there are retail or 'high street' banks for the masses. There are no savings and loan banks or mutual building societies operating as banks in the region. The services offered in other countries by these organisations are undertaken by the 'normal' banks in the Gulf.

An interesting aspect of Middle Eastern banking that you're unlikely to involve yourself with (unless you're a Muslim) is Islamic banking. The teachings of Islam ban interest or usury, and Islamic banking involves the centralisation of funds within a bank. These resources are then used, for example, to fund a construction project or other type of investment, which in turn produces returns, which are then shared out in proportion to input.

As a working expatriate, you're likely to open a standard current or deposit account with one of the many international banks found throughout the region. Banks such as Standard Chartered, Citibank, British Bank of the Middle East and others provide a reasonable service, bank charges are quite low and loan terms are competitive. (Banks are keen to attract customers and therefore eager to issue loans.) Banking in the region has now become highly automated compares favourably with banking in other advanced countries.

Some banks offer drive-in services, although doing business quickly is unnatural to the temperament of the region. Others provide mobile banking facilities for outlying villages and remote areas. Large industrial complexes often have banks on site for the convenience of their workers and this is also the case with some civil service organisations such as police training centres.

If you have a complaint against a bank and cannot resolve it through the bank's senior administration, the next course of action is to appeal to the Chamber of Commerce for advice, or perhaps the regulatory Central Bank; the civil court is your last recourse, but this is rarely necessary.

Opening Hours

There are variations in bank opening hours throughout the region. In general, banks are open from 8am to 1pm, Saturdays to Wednesdays, when many banks re-open in the afternoon from 4.30 to 6.30pm. On Thursdays, opening hours are usually 8am to noon, and banks (like other businesses) are closed on Fridays. Companies dealing in foreign exchange and money transfers usually work later in the evening, particularly those located in shopping malls and main shopping thoroughfares. At major international airports, bank facilities are usually open 24 hours. Public holidays are observed by banks, which conform to the holiday periods set by the governing administrations for private sector companies (see **National Holidays** on page 348).

In Saudi Arabia, work sometimes begins earlier, with a longer midday break and longer evening hours. During the holy month of Ramadan (see page 354), banking hours are shortened by 45 minutes in the morning and an hour in the afternoon.

Opening an Account

The formalities involved in opening a bank account in the Gulf are quite stringent and involve a considerable amount of paperwork. It's mandatory to have a residence visa, which demonstrates your right to be in the country. You also require a 'letter of no objection' or a 'no objection certificate' (NOC) from your employer. The employer's letter needs to stipulate your salary, to show the amount that will regularly be paid into the bank. Some banks will ask to see your tenancy agreement to establish your residential address, and most will ask for a photocopy of your passport. You should take copies of all these documents, as well as identity photographs.

A worker's dependants (e.g. wife and family) can open an account with his permission, as he's in effect their sponsor.

When moving to the Gulf to live and work, it's unlikely that you will close your bank account at home, particularly if you still have payments to make to cover commitments in your home country. In order to limit your tax liabilities there, however, the funds going into home accounts should be kept to a minimum. It's almost certain that you will also open an offshore bank account (see page 237).

Current Accounts

Cash is preferred for everyday transactions in the Gulf, where people are generally suspicious of cheques. In fact, although utilities companies and other major service providers accept personal cheques for regular payments, these are most unlikely to be accepted by local retailers, as they carry no guarantee of payment, even though issuing a cheque without the necessary funds in your account is a criminal offence in the region (see below). Most current accounts are therefore not cheque accounts, although these are also available.

All the standard banking services are offered by Gulf banks, including cheque clearance, standing orders, direct debits and credit card repayments. A certain number of transactions per year are usually free, after which there might be a charge levied, usually at the discretion of the bank manager. Charges vary between banks, as they do in other countries, so shop around before opening an account with a particular bank. Cash dispenser cards are issued as a matter of routine, with the standard security measure of personal identification numbers (PIN) to allow access to your money through ATMs. Personal credit and charge cards, most of them underwritten by Visa or Mastercard, might also be issued by a bank, but these must be negotiated with your banker and often have spending restrictions.

It might be in your interest to open an account with your employer's bank: favourable terms might be offered for group accounts and your salary might be accessible more quickly if the accounts are in the same system. If you wish to change bank, it pays to be honest and close your account instead of leaving a small amount in it to keep it active, as you're likely to incur charges. Current accounts pay little or no interest on account balances and, if they do, you must usually have a substantial balance to qualify. It's better to keep surplus funds in a savings or deposit account (see below).

The information shown on personal cheques is fairly standard (i.e. the name of the bank, the branch, your name(s), the date, etc.), and the layout of cheques is similar to UK or American cheques. The recipient's name is written on the top line, the amount written in words on the following line and the amount in figures entered in the adjacent box. You sign the cheque on the line at the bottom. An important point to remember is that Arab names are very similar, especially in their diminutive form, so you should be sure to write the full name of an Arab recipient. You aren't entitled to reimbursement for a 'misdirected' cheque if you've been careless and inaccurate when writing it, although banks are responsible if they've honoured a cheque which doesn't bear your proper signature.

Cheques are available for completion in English or in Arabic (which is read and written from right to left), and bank statements and correspondence can be provided in either language (your bank should use the appropriate language automatically). The business language of the region is English, and you should encounter no difficulties if you can communicate in Arabic or English.

Both crossed and uncrossed cheques are available. Crossed cheques (marked 'A/C Payee Only' at 45 degrees across it) can be paid only into the payee's account and are therefore safer. An uncrossed cheque can be paid into any account, although the bearer is normally asked to endorse the back of the cheque. To ensure that a cheque can only be paid into the account of the payee, you must add the words 'A/C Payee Only' between the crossed diagonal lines on the cheque. Uncrossed cheques made out to 'Bearer' or 'Cash' are treated as currency and can be cashed by anyone.

You should never overdraw your bank account unless you have authorisation from the bank. If you do so and the sum is small, your bank might pay the amount and inform you of the shortfall, or they might pay only the amount held in your account, or they might not honour the cheque at all. The last is unlikely, unless you're a new customer or have a poor record with the bank. In most cases of an unauthorised overdraft, you will incur a substantial charge and be questioned about the incident.

Note that issuing a cheque without the necessary funds in your account is a serious criminal offence in the region and the police will be notified at the discretion of the bank (or creditor) concerned. Prosecution isn't uncommon and punishments can be harsh.

A large transient expatriate population means that financial abuses aren't uncommon, and the banks protect their interests carefully, with the support of the judicial system.

It's important to understand that, in the case of serious financial difficulties, expatriates are unlikely to receive much in the way of sympathy and understanding, since their services in the country are viewed as expendable. In cases of criminal financial actions, penalties are likely to be harsh and might involve confinement for indeterminate periods while the judicial process takes its tortuous course, especially in the more conservative states.

If your cheque book is lost or stolen, you must notify your bank by telephone immediately and confirm the conversation in writing. Once you've informed the bank of the loss, any cheques written after that point cease to be your responsibility. It's possible to stop payment of a cheque, but you must be in a position to persuade the banking administration that the cause is genuine and pressing.

When buying a major item such as a car on credit, the bank funding the loan is likely to issue you with a series of post-dated monthly cheques, to be passed to the vendor, who will present the cheques on the appropriate dates for settlement. You should ensure that the cheques are correct in every detail and that you keep any receipts issued. Make sure also that there are sufficient funds in your account to meet the payments. If you're unable to meet a payment, you must notify your bank in advance to make an appropriate arrangement. Banks are usually helpful in such cases (as no bank wants to acquire second-hand cars in default of payment). In the case of a motor vehicle purchase, the official registration of the vehicle might show the bank as the official owner until the loan has been repaid in full (see **Vehicle Registration** on page 171).

For utility bills, direct debits can be arranged with your bank to cover regular payments, but make sure that you check your statements to ensure that these instructions are being carried out. Alternatively, you can pay utility bills in cash at any bank, irrespective of whether you have an account there.

You can of course pay cheques drawn on foreign banks in major currencies into your local account. You might be credited with the amount straight away, but some banks wait for clearance, which can be a lengthy process. If you're expecting regular payments of this kind, check whether your local bank has correspondent status with the foreign bank involved, which will precipitate payments. If not, you might need to find a quicker method of being credited with the money (see **Importing & Exporting Money** on page 227).

Savings & Deposit Accounts

You can open a savings or deposit account with any retail bank in all of the Gulf states. There are no specific savings banks such as thrifts or S&Ls in the USA or building societies or 'mutual companies' in the UK. Although savings accounts offer lower interest rates than deposit accounts, they have the advantage of easy withdrawal at any time. Savings account holders might receive a passbook in which financial transactions can be recorded, but more usually a monthly statement is issued in order to record the progress and details of the account.

Holders might also be issued with a cash card for use in ATMs, a cheque book and a credit card, depending on the type of account.

There are many types of deposit account available, offering varying rates of interest according to the amount on deposit and minimum deposit period. This is usually a month, although some banks pay interest after a week – generally on large amounts only. High interest accounts are available but require substantial amounts to be deposited in order to qualify for the higher levels of interest. Some banks offer standing order facilities with these accounts and issue cheque books, but there might be maintenance charges and a limit on the number of cheques that can be issued annually.

In many Gulf banks, you can open savings accounts designed for major foreign currencies, predominantly US$ and GB£. Most expatriates, however, wish to export the majority of their income to accounts outside the region (see **Foreign & Offshore Banking** below).

Cash & Debit Cards

All banks in the region offer customers cash and debit cards, which can be used at any branch of the same bank and, by arrangement, at other banks. Purchases and cash withdrawals are automatically debited and deducted from your savings or cheque account and details of withdrawals are shown on your monthly statement. You're limited to the funds in your account and may not overdraw your account (see page 234).

Cards usually have a limit on the amount that can be withdrawn in any one day from ATMs: generally around $450 to $700 (£300 to £500) in local currency. Account balances and mini-statements can usually be obtained from these machines. Most ATMs accept a substantial number of both regional and international cards, invariably illustrated on the machines themselves, although there's usually a fee for using ATMs operated by banks other than your own. There are plenty of ATMs throughout the region: as well as those inside and outside banks, you will find them in shopping malls, supermarkets and hypermarkets.

Most machines provide instructions and information in Arabic and English. Note that with some machines you must remove your cash quickly or it will vanish before your eyes, back into the machine! If you request more than your current account balance, you will be asked to request a lesser amount or the transaction will be terminated.

Transactions will also be terminated and an appropriate message displayed if you select a service that's unavailable. You can use the 'cancel' button at any time to terminate a transaction. Your card will (hopefully) be returned to you and you can start again, if needed. If you lose your card during a transaction (or at any other time), you must notify your bank as soon as possible. Take note of the name of the official that you notify and the time and method of notification. You will probably be asked to come to the issuing bank and complete an appropriate form in order to obtain a replacement card.

Foreign & Offshore Banking

In many cases, foreign workers in the Gulf find that they're able, for the first time, to save part of their income for the future. You should therefore investigate the best ways to obtain (safe) returns on the money invested and (legal) ways to avoid tax. Before leaving your home country, declare your trip to your home tax authorities. Provided you establish non-resident status in the Gulf country in which you're working, you will normally be outside the remit of your home country's tax regulations and will therefore minimise (or avoid altogether) tax penalties. If you keep your home bank account open in order to pay expenses (e.g. related to a property), the money that you remit to this account should be kept to a minimum. If you're also earning income in your home country (e.g. from property rental), you may be liable for tax on this and you should check with your home tax office or a financial adviser. US citizens must also pay home tax on their overseas earnings.

An offshore bank account may be advantageous if you want to earn interest while keeping funds reasonably fluid in the short to mid-term. An offshore account can be used as a central source from which to send funds to other locations, including an account in your home country. Other attractions are that money can be deposited (and maintained) in a wide range of currencies, customers are usually guaranteed anonymity, there are no double taxation agreements, no withholding tax is payable and interest is paid tax-free.

There are over 50 official 'tax havens' offering offshore banking, including the Channel Islands (Jersey and Guernsey), the Isle of Man, Gibraltar and the Virgin Islands. A large number of American, British and other European banks and financial institutions provide offshore banking facilities in one or more locations. Most expatriate financial publications, such as **Resident Abroad**, carry advertisements for offshore banks and their services.

Most institutions offer high interest deposit accounts for long and mid-term savings and a variety of investment plans. Accounts have minimum deposit levels that usually start at around $1,500 (£1,000), with an upper limit of around $150,000 (£100,000), above which you may be able to negotiate a special interest rate. The major disadvantage of offshore ccounts is that there are usually stringent conditions relating to withdrawal periods and penalties for early withdrawals. You can deposit funds with instant access or for a fixed period, for example from 30, 60 or 90 days up to a year or more. Interest is usually paid monthly but can be paid annually, in which case interest payments are slightly higher. There are usually no charges if you maintain the minimum balance in the account. Some accounts offer a cheque book but are likely to impose a limit on the number of cheques that you can issue in any year, after which you must pay charges. Cash or credit cards are frequently offered, usually underwritten by Visa or Mastercard, and these can be used in ATMs worldwide.

When reviewing financial institutions and offshore banking centres, your first consideration should be the security of your money. Offshore branches of larger companies are in most cases separately formed companies, with rules and regulations applying to the countries in which they're formed and operate within. In the event of any difficulties, the parent company is likely to bail out its subsidiary, but might not be legally required to do so. Nevertheless, big is generally best when it comes to selecting a home for your money. The major international banks are hardly likely to fold and you might feel more comfortable with those that you already know. **If you're offered unrealistically high terms of interest, the chances are that they're just that – unrealistic.** However, some of the northern European banks, e.g. those in Finland, offer much higher rates than average, presumably to attract funds, and they've been operating safely for a number of years.

Many banking centres offer a protection system whereby a percentage of bank deposits up to a maximum sum is guaranteed in the event of a financial institution becoming insolvent (Guernsey, Jersey, the Isle of Man and other offshore centres operate such a protection scheme). You can check the level of deposit insurance offered by the various financial institutions with Moody's Investor Service or via your financial adviser; you can also verify their credit ratings. All banks have a credit rating, from the highest of triple 'A' downwards, and most are happy to tell you about it, particularly if they have a high rating. Ratings just below 'AAA' don't necessarily mean that the financial institution's status is doubtful.

Some people regard savings and deposit accounts as attractive only to the smaller investor. Those with larger amounts to invest, who are seeking greater returns, might consider other types of investment (see below).

INVESTMENT

Before making any sort of investment – whether you have a lump sum at your disposal or wish to make regular contributions to an investment fund – you should take financial advice. There are plenty of financial advisers, investment bankers and insurance agents in the region. Knowledgeable colleagues are a valuable source of advice as to who to deal with, although you should also do your own research. Note, however, that you will have difficulty finding an adviser who is completely independent, as many are representatives of companies seeking investment funds. It's important to discover how an adviser is remunerated. If he's paid by commission from a particular investment house, he will obviously be biased towards their products. This isn't necessarily a bad thing, but you might be missing better opportunities for your money. If the adviser works on a fee basis (usually related to the amount of funds being managed), you're likely to be given a more independent, unbiased viewpoint, but this isn't of course a guarantee of success. You might find that some 'advisers' are nothing more than general salesmen without specialised knowledge of the financial market. If you're doing business with a bank or financial investment company, it may be easier to make a judgement by looking at past performance, although past performance is no guarantee of future gains.

You must also consider the amount of risk that you're prepared to take with your investments. Indeed, this is one of the first points that a financial adviser will want to establish and it's important to take guidance on this. If you're young and have few responsibilities, you might be inclined to take high risks in the pursuit of greater gains. Fixed interest investments, either short or long-term, are more suitable for the conservative investor, your capital being returned on maturity, although obviously the value can vary during the agreed period. Most advisers balance your investments, with a mixture of fixed interest and capital growth to ensure decent progress with protection. Unit trusts and similar types of investment allow for a spread of financial and commercial activity based on volume funds and mean that the smaller investor can participate in this sector. If you have a lot of money to invest, you may want to use a private investment bank to manage your investments. The minimum investment is usually around $375,000 (£250,000), although many private banks have higher limits.

Whatever type of investment you're considering, you should note the following points:

- Satisfy yourself that any advice you receive is sound and reasonable. If you have any doubts, don't proceed.

- If you're acting independently, make sure that the company/investment opportunity has professional standing and a record of acceptable performance.

- Devote time and thought to the degree of risk you're prepared to take.

- Talk to knowledgeable colleagues and/or your bank manager.

- Don't pay any money to investment advisers.

- Check the ownership of any holdings being made for you and the status of nominees.

- If you have a portfolio of investments, be clear at the outset as to whether you want discretionary on non-discretionary status. Many institutions only accept non-discretionary status, which allows them complete freedom to move your funds at their discretion.

- Make sure that you fully understand the fees that will be levied on your investments.

- No reputable company will indulge in 'churning' (i.e. switching investments regularly to earn transaction fees). If you find too much activity on your portfolio, check it.

- If you find that you've been transferred out of a high performing fund, ask why.

- Finally, remember the law of gravity: what goes up, must come down. And a competent investment company should know when the time comes to move funds.

CREDIT & CHARGE CARDS

A credit card provides access to funds on credit up to a particular limit, upon which an interest charge is made, depending on the particular conditions of repayment. A charge card offers a similar facility but restricts the credit period (usually to a month). Visa and Mastercard are the most widely accepted credit cards worldwide and are the most commonly issued by banks on the Arabian peninsula. The presence of the Visa or Mastercard name on an unrecognised Arab bank card is important when travelling to other regions. Charge cards such as those issued by American Express and Diners Club are also available in the Gulf and are fairly widely accepted, although less so than the major credit cards, mainly because of the higher commission charged to the supplier of the goods or services.

The annual fee for a credit or charge card varies with the issuing bank but is usually around $15 (£10) for a standard card, fees rising for gold cards, which provide higher levels of credit. Some cards come with additional benefits, such as travel insurance or life insurance when the card is being used for travel arrangements. Others offer a points system that increases with the amount of purchases, the points being redeemed for consumer goods, travel discounts, etc.. Using a credit or charge card in some countries offers protection against a company going bust or the purchase being faulty. Most major purchases should be transacted with a card if this type of protection is offered. **Shop around, as fees, interest charges and benefits vary enormously**.

When making purchases in the Middle East, haggling is invariably expected. But the production of a credit or charge card will wipe out any beneficial terms that you might have negotiated. In fact, there might actually be a surcharge if you want to pay with a credit or charge card, particularly if you're buying from a small trader.

You can of course use a foreign credit card in the Gulf and you might benefit from delayed charging, but not if you withdraw cash, for which charging starts immediately. You might, however, find it more convenient to receive your bills in local currency and pay from local funds, rather than to be subject to fluctuating currency conversion rates. The western practice of major department stores issuing their own credit cards is uncommon in the Gulf, largely because of the cash culture that still prevails in the region.

All credit and charge cards allow you to access cash from ATMs and you might gain some advantage from the rate of exchange between the tourist or commercial rate, although you're likely to incur a charge for a cash transaction. There are also occasions when a credit card isn't only useful but a necessity, for example when renting a car or booking into a hotel.

If your card is lost or stolen, make sure that you report it immediately by telephone to the issuing company or bank and confirm it in writing or in person. It's important to keep the telephone number of the card company to hand for speedy notification. Your liability is usually limited until you report the loss; after that, no liability applies. In the case of theft, you should also report the matter to the police.

LOANS, OVERDRAFTS & MORTGAGES

Your employer might have a scheme to lend staff money to pay for significant purchases, to be repaid by deductions from their monthly salary. But this benefit is becoming rarer. Banks, however, are quite happy – even enthusiastic – to offer loans and provide overdrafts for their customers. Loan conditions vary from bank to bank and you can of course approach banks other than your usual one, although the background checks are likely to be more stringent if you approach a bank where you're unknown. Your income will be checked with your employer, who, as your sponsor, will already have given a 'letter of no objection' or a 'no objection certificate' (NOC) in order for you to open a bank account and will probably be liable for any financial default on your part.

Mortgages usually apply to the purchase of property, but this isn't the case in the Gulf, where foreigners aren't allowed to own property or land. A mortgage in the Gulf means a loan for the purchase of an item such as a car and constitutes a fixed amount to be repaid in set instalments over a fixed period. The amount that you can borrow depends on a number of factors, such as your income, your employment status, your employer's approval and your ability to meet the commitment. With a major purchase, the bank might require you to pay 10 per cent of the price, supplying the remaining 90 per cent themselves.

It's unlikely that local banks will offer mortgages or significant loans for purchases being made outside the region. However, your home/foreign/offshore bank might have a branch in your Gulf state and might be persuaded to offer you a deal. If you need a loan, you should shop around and seek advice from colleagues, particularly the 'old hands'.

In the event of your being unable to meet your repayments, don't default and ignore the situation. Go to your banker and discuss the matter; payments can usually be rescheduled. If you default on a loan, the item involved is likely to be repossessed, but you might still be involved in litigation, which should be avoided at all cost. Note that defaults in paying off loans and overdrafts are viewed gravely, so such agreements shouldn't be entered into lightly. Overdrafts also bring interest charges, and exceeding the limit of an agreed overdraft attracts punitive charges while the matter is being addressed.

INCOME TAX

There's currently no personal income tax in any of the Gulf states; nor are there social security contributions to be made. Saudi Arabia, however, has for some time been investigating the viability of introducing a personal tax (a rate of 5 per cent is usually quoted) and more recently there has been a draft proposal to tax all foreigners 10 per cent on all income over $1,000 (£675) per month, although recurring concerns over Iraq and possible regional conflict look set to delay the introduction of any such scheme. The Saudi Arabian government has tried previously to introduce taxes but the legislation was quickly withdrawn when it became clear that there would have been a mass exodus of foreign expatriates, particularly those from western countries, upon whom Saudi Arabia is dependent in vital areas of its administration and economy.

UK expatriates who have established 'non-resident for tax purposes' status in their home country aren't required to pay tax on their earnings overseas, provided that they adhere to the annual time limit (a maximum of 183 days) for stays in the UK. However, if you're also generating income within the UK (e.g. from property rental), you may have tax liabilities there. US citizens are liable for tax in the USA on their foreign earnings, and all workers returning to their home country after completing employment abroad are obliged to inform their respective tax authorities.

COMMERCIAL TAXATION

This is a complicated subject, and anyone giving serious consideration to starting their own business in the region needs to carry out extensive research into the particular rules and regulations in the relevant state or states. Rules applying to sponsorship and degree of ownership vary, and consultating with the local Chamber of Commerce and securing reliable legal advice are vital. There's a wealth of information and professional advice available to those wishing to start a new venture in the Gulf and, if the project is in one of the favoured industries, assistance might be available in the form of investment capital, tax breaks, etc.. If you're looking for a sponsor, which in most cases is necessary, and you have a favoured project, a member of the Chamber might well sponsor you himself.

General information on commercial taxation in each of the states is provided below.

Bahrain

Those running a business must pay an annual commercial registration fee, depending on the type of business and the basis upon which the company was formed and is operating. The only commercial taxes are those relating to businesses connected with the oil industry. Otherwise, those who are used to withholding taxes, sales tax, capital gains taxes and other levies will be pleasantly surprised to find that profits can be transferred without deduction.

Kuwait

Companies which have foreign participation are taxed on profits and capital gains, while wholly Kuwaiti-owned companies are free from these encumbrances. However, there are tax breaks for certain new companies, e.g. high technology companies which assist the national policy of diversification away from an oil-based economy. These enterprises might enjoy zero taxes or perhaps a tax holiday for a start-up period of up to ten years as well as being able to freely export funds and capital. There are also certain import duty exemptions on equipment and other items for new companies.

Oman

There's taxation on corporate activity in Oman, where higher rates are levied if there's foreign ownership participation. However, there are exemptions for companies engaged in certain occupations, such as tourism, agriculture, animal breeding, fishing and fish processing, the export of local products and mining. These exemptions apply for around five years, although extensions are possible.

Qatar

Corporation tax is levied, but there are exemptions for favoured activities, particularly those deemed to be of special importance to the state and involving new technology.

Saudi Arabia

Foreign-owned companies must pay tax on their income, while Saudi-owned companies pay Zakat, an Islamic form of taxation. Certain new industrial and commercial ventures receive tax incentives and sometimes help with start-up investment.

United Arab Emirates

Foreign banks and some companies in oil-based activities are liable for corporation tax.

OTHER TAXES

Expatriates cannot own property in the Gulf and this is likely to remain the case for the foreseeable future. There are therefore no property taxes to be paid, but in some states local 'rates' (*baladiya*) are levied for expenses such as refuse collection and road maintenance, although these are often payable by the property owner rather than the lessee. There are no personal capital gains tax liabilities, although businesses sometimes attract a CGT levy (see above). There's no value added tax or sales tax in the Gulf; nor is there wealth tax, inheritance tax or gift tax.

WILLS

You should make a will to ensure that your final wishes are made clear to your relatives and dependants, who will otherwise have to deal with the problem of your dying intestate. As a foreigner and non-national in the Gulf, you won't own land or property, although you might have a shareholding in a company that should be disposed of in a will, which might be covered in the company's articles of association or documentation of formation and closure. Even if you have no assets in the Gulf, having a will based on your estate in your home country is important, since your country of domicile is likely to be the place of probate.

If you die in the Gulf, the local authorities will require instructions as to the disposal of your remains. Note that the Saudi authorities don't allow the burial of non-Muslims in their territory and require the removal of the body for burial or cremation elsewhere (see **Births & Deaths** on page 209).

COST OF LIVING

The overall cost of living in the Gulf is similar to that in most European countries, if you're living in the style of the average western expatriate. But the general lack of taxation in the Gulf states has a significant impact on the cost of certain items, e.g. cars. On the other hand, the cost of accommodation is sometimes high, as is that of certain food items, particularly imported foods. If you buy internationally recognised branded foods and household goods, you might pay higher prices than in your home country, but there are usually plenty of cheaper locally and regionally produced alternatives that are of excellent quality. Clothing can also be expensive if you favour designer labels – this isn't peculiar to the Gulf – although there's little need for winter clothing.

The price of wines and spirits, where these are permitted, is slightly lower than in the UK but higher than average European prices. Electronic goods, such as televisions, hi-fis, DVD players, photographic equipment and computer hardware and software, are generally less expensive than in Europe, mainly because of lower import duties. Recently published figures for consumer price inflation range from 0.3 per cent in Saudi Arabia to 3 per cent in the UAE.

Utilities, such as electricity, water and gas, are subsidised to some extent by the region's governments, which own the services (except for bottled gas supplies) in order to provide inexpensive electricity and water, mainly for the benefit of the local population. Utilities are therefore cheaper than in most European countries. However, at the height of summer, air-conditioning costs will escalate, rather as the cost of heating increases in winter in colder climates. Newcomers sometimes make the expensive mistake of keeping their air-conditioning on even when they're out, but this is unnecessary, as air-conditioning systems reduce the temperature in your accommodation quickly when activated on your return home.

You should also allow for the cost of international telephone calls, although these are kept low by Gulf governments, who want to encourage international business and investment in the region. Most Gulf states also waive charges for local calls, which can lead to considerable savings.

Your cost of living will obviously depend on your lifestyle, and costs vary to some extent between the six states, Bahrain being generally the most expensive and Saudi generally the cheapest. When you're negotiating a work contract, it's usual for your prospective employer to produce detailed cost of living figures for his country, which are useful in helping you to decide whether the proposed job is financially attractive or not. Average monthly major expenses for a single person, couple and family with two children are shown below (numbers in brackets relate to the notes following the table).

Monthly Costs ($/£)			
Item	Single	Couple	Couple with 2 Children
Housing (1)	900/600	1,050/700	1,200/800
Food (2)	450/300	750/500	1,050/700
Utilities (3)	225/150	300/200	450/300
Leisure (4)	450/300	450/300	600/400
Transport (5)	75/50	150/100	150/100
Insurance (6)	100/65	150/100	225/150
Clothing (7)	150/100	300/200	450/300
Totals	2,350/1,565	3,150/2,100	4,125/2,750

1 Rental costs for a one-bedroom apartment in a modern block, probably unfurnished, a two-bedroom apartment in a similar block and a two or three-bedroom apartment or a modest villa. Apartments might have air-conditioning included in the rent. Satellite television is probably provided but is unlikely to include all channels. A swimming pool and/or gym are usually provided.

2 Doesn't include luxury food items or alcohol.

3 Includes electricity (and air-conditioning), water (and usually sewage if charged in conjunction with the water, as is normal) and an allowance for telephone charges.

4 Includes entertainment, dining out, sports, newspapers and magazines but not holidays (air fares are often included in work contract terms).

5 Includes running costs for an average family car plus third party insurance, petrol, servicing and repairs, but exludes depreciation and credit purchase costs.

6 Includes private health, travel, car and contents insurance. Note that property is rented, so building insurance is usually unnecessary (see **Chapter 5**).

7 Lots of clothing is unnecessary in the region's hot climate. Office wear for men is a shirt and tie, except for formal occasions.

15.

LEISURE

Living in the Gulf isn't simply long hours of hard work, and the choice of leisure pursuits available to foreigners is wide. Indeed, the growth of tourism in the region has been helped by the Gulf's varied leisure facilities, many owing their existence to the interest of the expatriate community. In the early 1970s, before the oil boom, the local population's entertainment was limited to traditional pursuits like swimming, watching camel racing and, occasionally, falconry. And access to the last two was only by courtesy of the wealthy merchant families and perhaps members of the ruling families. Sporting activities were undeveloped and even the current fanatical support for football didn't exist.

Things changed rapidly and forever with the oil boom and the massive influx of foreign workers in search of activities to fill their free time. An obvious leisure opportunity was provided by the Gulf's many miles of clean, safe, sandy beaches and warm waters. The natural beauty of much of the terrain was another attraction and both were exploited. This helped the budding tourist industry, which has now expanded to become a major source of revenue. The development of tourism is seen as important in the Gulf, as the authorities try to direct their economies away from an almost total reliance on oil. The Gulf states aren't looking for mass tourism, however, which might put an unwelcome strain on the environment as well as bringing 'undesirables' into what are still traditional, conservative societies. The general thrust of the tourist drive is up-market, and the various tourist organisations work hard to encourage affluent visitors.

As well as beach activities, desert safaris have become popular, as have shopping expeditions to the souks (see page 319) to haggle with the traders. There are excellent restaurants throughout the region, covering most of the world's cuisines. Where alcohol is allowed, hotel restaurants and bars are licensed, but few outdoor restaurants are permitted to serve alcohol. In the more liberal states, there's plenty of night-life, with hotel bars and discos to cater for tourists and expatriates.

Note that during the holy month of Ramadan (see page 354), you shouldn't eat, drink or smoke anywhere where you can be seen by Muslims during the hours of daylight (especially in Saudi Arabia) or engage in any noisy activity or kiss anyone in public. In other words, you musn't be seen to be enjoying yourself while locals are enduring a month-long fast and abstention from bodily pleasures.

Each of the Gulf states has its own character, although the common threads that bind them together are the Islamic faith and their Arab customs, beliefs and traditions. There are more similarities than differences.

Bahrain & Dubai

Bahrain and Dubai have a more open and tolerant attitude to foreign cultures and attitudes than the other Gulf states and are keen to provide a wide range of amenities to attract visitors. Both also allow the consumption of alcohol. Hotel bars and some clubs and restaurants are licensed to sell alcoholic drinks to non-Muslims, and established expatriate workers can apply for a liquor licence, which allows them to buy alcohol at special 'off-licences'. The consumption of alcohol, however, is banned during the holy month of Ramadan (see page 354) and on one or two holy days, such as the Prophet's Birthday. (Some time ago, the start of Ramadan coincided with the Gregorian calendar's New Year celebrations, which upset tourists expecting to celebrate the event in the traditional way!)

As well as bars and clubs, which thousands of people from the neighbouring Gulf states (particularly Saudi Arabia) come to enjoy, Bahrain offers plenty of fine restaurants and hotels and numerous sporting activities (see **Chapter 16**). What's more, Bahrainis are genuinely hospitable, friendly people.

Kuwait

Kuwait lacks the exhuberance of Dubai and Bahrain. It's an affluent society and Kuwaitis are conservative, business-like and, according to some people, arrogant. They're nonetheless hospitable and can provide a traditional Arab welcome. The country and its people suffered a great deal during the conflict with Iraq, but recovery has been swift and normal life has resumed. Kuwait lacks leisure facilities, however, and has a limited range of hotels. Currently, tourism is not a priority, although there are developments afoot that might change this in the future. The consumption of alcohol is banned in Kuwait, where expatriate entertaining tends to be at home. Some expatriates brew their own alcoholic beverages, although the penalties for being caught can be severe.

Oman

In the past, the Sultanate of Oman restricted the development of tourism as it sought to build its economy. In fact, for many years it was quite difficult to visit Oman, even on business. This situation has changed and the tourist industry and leisure facilities are now being developed. The country offers excellent hotels, the consumption of alcohol is allowed in licensed premises, and expatriate residents are allowed to buy alcohol for private use. Leisure activities aren't as extensive as they are in Dubai or Bahrain, but ambitious plans include doubling the number of hotels and the extension of tourist facilities, which are currently centred on the capital Muscat. The Tourism Directorate is also planning major sporting competitions and shopping festivals to attract visitors.

The climate is excellent for much of the year and the countryside is very beautiful, with a great diversity of terrain — from spectacular mountains to superb coastlines and fertile valleys. Omanis are hospitable and perhaps more relaxed than some of their neighbours. Expatriates tend to stay a long time in Oman — an indication of how enjoyable a country it is.

Qatar

Like Saudi Arabia, Qatar is a 'closed' culture, and expatriates are attracted by the range of work available rather than the lifestyle. The country is very flat but has a pleasant coastline on the Arabian Gulf. Desert sports and watersports are practised. With major development programmes under way, however, more leisure facilities are being built. There are excellent hotels in the capital, Doha, and they offer entertainment, good food and sports. There's also an impressive building plan for new international hotels by the Hilton, Four Seasons and Ritz Carlton groups.

Licensed bars and hotels are permitted to sell alcohol, and the range of food on offer in the various restaurants makes dining out a pleasure. As in Kuwait and other more formal Gulf societies, however, the expatriate communities tend to entertain in their own homes. Resident expatriates can apply for a liquor licence to purchase supplies at designated retail outlets.

Saudi Arabia

The Kingdom of Saudi Arabia is perhaps the most conservative Gulf country, with strict laws rigidly enforced. It takes its position as the birthplace and centre of the Islamic faith very seriously and abides by Islam's Sharia law as laid down in the Koran, which isn't simply a religion but also dictates the law and ethics of its followers. This leaves little room for entertainment in the western sense, and there are no clubs, associations, cinemas or other places of entertainment in Saudi Arabia. However, it does allow — and indeed encourage — sporting activities, for which there are extensive facilities, particularly for native citizens (see **Chapter 16**).

The Kingdom boasts a long coastline with reasonably attractive beaches, fertile agricultural valleys and plains, and majestic mountainous regions. There are also vast desert areas, such as the aptly named 'The Empty Quarter', traversed by the nomadic Bedouin. Nevertheless, there's currently no general tourist industry in the country and, although some of the obstacles to it are slowly being lifted, it will be a long time before Saudi Arabia becomes a significant tourist destination. Pilgrims entering the Kingdom as part of their Islamic duties form the main 'tourist' trade, as they proceed to Mecca (Makkah in Arabic) for the annual pilgrimage (Haj — see **Religion** on page 355).

The centres of the three main provinces are the cities of Jeddah (to the west, on the Red Sea), Riyadh (the capital, in the central province) and Al-Khobar and Dammam (to the east, on the Arabian Gulf). These cities have fine hotels belonging to major international chains and offering swimming pools, tennis courts, gymnasia, etc.. Women might not be allowed to use the swimming pools; if they are, it will be at a different time from men.

The expatriate communities spend most of their leisure time within the confines of the housing compounds where they live. Some of these compounds are very large, with many housing units and apartment blocks. The facilities are usually extensive, with large swimming pools, where mixed bathing is allowed, and often squash and tennis courts, a gymnasium and a restaurant.

Although the possession and consumption of alcohol is strictly prohibited throughout the country, many expatriates make their own alcoholic drinks, within the relative 'safety' of their compounds. The authorities might 'turn a blind eye' provided that the activity is discreet but, if they don't, the penalties are severe: a jail sentence, lashes and expulsion from the country. Selling or providing alcohol to a Muslim is a particularly serious offence.

Women aren't allowed to drive cars in the Kingdom, which restricts their movement very considerably. Travelling in a car with a female other than your wife or a very close relative is also prohibited and carries substantial penalties, including jail while the matter is dealt with.

Shopping is one of the major pastimes for all residents of Saudi Arabia, mainly because there's so little else to do. Shopping malls are modern, and the shops themselves offer goods to suit all needs and tastes. A frustration for non-Muslims and possibly some Muslims is the requirement that shops should close during prayer times (i.e. at noon, in mid-afternoon and at sunset – see page 354). Similarly, restaurants don't allow anyone to enter or leave during prayer times (see page 286), and there are separate sections and entrances for single males and families.

Satellite dishes are officially banned, although all compounds and most hotels provide coverage and usually broadcast videos on their internal channels. However, films are censored for sexual content and erotic films are illegal.

Although leisure activities are confined to sports and entertaining at home, expatriates in settled jobs tend to stay for many years in the Kingdom. Not only do Saudis usually pay the highest salaries in the region but, because there's so little to do, it's easy to save most of your money. You might have an opportunity to meet and mix with Saudis, and if you're invited to their home, you should accept. Saudis are generally hospitable and capable of giving a warm Arab welcome to foreigners, but in return you must respect their customs and traditions.

United Arab Emirates

The seven Emirates vary considerably as to their leisure facilities. Expatriates far outnumber the local population, and the mix of cultures makes for a variety of leisure activities.

Abu Dhabi: The largest of the Emirates and the capital of the Federation, Abu Dhabi has many fine hotels. These have good restaurants serving a wide range of international cuisines, although you cannot purchase alcoholic drinks with your meal; only pubs and bars are licensed. Resident expatriates can also apply for a liquor licence to buy alcohol at specific retail outlets. There are many social and sports clubs, but as in other Gulf countries, home entertainment plays an important part in everyone's social life. Abu Dhabi is primarily the centre of government and a thriving commercial centre, and the general atmosphere is more restrained than in its neighbour Dubai.

Touring the desert is a popular leisure activity, including 'wadi bashing' in four-wheel drive vehicles, sedate camel rides and desert barbecues, sometimes accompanied by belly dancing.

Ajman: The smallest of the Emirates has a pleasant corniche beach, some historic sites and a peaceful atmosphere. Leisure facilites include hotels, beach clubs and a museum. Alcoholic drinks are available, served in teapots; ask for 'special tea'.

Dubai: The liveliest Emirate in the Federation, Dubai is the tourist centre of the region and probably the favourite destination for expatriates. It covers a small area and consists mainly of the city of Dubai itself. However, there's no shortage of luxury hotels, marinas and shopping malls along the superb beaches extending towards Abu Dhabi. The recently extended airport is superb, with world-famous duty-free shopping. As well as having all the sporting facilities you could wish for (see **Chapter 16**), Dubai is home to the annual 'Million Dollar' (actually more like $3 million!) horse race, at the Nadd Al-Shiba racecourse.

Shopping in the numerous modern malls, with their wide range of designer goods, provides tremendous opportunities for bargains. The gold souk is also famous, with streets of shops selling gold jewellery. Haggling is part of the enjoyment, and you can negotiate attractive discounts. On the Creek, you can watch traditional trading boats (dhows) loading and unloading their cargoes for Africa and India, as they've done for centuries.

Expatriates and tourists are spoiled for choice in Dubai. You can 'disco' until the small hours, and bars in the hotels are fully licensed. Home entertainment isn't as prevalent as it is in other Gulf states, mainly because there are so many things to do.

Fujairah: Fujairah is located on the Gulf of Oman coast and attracts many visitors because of its diverse scenery. Spectacular mountains and passes provide a welcome contrast with the flat desert landscape, and its beaches are unspoilt. Tourism has yet to be fully established but there are plans to develop it, although not at the expense of the natural attractions of the area. Along the road from Dubai are the beautiful natural water springs at Masafi and the pottery market near Dhaid. Fujairah can claim to have the only bullfighting in the Gulf, but no bullfighter is involved: two bulls wrestle until one of them decides to call it a day. Alcoholic drinks are available in licensed bars and restaurants and at a limited number of retail outlets, where you require a liquor licence (see page 318).

Ras Al-Khaimah: Ras Al-Khaimah is a quiet town with a long and interesting history and is an attractive place to visit. Visiting it is like stepping back in time. Traditional fishing dhows are still built, and the yards are well worth a visit. There are good beaches, where swimming and watersports are enjoyed (see **Chapter 16**), as well as parks and gardens. Home entertainment is a favoured pastime among the expatriate population, which is small compared with neighbouring Emirates. Resident expatriates are allowed to purchase alcohol, and alcoholic drinks are also available in one or two hotel bars.

Sharjah: Sharjah has a total ban on alcohol, which has not encouraged tourism, but because of the lower costs in the Emirate, many people use it as a dormitory, commuting to Dubai for work and entertainment. Sharjah was an important ancient sea port and has a long tradition as a seafaring nation. It has a great deal to offer culturally and has many fine beaches, notably at Khor Fakkan. Wildlife conservation is important, and the state's large mangrove swamp attracts migratory birds and other wildlife. Shopping in the famous souk, a remarkable piece of architecture, is an interesting outing for those ready to bargain for 'antiques', carpets and bric-a-brac.

Umm Al-Quwain: The small Emirate of Umm Al-Quwain is quiet and undisturbed, with a tradition of fishing and no oil exploitation. Visitors, most of whom are expatriates working in the other Emirates, are attracted to its beaches and wildlife. There's also a horse-riding centre, which teaches dressage. Alcohol is available in some bars and restaurants.

TOURIST OFFICES

With tourism growing in importance, the region's administrations are setting up tourist offices and promoting the states internationally.

Each state now has a governing body to supervise the development of tourism, whether a specific government office, a combined one such as a Ministry of Tourism and Industry, or a section of the Ministry of Information.

The overseas embassies of all Gulf states (including the Kingdom of Saudi Arabia) provide information about tourism in their country, although in the case of Saudi Arabia this is very limited. Their websites also provide information and assistance (see **Appendix C**). National airlines such as Emirates, Gulf Air and Saudia also supply information at their offices throughout the world, as do major tour operators.

Bahrain: The Tourism Directorate within the Ministry of Cabinet Affairs and Information can be contacted at PO Box 253, Manama, Bahrain (☎ 973-211 026) and there's an information desk at the arrivals hall of Bahrain International airport. There are also helpful local publications in English, such as *This is Bahrain*, and hotels have pamphlets and brochures listing tours and excursions.

Kuwait: Kuwait's tourist industry is in the early stages of development and there are no local tourist offices, but information is available from the Department of Tourism at the Ministry of Information, PO Box 193, Safat, Kuwait (☎ 965-243 6644). Tour operators, embassies and airlines (Kuwait Airways) can also provide information.

Oman: Oman has no tourist offices, but information can be obtained from the Directorate General of Tourism, at the Ministry of Commerce and Industry, PO Box 550, Muscat, Sultanate of Oman (☎ 968-771 7085).

Qatar: Qatar doesn't have an official department or local office to look after tourism, and the main source of information is the embassy in your country.

Saudi Arabia: Saudi Arabia has severe restrictions on tourism, particularly on non-Arab, non-Muslim travellers. Visas are very difficult to obtain, even for business visitors. Indeed, even expatriates residing in the Kingdom must seek permission to travel from one province to another. One British tour operator managed to organise a cruise visit to Jeddah recently, but with many restrictions. Although the long-term intention is to develop tourism, little tourist information is currently available.

UAE: Dubai is currently the most active Gulf state in promoting itself as a holiday destination, and international newspapers are full of advertisements extolling its virtues. Further information is available from the Dubai Department of Tourism and Commerce Marketing, PO Box 594, Dubai (☎ 971-4-223 0000). Emirates Airlines works closely with its tour operator DNATA and there are tourist offices in the UK, Ireland, France, Germany, Hong Kong, Japan and the USA, listed in telephone directories under the title 'Dubai Commerce & Tourism Promotion Board'. There are no designated tourist offices in any of the other Emirates.

HOTELS

The demand for hotel accommodation in the Gulf took off in the 1970s, particularly in Saudi Arabia. Standards of accommodation and staff efficiency and civility weren't very high initially, but that has changed. There's now a wide selection of hotels throughout the region, ranging from super-luxurious establishments to budget hotels in old souk areas. However, while there are plenty of five, four and three-star establishments, there are few at the cheap end of the scale. The international hotel chains are well represented, including the Intercontinental, Sheraton, Hilton, Radisson, Ramada and Holiday Inn. Rooms are generally large by European standards.

Dubai has the most luxurious hotels in the region, including the Ritz Carlton and the locally developed, spectacular Jumeirah Beach Hotel, with its opulent off-shore complex. Advance publicity claimed that entrance to this complex would be restricted to those with Rolls-Royces and helicopters, which was untrue of course but indicated the type of customer that it's aimed at. It's currently the top Gulf hotel, but things don't stay the same in the region for very long and there's a competitive spirit between the states and corporate hotel groups to outdo each other.

Hotel staff are invariably friendly and efficient, many of them being from India, Pakistan, the Philippines and other parts of Asia and North Africa. (Although not highly paid by local standards, they're earning far more than they could at home and are therefore keen to keep their jobs, which are much in demand.)

Residential hotels are unknown in the region, for two reasons. First, Arabs are tribal by nature, with a culture of the extended family, so travellers invariably have relatives to stay with. And second, most of the Gulf's non-Arab residents are expatriate workers, who have their own rented accommodation.

Room rates aren't fixed by government, but are set by the operating company. Generally, rates are high, and tourists are advised to travel in a group, as the group rate is invariably much lower than individuals can negotiate. Also, there are few single rooms, so single occupants must pay the same rate as two people sharing a room. In Dubai, for example, the full room rate in a four or five-star hotel is around AED500 to 800 ($135 to 220) per night, plus 10 per cent for service and local tax.

There are several permutations of hotel rates and discounts, including the standard full-rate, group corporate company rate, group tourist rate, duration discount, weekend rate and others. You can often negotiate a discount, and seasoned visitors rarely accept the first rate offered. Beach-front hotels sometimes charge a premium for a room with a sea view and, if you would rather save money than look at water, book a room at the side or back of the hotel. If you arrive in the evening and the hotel still has vacancies, you can usually negotiate a substantial reduction.

Many hotel chains run special clubs and facilities for regular guests, and these are much in evidence in Gulf hotels. Special floors with breakfast rooms, butler service and other concessions are common. Some clubs offer free drinks during 'happy hours' for their privileged guests. In almost every case, guests receive a fruit basket on arrival and a free newspaper in the morning. Children usually stay for free if they're sharing their parents' room and extra beds/cots are available. It's wise to ensure that all of your requirements are made clear to the hotel when booking. Most hotels keep a note of their regular guests' requirements and adjust their bookings accordingly.

All the region's hotels, except perhaps the cheapest, are well appointed, with good-quality furniture, bed linen and towels. Air-conditioning is standard, and there's usually a temperature control in each room. There's invariably a television, with a wide choice of satellite channels, including BBC, CNN, Sky and many other international and local channels in English, French and Arabic. Many hotels have their own video channel, informing guests about in-hotel entertainment, local attractions, excursions and, in particular, the hotel's restaurants and their opening times.

In states where alcohol is permitted, it's often allowed only in hotel bars and restaurants, and so hotels are often centres of entertainment in the region. (There are exceptions to this, e.g. some of the expatriate clubs, although these aren't usually open to non-residents or non-members.) It's usual for hotels to provide live entertainment, and most luxury hotels in the more liberal states have discos and night clubs, open into the small hours. Alcohol prices are likely to be considerably higher than you would pay at home, particularly in the top-class hotels, and higher than in most expatriate clubs. The mini-bar in your room will also provide a wide selection of drinks and light snacks, but at premium prices.

In one or two states, the downmarket hotels (as well as some of the better ones) have female 'visitors' from the former eastern bloc countries, the CIS and Africa, who work in what is renowned as the oldest profession. In some cases, the number of prostitutes is astonishing, showing how large the demand must be.

Hotel restaurants are usually excellent, offering a wide variety of international cuisines. There's often a choice of different types of restaurant, including buffets, pasta and pizza bars, bistros and more formal eateries. The ubiquitous 'breakfast room' will serve meals all day, at the hotel's most reasonable prices, and room service is usually available on a 24-hour basis, certainly in the better hotels. For the health-conscious, there's invariably a hotel gymnasium, swimming pool and sauna, and in many cases golfers are able to sign into a local golf club as a hotel guest member.

You will be required to show your passport, travel visa or residence visa when checking in to a hotel. Your documents might be held while a photocopy of the necessary visa stamps is taken; your passport will then be returned to you. You're recommended to carry photocopies of your travel documents to guard against their loss. Losing your passport in certain Gulf countries (especially Saudi Arabia) can present severe difficulties.

Travellers who are unfamiliar with the region should always book well in advance (and preferably have a faxed confirmation of the booking), particularly for special occasions, such as the annual shopping festival in Dubai (see page 279) and the Eid holidays (see page 348), when Saudis come across the Bahrain-Saudi causeway to enjoy relative freedom and entertainment.

Budget Accommodation

There isn't an abundance of budget accommodation in the region; the Gulf isn't backpacker territory and few locals use hotels, preferring to stay with relatives, although the concept of the extended family is beginning to lose its appeal among the younger generation. With the growth of tourism, budget hotels have found themselves much in demand, particularly from tour operators arranging visits for travellers from eastern Europe, CIS and other countries within the former Soviet Union. Most cheaper accommodation is located in souk areas or older, more traditional parts of cities (which also tend to be the noisier areas), but they're nevertheless likely to be well serviced, clean and safe. A room in a mid-range hotel room costs around $100 (£65) per night.

When newcomers arrive in the Gulf, they sometimes need short-term accommodation while they look for a 'permanent' home. Furnished one, two or three-bedroom units, with kitchen and laundry facilities, are available in most cities. Daily room rates are around $55 (£35), including 10 per cent tax, with a minimum stay of a week.

Selected Hotels

The following list of Gulf hotels includes some cheaper accommodation, as indicated.

Bahrain

- Ad-Dewania Hotel, Manama (☎ 973-263 300). A small, clean, friendly, budget hotel.

- Al-Jazira Hotel, Manama (☎ 973-211 810). A friendly, attractive, mid-priced hotel.

- Al-Kuwait Guest House, Manama (☎ 973-210 781). A small, basic, well-located, budget hotel.

- Bahrain Hotel, Manama (☎ 973-227 478). A quiet, budget hotel.

- The Diplomat, Manama (☎ 973-531 666). A well-located, upmarket hotel.

- Sahara Hotel, Manama (☎ 973-225 580). A decent, mid-priced hotel.
- Sheraton Bahrain, Manama (☎ 973-533 533). One of Bahrain's top hotels, located.

Kuwait

- Carlton Tower Hotel (☎ 965-245 2740). Respectable and mid-priced.
- Kuwait Plaza Hotel (☎ 965-243 6686). A well-located, relatively inexpensive five-star hotel.
- Le Meridien Kuwait (☎ 965-245 5550). Another relatively-affordable top-end hotel.
- Oasis Hotel (☎ 965-246 5489). A respectable, mid-priced hotel.
- Second Home Hotel (☎ 965-253 2100). A reasonable, clean, good-value hotel.

Oman

- Al-Naseem Hotel, Mutrah (☎ 968-712 418). A respectable, clean, budget hotel.
- Bowshar Hotel, near Ruwi (☎ 968-501 105). A reasonably priced, mid-range hotel.
- Hyatt Regency, Shatti Al-Qurm (☎ 968-602 888). A beautifully decorated luxury hotel.
- Nizwa Tourist House, Nizwa (☎ 968-412 402). A simple, clean, good-value hotel.
- Qurm Beach Hotel (☎ 968-564 070). A clean, peaceful budget hotel.
- Salalah Tourist Hotel (☎ 968-295 332). A good-value hotel.
- Sohar Beach Hotel (☎ 968-841 111). A good, mid-priced hotel.

Qatar

- New Capital Hotel, Doha (☎ 974-445 445). A well-located, clean, mid-priced hotel.

- Qatar Palace Hotel, Doha (☎ 974-421 515). A good, central, mid-priced hotel.
- Safeer Hotel, Doha (☎ 974-353 999). Also a good, central, mid-priced hotel.

Saudi Arabia

- Al-Maseef Hotel for Tourists, Taif (☎ 966-2-732 478). A mid-range hotel.
- Hotel Alrajehi, Riyadh (☎ 966-1-412 3557). A good-value, mid-range hotel.
- Hotel Makkah, Jeddah (☎ 966-2-647 7439). A good, mid-priced hotel.
- Mamora Hotel, Riyadh (☎ 966-1-401 2111). A good, mid-priced hotel.
- Shaheen Hotel (☎ 966-2-642 6582). A popular budget hotel.

United Arab Emirates

- Ajman Kempinski Hotel and Resort, Ajman (☎ 971-6-451 555). An impressive, upmarket hotel.
- Golden Beach Motel, Sharjah (☎ 971-6-281 331). A spacious, mid-range hotel with self-catering facilities.
- Holiday Inn Resort, in Sharjah (☎ 971-6-371 111). A top hotel with attractive weekend rates.
- Jumeira Beach Hotel (☎ 971-4-480 000). A famous landmark, with a spectacular tower rising from the waves – and prices to match.
- Panorama Hotel, Dubai (☎ 971-4-518 518). A reasonably-priced hotel.
- Hotel Regency, Abu Dhabi (☎ 971-2-765 000). One of Abu Dhabi's better value hotels. You can use the beach and health club at the nearby Sheraton.
- Tourist Hotel, Dubai (☎ 971-4-229 388). A good, mid-range hotel.

YOUTH HOSTELS

There are few youth hostels in the region, for the same reasons that there are few budget hotels: that local travellers have traditionally been accommodated by relatives, and that tourists on a budget are discouraged. The majority of hostels are in Saudi Arabia, although these are open only to men. However, they're of good quality and cheap (around $2/£1.35 per night). To stay at a Saudi hostel, you must have a Hostelling International card. Hostels are at Abha (☎ 966-7-227 0503), Dammam (☎ 966-3-857 5358), Hail (☎ 966-6-533 1485), Hofuf (☎ 966-3-580 0028), Jeddah (☎ 966-2-688 6692), Najran (☎ 966-7-522 5019), Riyadh (☎ 966-1-405 5552), Sakaka (☎ 966-4-624 9333) and Taif (☎ 966-2-725 3400).

Bahrain has a single hostel (☎ 973-727 170), costing around $10 (£6.50) per night (half as much for members of the Youth Hostel Association), and there are two in the UAE: at Dubai (☎ 971-625 578), where the prices are similar to Bahrain, and Sharjah (☎ 971-225 070), whose hostel is slightly cheaper at around $8 ($5.50) per night.

SELF-CATERING

Most Gulf cities have a limited amount of rented, short-term, self-catering accommodation, usually in purpose-built apartment blocks or in a hotel annexe. The more luxurious accommodation tends to be linked to a hotel and offers access to the hotel services and facilities. In all cases, an inventory is taken on your arrival and a similar check made on departure; any losses or damage must be made good. Information about this type of accommodation can be found in the yellow pages and local newspapers and from tourist and airport information desks. Booking is recommended in view of the limited availability.

CARAVANNING & CAMPING

There are no camping or caravan sites in the region. The climate doesn't lend itself to either, as air-conditioning is necessary for most of the year. The few Bedouin continue to lead a nomadic life in their encampments, but this has little in common with camping as a leisure activity. The only other camping activity is when Arab families and expatriates venture out in their four-wheel drive vehicles at weekends and pitch tents in the desert.

MUSEUMS & ART GALLERIES

There are plenty of museums and galleries throughout the Gulf. Arabs are at pains to inform foreigners about their rich heritage and way of life before the discovery of oil in the region, and their museums reflect this. The seafaring traders of the Gulf were noted explorers and covered great distances, while people from the coastal regions engaged in pearl collecting, fishing and farming. There are no outstanding centres of world art in the Gulf region, but plenty of regional collections, with exhibitions usually put on by the artists themselves. Most of the graphic arts feature scenes of everyday life, flora and fauna. There's a particular love of equestrian art, while pictures of falconry and hunting birds are also popular.

Because of the crucial importance of Islam in people's lives, mosques are the highest expression of Arab artistic expertise, and they display some of the world's most impressive architecture, particularly their majestic domes and spires. As a non-Muslim, you might be allowed to enter some mosques, provided that you've asked for permission beforehand, but you must be properly dressed and observe the protocol, including removing your footwear. If you want to take photographs, even of the exterior, it's wise to seek permission first. Mosques that are especially worth visiting are listed under **Other Places of Interest** on page 269.

Many of the region's museums come under the authority and sponsorship of the various Ministries of Heritage and Culture or departments of the Ministries of Information, and are well-funded and maintained. The major museums in each state are listed below.

Bahrain: The National Museum in Manama is one of the region's best museums and houses some fascinating finds from the Tumuli burial mounds (see **Other Places of Interest** on page 269). Labels and descriptions are in English as well as Arabic, and the museum costs just 500 fils ($1.30) to enter. It's open from 7am to 2pm on Saturdays, Sundays and Tuesdays, from 8am to 2pm and from 4 to 8pm on Wednesdays and Thursdays, and from 3 to 8pm on Fridays. The Beit Al-Quran (House of the Koran) in Manama is a museum and research centre, with a large collection of Korans and interesting displays of Islamic calligraphy. It's open between 9am and noon and from 4 to 6pm from Saturdays to Wednesdays, and from 9am to noon on Thursdays.

Kuwait: Kuwait's museums used to be renowned for their collections of Islamic art, but the Iraqis looted some of them during the 1990 invasion and caused a great deal of damage. The National Museum's pride and joy used to be the Al-Sabah collection, including some of the world's most important Islamic art. The Iraqis have returned much of it, but many of the pieces were damaged. The Tareq Rajab Museum in the Jabriya district of Kuwait City is a private collection of Islamic art. The Science and Natural History Museum isn't one of the world's greatest, although it contains plenty of stuffed animals. Sadu House, which is near the National Museum, is a museum of Bedouin arts and crafts. The house itself is also of interest, being built of coral and gypsum.

Oman: Oman has a variety of museums. Ruwi offers an Armed Forces Museum, while the Bait Al-Zubair in Muscat has a collection of weapons, clothing and jewellery. The Omani French Museum in Muscat celebrates the links between France and Oman, while the Natural History Museum features the wildlife of the country, including the Arabian oryx and lynx. The Oman Museum in Muscat traces the history of the country from the third millenium BC, and the Children's Museum at Al-Qurm Park has interactive exhibits. The town of Sur has a Marine Museum, while Salalah's Museum includes some interesting photographs of Arabia in the 1940s and 1950s by the famous explorer and traveller Wilfred Thesiger.

Qatar: Qatar is not renowned for its visitor and cultural attractions, but Doha offers a National Museum, Ethnographic Museum and a Postal Museum. The National Museum is the city's main attraction, with plenty of exhibits about all aspects of the country, labelled in English as well as Arabic.

Saudi Arabia: Riyadh's impressive museum is particularly rich in archeological exhibits. Entrance is free and it's open from 8am to 2pm, Saturdays to Wednesdays. King Saud University Museum in Riyadh also has a modest archaeological collection. You need to make an appointment to visit, (☎ 966-1-467 8135). Jeddah Museum is worth visiting and is especially strong on the region's archaeology and ethnography. The city also has The Museum of Abdul Raouf Hassan Khalil, an interesting private collection in a series of gaudy houses. Dammam contains the Eastern Province's Regional Museum of

Archaeology and Ethnography, but Hofuf's Museum is stronger on the eastern region's archaeology. The Aramco compound at Dhahran incorporates what is regarded as Saudi Arabia's best museum, covering everything to do with the oil business in an interactive format.

UAE: In **Abu Dhabi,** you can visit the national archives at the Old Fort, while the Cultural Foundation displays the history of the UAE and is also a centre for art. The Heritage Village shows traditional life from former years, while the Petroleum Exhibition depicts the history and development of oil discovery and production. The Al-Ain museum at the old Eastern Fort is the birthplace of the Ruler Shaikh Zayed (Abu Dhabi) and has exhibits about the history of the UAE, as well as depicting the ancient lifestyle of the Bedouin. Flora and fauna of the region can be studied at the University of Al-Ain.

In **Dubai,** places of interest include the Dubai Museum with its archaeological finds, the Shaikh Saeed Al-Maktoum House and Museum with scenes of everyday life, and the Majlis Art Gallery in a beautifully restored house, with work from both local and international artists.

Sharjah has a plethora of old buildings, restored in such a way as to show what the region was like before modernisation. The Emirate also has plenty of museums: The Sharjah Art Museum, Sharjah Fort, Heritage Museum, Islamic Museum, Archaeological Museum, an impressive, modern Natural History Museum and an enjoyable, interactive Science Museum and Planetarium. **Ajman,** the smallest Emirate, has one of the region's better museums, while **Fujairah** has two.

OTHER PLACES OF INTEREST

Bahrain

Manama

- The **Heritage Centre** has collections of antique weapons and traditional costumes, as well as displays about pearl diving, seafaring and date palms.

- The **Al-Fatih Mosque** is the country's largest building, covering around 6,300m^2 (68,000ft^2) and accommodating for 7,000 worshippers. It welcomes non-Muslim visitors between 8am and 2pm on Saturdays to Wednesdays.

- The **Friday Mosque** has an impressive mosaic minaret and its position next to the modern Bahrain Tower provides an interesting contrast between the traditional and the modern.

- Dotted around the town are historic **wind towers**, designed to harness breezes and direct them down into surrounding buildings.

Rest of Bahrain Island

- Bahrain is home to an amazing 100,000 ancient burial mounds, the most interesting of them near the village of **A'ali**. Many date from the Dilmun period of 2,800 to 1,800BC and some are 45m (150ft) across and 15m (50ft) high. A'ali also has Bahrain's best pottery workshop.

- The **Ad-Diraz Temple** dates from between 2,000 and 1,000BC.

- **Adhari Park**, south-west of Manama, is a garden with natural springs, a pool and amusements, making it an attractive haven from the urban bustle. It's open daily from 8am to noon and 3.30 to 9pm.

- **Al-Areen Wildlife Park** is a small wildlife park, featuring nearly 250 species of mammals and birds native to the region. Bus tours are available. Telephone ☎ 973- 836 116 for details of opening times.

- At the west of Bahrain island, the village of **Al-Budayyi** commands excellent views of the King Fahd Causeway to Saudi Arabia.

- **Barbar Temple** is in fact a group of three temples, dating from around 3,000BC, dedicated to Enki, God of Wisdom.

- West of Manama, the **Qala'at Al-Bahrain** fort dates from 2,800BC and is historically if not visually impressive.

- **Riffa Fort** dates from the 17th century and stands over the Riffa Valley, affording magnificent views.

- **Sar** is another ancient burial site, with hundreds of burial mounds, currently being excavated.

Muharraq

- **Beit Sheikh Isa Bin Ali** and **Beit Seyadi** are two houses dating from around 1800, giving an interesting impression of what life in old Bahrain must have been like.

- **Qala'at Abu Mahir** is a 16th century fort.

- **Qala'at Arad**, a Portuguese fort from the 15th century, offers attractive views.

Kuwait

Kuwait City

- Kuwait's major landmark is the **Kuwait Towers**, opened in 1979. The tallest of the three reaches 187m (617ft), with an observation deck which is open from 9am to 11pm every day. Admission costs 500 fils ($1.60).
- The **National Assembly Building** was designed by the Dane Jorn Utzon, who was also responsible for Sydney's Opera House. Its roofs imitate Bedouin tents.
- The **Grand Mosque** dates from 1986 and can accommodate 5,500 worshippers.

Rest of Kuwait

- The **Al-Ahmadi oil refinery** includes displays about the industry and a modest, pleasant public garden.
- **Failaka Island** is the most historical part of Kuwait, with remains dating back to the Bronze Age. The small island is a one-and-a-half hour ferry ride from the mainland and is a must for those interested in the country's archaeology.

Oman

Greater Muscat

- The **National Aquarium** is regarded as the best in the Gulf. The descriptions are in English as well as Arabic, entrance is free and it's open between 7.30am and 2.30pm, Saturdays to Thursdays.
- The **Mutrah Souk** is thought to be the best in the Gulf.

Musandam Peninsula

- **Khasab**, the peninsula's capital, is a lively town, but without many historic sites.

- **Khumzar** is a village set on a cove at the north of the peninsula, but the scenery is the main reason for visiting.
- **Tawi** is a village with prehistoric cave carvings and an ancient well.

North Oman

- The town of **Bahla** is the main source of pottery in Oman, as well as boasting an attractive souk and a UNESCO-listed fort.
- **Barka's** attractions include a fort and a restored old merchant house (Bait Nua'man). For those who find it attractive, there's also bull butting, where two bulls are set to fight each other (every second Friday in winter).
- **Nakhal** is an attractive town, with a fort and a spring.
- **Nizwa**, one of Oman's main attractions, is the old seat of the Imams, with plenty of atmosphere and much to see.
- **Ras Al-Jinz**, at the eastern tip of the Arabian Peninsula, is a protected area where 10,000 turtles nest on the beach each year between June and August.
- **Rustaq**, Oman's capital in the Middle Ages, has several historical sites and an impressive new souk.
- **Sohar**, the legendary home of Sindbad the sailor, Sohar offers a fort, souk and other historic attractions.
- **Sur** is a relaxing town offering beaches, forts and a dhow-building yard among its attractions.

South Oman

- **Job's Tomb**, known as Nabi Ayyub in Arabic, is impressively located on a hill overlooking Salalah and is worth visiting for the views alone.
- The ruins of an ancient port of **Khor Rouri** are also in an impressive setting.
- **Mughsail** is the site of great beaches, frankincense trees, beautiful scenery and marine blowholes.
- **Salalah** is Oman's second city and the birthplace of the ruler, Sultan Qaboos. It's wet and green between June and September as a result of its summer monsoon. There's a lot to see and it offers good shopping for traditional crafts.

Qatar

Doha

- **Al-Corniche** is 7km (4mi) of pleasant walkways, jogging tracks and plants.
- **Aladdin's Kingdom** is a park with amusement rides.
- **Doha Fort** is an attractive 19th century fort built around a large courtyard and garden and housing displays about Qatari history.
- **Palm Tree Island** is a small island in the bay, with beaches and sports.

Rest of Qatar

- The town of **Al-Khor** has a museum and some watchtowers, and its gardens are a green haven in which to escape the monotony of the desert.
- There are attractive beaches and winter flamingo roosts south of the village of **Al-Wakrah**.
- The town of **Al-Zubara** has a museum but is most noted for its views of the surrounding desert.
- The village of **Ash-Shahhainiya** has a camel-racing stadium, and you can drive along the race track during races to keep up with the action!
- **Khor Al-Adaid** is Qatar's premier attraction — described as an inland sea, but actually a large lake, surrounded by impressive sand dunes. It's only accessible by four-wheel drive vehicles.
- **Umm Salal Ali** is a series of 5,000-year-old burial mounds.

Saudi Arabia

Riyadh

- The **Masmak Fortress** is a dried mud fortress with a small museum about Abdul Aziz, a Saud family hero.
- The **Murabba Palace** was built by Abdul Aziz in the 1940s.

- The **King Faisal Centre for Research and Islamic Studies** has displays of manuscripts and art.
- The **Al-Thumairi Gate** is an impressive site.
- The **Camel Market** on the city's outskirts is intriguing.
- **Dir'aiyah,** also on the outskirts of Riyadh, is the ruined capital of the Al-Sauds and the country's most visited archaeological site.

Central Region

- **Hail,** in the centre of Saudi's main agricultural area, has a handful of historic forts and towers.
- **Jeddah,** halfway down the west coast, a bustling port whose attractions include walks along the route of the old city walls and Shorbatly House, a good example of traditional architecture. Naseef House belongs to one of Jeddah's most famous merchant families.

Eastern Province

- **Hofuf's** main attraction is its situation in the Al-Hasa oasis, one of the world's largest. Qasr Ibrahim, an Ottoman fortress, and the souk are worth visiting.
- The village of **Nairiyah** has an interesting Bedouin market on Friday mornings.
- **Tarut Island** has a much-visited Portuguese fort, on a site in use since ancient times. The small island is connected to the coast by a causeway.

North-west Region

- **Domat Al-Jandal** is a small town with two interesting historical sites: Qasr Marid and the Mosque of Omar. The former is a fortress, parts of it dating from Nabataean times, the latter one of the country's oldest mosques.

South-west Region

- **Abha,** the capital of the province of Asir, enjoys milder weather than much of Saudi Arabia, sitting in attractive, forested, mountain scenery. You can visit the Shada Palace, but the main local attraction is the Asir National Park, covering around 450,000 hectares (over 1 million acres).

- **Habalah,** an impressive, deserted cliffside village, reached by cable car.
- **Najran's** interesting architecture has a strong influence of nearby Yemen. There's also a fort and palace to see.

Western Region

- **Madain Salah** is a series of impressive, 2,000-year-old rock tombs built by the Nabataeen people and is one of Saudi Arabia's best-known archaeological sites.
- **Taif** offers a relatively cool, fresh haven from the rest of the country's summer heat, as it sits in the mountains above Mecca. The surrounding scenery is also an attraction, as are the Tailor's Souk and the Abdallah bin Abbas mosque.

United Arab Emirates

Abu Dhabi

- **Al-Ain** and **Buraimi** are in an oasis area on the border with Oman – a cool, fresh, verdant change from the rest of the country. There are also interesting livestock and camel souks, and Al-Ain also has a good zoo. The Round Structure is a 5,000-year-old tomb.
- **Al-Hosn Palace** is Abu Dhabi's oldest building, dating from the late 19th century; most of the country's architecture is barely a quarter of a century old.
- **The Cultural Foundation** is the home of the National Archives, the National Library and the Institution of Culture and Art, and also hosts art and history exhibitions and concerts.
- **Liwa** is an oasis on the edge of The Empty Quarter, with amazing sand dunes.

Ajman

- The **Iranian Souk** is more a market for general items than souvenirs, but makes for an enjoyable stroll.

Dubai

- The **Bastakia Quarter** is around 100 years old and a conservation area, with old merchant and windtower houses.
- **The Creek**, which splits Dubai, is the waterfront region and well worth touring, both by boat and on foot.
- Dubai's **Diving and Heritage Villages** have displays about pearl diving and traditional Bedouin life.

Fujairah

- **Badiyah** is said to be the oldest town in the Gulf, inhabited continuously for 5,000 years. It's best known for its mosque, dating from 640 and the oldest in the UAE.
- **Dibba** is the site of a famous battle in 633, and the resulting graveyard, with thousands of headstones, is an arresting site.

Ras Al-Khaimah

- **Shimal** is one of the region's most important archaeological sites, dating back 5,000 years and the location of the Queen of Sheba's Palace.

Sharjah

- The **Al-Hisn Fort** dates from 1822 and has an interesting collection of old photographs, showing the contrast between old and new Sharjah.
- The town of **Kalba** has Arabia's oldest mangrove forest, which you can canoe through, spotting wildlife.
- **Khor Fakkan** is reputed to be the UAE's most attractive town.
- Sharjah also has a number of **souks**, including the Al-Arsah and Sharjah souks, and an animal and a plant.

Umm Al-Qaiwain

- **Ad-Dour** is a Hellenistic site dating from 200BC, with the remains of a fort, a temple and tombs.

● **Aquapark Dreamland** is a modern waterpark with the usual rides and slides.

CINEMAS

Cinema attendances are growing rapidly in most Gulf states, particularly Bahrain, Kuwait and the UAE. There are no cinemas in Saudi Arabia, however, with its almost total ban on entertainment. Previously, cinema audiences were mainly Asian expatriates and cinemas were pretty basic. These have now improved, with the arrival of the latest sound and projection systems in comfortable, air-conditioned cinemas and luxurious new multiplexes, although the Asian population still makes up the bulk of the cinema-going public, and cinema is beginning to prove more popular than home video.

Tickets are cheap, but mobile phones are an annoyance in the region's cinemas, with incoming and outgoing calls common, despite the cinema management's requests to turn them off. Local Arab youths are the main offenders. Many cinemas managers are Asian and some undoubtedly feel intimidated by the thought of trying to control Arab locals.

Films shown are from the USA, Egypt, Great Britain and, in vast numbers, from India's 'Bollywood' studios. Some cinemas feature Indian films exclusively and these often attract the largest crowds. The majority of films aimed at the local Arab population originate from Egypt, which has a large, productive film industry.

Egypt has 10 or 15 top actresses, who are as popular in the Arab world as Hollywood stars are elsewhere. The Egyptian film industry's glory days seem to be behind it, however. Cairo's studios used to produce over 100 films every year, but that number has dropped to around 15 or 20. And their quality is generally poor, with much over-acting and infantile humour. A notable exception is the work of the director Yousef Chahine, who received a lifetime achievement award at the 1997 Cannes Film Festival.

Syria and recently Lebanon have also developed film industries and export their films to the region. Lebanon is becoming a beacon in the Arab film world. Director Ziad Doueirim was previously a cameraman for Quentin Tarentino on some of Tarantino's most successful films. Maroun Baghdadi has enjoyed success at Cannes, while the work of film makers Samir Nasri, Jocelyn Saab and Mohammed Sweid is well worth seeking out. A surprise to many is the fact that Iran has also been making some internationally acclaimed films, this despite the obvious strictures that apply there. Some Iranian films, however, put many of Egypt's efforts to shame, being sophisticated cinema with international appeal. Particularly recommended are directors Abbas Kiaorstami (winner of the 1997 Palme d'Or at the Cannes Film Festival), Mohsen Makhmalbaf and Jafar Panahi.

While Saudi Arabia has no cinemas, there's a large market for home videos, and rental shops are found everywhere, all doing brisk business. The subject matter of the films must be innocuous, with no explicit or implicit sexual activity allowed. Perversely, there appears to be no restriction on violence or the use of English language which would be deemed obscene or offensive elsewhere and warrant a warning. Smuggled, sexually explicit videotapes sometimes circulate within expatriate compounds, but it's dangerous to try to bring them into the country because of the stringent customs checks and penalties (see page 85).

THEATRE, OPERA & BALLET

These three forms of entertainment are rare in the Gulf region, which is something of a cultural wilderness in this respect. The little that is available is aimed primarily at western expatriates. There's some tradition of theatre in the Arab world, focused on Egypt, but historically it hasn't been a feature of Arab life in the region. Most Gulf Arabs are happy to watch this type of entertainment on video or via satellite television from the Egyptian Satellite Channel (ESC).

Theatrical productions are staged mainly in hotels and usually in combination with a dinner. British Airways is a notable sponsor of light comedies and typical British farces, flying out the cast on a circuit that usually involves several Gulf locations and then moving on to Singapore and perhaps Australia. There's little or no serious theatre and theatres as such don't exist, some shows being staged in conference halls. There are amateur theatre groups in most states, however, notably in Saudi Arabia, where expatriates must make their own entertainment. Popular productions take place occasionally at the US Consulate in Jeddah, where it's possible to obtain a limited number of alcoholic drinks during the shows (which no doubt contributes to their popularity).

Ballet and opera are also rare, there being no facilities for major or sophisticated productions. Traditional dancing (including belly dancing) is usually performed at Arab parties (although not in Saudi Arabia), to which you may be invited if you make friends among the native population.

MUSIC

In the more liberal Gulf countries, such as Dubai and Bahrain, there's plenty of musical entertainment, which consists mainly of rock and pop concerts and feature a surprising number of top international stars, usually on their way to the Far East and Australasia. These are invariably held outdoors, sometimes in sports complexes or stadia, and can attract very large crowds, from both the local and foreign populations. With alcohol available, there's little difference between these concerts and similar events in the west, although unruly or anti-social behaviour is very rare in the region and never allowed to continue should it occur.

The Arab world has its own musical stars and their shows are also enthusiastically attended in the Gulf . The famous Lebanese singer, Fairouz, noted for her distinctive, haunting voice, appeals to the heart of many Arabs (particularly those oppressed in their own homelands) and attracts sell-out audiences wherever she goes.

Music of all kinds is broadcast on the radio throughout the region (see page 136).

FESTIVALS

There's a successful month-long shopping festival in Dubai every spring, one of its main attractions being the daily raffle of luxury cars. During the festival, the national airlines offer cheaper rates and the hotels also encourage visitors with discounted room rates. The festival's success has led to a further innovation in Dubai, the 'Summer Surprises', which lasts for two weeks and takes a specific theme, with related performances and shopping opportunities. Other Gulf states have trade shows, motor shows and the like, but no festivals in the accepted meaning of the word. In Saudi Arabia, public congregation is prohibited.

SOCIAL CLUBS

There's a wealth of expatriate clubs and associations throughout the region and they form a vital part of Gulf life. During the great rush of workers to the area in the 1970s, most expatriates were men, whose contract called for them to live as if they were single, whether they had a family or not. A few did bring their wives, but they had to pay for the tickets themselves; only senior personnel were allowed to bring their wives and families to the region at the company's expense. With so many single men in the region and virtually no local entertainment, there was a need for clubs where they could relax and socialise.

As the majority of western expatriates were British, they formed 'British Clubs', which still exist in many Gulf states. In those countries that permitted the consumption of alcohol, these clubs were usually based around bars with a pub atmosphere. Members could also play football, cricket and darts, etc.. Workers from the sub-continent formed 'Indian Clubs'.

Later, as companies found it necessary to allow workers to bring their wives and families to the Gulf in order to attract qualified, skilled people, schools, social clubs and associations were formed to meet the demands of a much larger and more diverse expatriate population.

Sport is an important feature of life in the region (see **Chapter 16**), and a wide range of sports clubs have been formed, many with an active social side. There are also plenty of clubs for women, including keep fit and dancing groups, and a multitude of special interest clubs such as historical societies and archaeology groups. International associations such as the Lions Club, Rotary Club, American Women's Club, St. George's Society, Caledonian Society, Hibernians and others are also represented in the region. Commercial associations include the British Businessmen's Club, the American Businessmen's Club and various Anglo/Arab associations.

Clubhouses usually have bars, one or two restaurants, a swimming pool, tennis courts, snooker tables and other facilities. There tends to be a fairly informal membership protocol, both to satisfy local regulations and to provide a code of conduct. In some cases, the long-established clubs have waiting lists, but the turnover of members is quite rapid because of the transient nature of the region's expatriate population, so waiting times aren't usually long.

In Bahrain and Dubai, there are a few commercially run expatriate bars and restaurants that are independent of a hotel (unlike most of the region's bars). The regulations call for these premises to be operated as members' clubs and there might be a waiting list, but the regulations aren't normally strictly enforced, although identification cards are issued. For those working in Saudi Arabia, the situation is different, with an almost total dependence on the housing compound for leisure and entertainment. There are sporting associations (see **Chapter 16**) but little else.

Joining a club is one of the best ways for newcomers to meet fellow expatriates and allows them to integrate into the foreign community. The advice and information that you have access to by joining one or more of these clubs is extremely valuable. Local English-language magazines such as **What's On** in Dubai and Oman and **This is Bahrain** list these clubs and associations.

NIGHTLIFE

Given the generally young expatriate population in the region, there's a lively nightlife in those countries where it's allowed. Dubai and Bahrain are the front runners when it comes to evening entertainment. Other Gulf states and the smaller Emirates don't have the thriving nightlife of Dubai and Bahrain. Nor do they have the wide range of hotels to offer the facilities, but they do offer some entertainment, geared more to local than expatriate tastes.

There tend to be two distinct groups in search of nightlife: young, predominantly western expatriates and affluent Arabs, who sometimes favour their own clubs, which offer Arab floorshows. Many nightclubs are located in hotels. The ranking, style and quality of the hotel naturally has an influence on the type and cost of the nightlife on offer. The five-star hotels have discos and nightclubs with cabarets and singers to suit both expatriate and local tastes. As you move down the class of hotels, the quality of the nightlife degenerates, and the region has some surprisingly squalid places.

GAMBLING

Gambling isn't permitted in the Gulf, owing to an Islamic stricture against it. Human nature being what it is, however, you can find unofficial gambling, particularly off-course betting on horse races. As with many things in the Middle East, you can indulge but must take care not to be caught. There are occasional rumours of schemes to provide gambling in offshore casinos on ships, but they don't seem to materialise.

The British lottery winning numbers are published weekly in the English-language press in the region. The Canadian and Australian lotteries constantly mail expatriates in the Gulf, but as these mailings are carried out by middle-men acting as agents, the cost is higher than in the originating country.

FOOD

The region isn't internationally renowned for its cuisine, but eating there can be an enjoyable experience, especially if you're invited to dine with locals. At typical Arab feasts, great amounts of food are served and everyone eats from the same dish. Food is always accepted and taken with the right hand in Arab countries and this must be strictly observed when eating with Arabs. The left hand is considered unclean. Should you make a mistake, you will be gently reminded to use only your right hand.

It's still possible to find a traditional Arab feast, especially at weddings and other important occasions. If you're very lucky (?), you might be served the old favourite of a camel stuffed with a sheep, a goat and chickens. You're much more likely, however, to be confronted by the traditional Bedouin dish of kabsa served at important events, comprising a whole sheep stuffed with spices and eaten with rice.

Whether at home or in a restaurant, hosts are usually very attentive to their guests and select choice pieces of meat for them. In fact, newcomers to the Arab world sometimes misunderstand why an Arab keeps offering more and more food, which they feel obliged to accept. The host's attitude is that he must always offer an abundance of food, while the newcomer's interpretation is that he cannot refuse. It's perfectly acceptable, however, to thank your host when you've had enough, or the meal might continue all night. On formal occasions, food is usually eaten quickly, with little if any conversation and certainly no discussion of business matters. Incidentally, despite the well-worn joke, you won't be offered a sheep's eye.

Breakfast

Breakfast isn't an important meal in the region and, if taken, is frequently continental, consisting of croissants, Danish pastries, brioches or muffins, served with tea or coffee. Top hotels offer a range of breakfasts, including the full English/American type. Sausages are likely to be beef, although pork sausages are available in some states; the meat content is specified on the packaging in view of the general prohibition against pork (see page 314).

Lunch

Lunch is the most important meal of the day for Arabs and consists of a starter, usually soup (lentil soup is a favourite, served with lemon), a main course of meat or fish served with rice, and then perhaps fresh fruit or an Arab milk-based dessert such as *mahallabia* or *om ali* (a type of bread and butter pudding). Note, however, that the weather in the Gulf isn't conducive to a combination of heavy lunches and work in the afternoon, despite air-conditioning.

Dinner

Dinner tends to be similar to lunch but lighter. Formal Arab dinners tend to begin quite late in the evening (i.e. after 9pm). Although you may be invited to arrive earlier than the time of the meal itself (for introductions and aperitifs), you shouldn't be late, as (contrary to popular belief) meals start on time. Soft drinks, water and sometimes containers of milk are placed in front of you, to drink during your meal. Arabic coffee is served after the meal, and guests leave shortly afterwards. It's considered impolite to leave before coffee is taken. Before departure, smouldering incense in traditional burners might be wafted over guests or rose water might be offered for the hands.

RESTAURANTS

Dining out can be a pleasure in the Gulf, with a wide choice of restaurants to suit all tastes. Indeed, visiting restaurants is an important form of relaxation in the region, while business entertaining in restaurants is also popular. Strangely, it's often difficult to find restaurants that serve food specific to the host country. This might be because many restaurants serve more general 'Arab' cuisine, designed to appeal to as many people as possible, rather than esoteric local specialities.

Far more common than establishments offering formal, traditional Arab meals are restaurants serving Lebanese food. Lebanese cuisine sets the standard among Arab restaurants, whether they're owned by Lebanese or other Arabs. Almost all hotels have a restaurant serving Lebanese food, which isn't only delicious but is usually well balanced and nutritious. Many spices are used in its preparation, invariably including cayenne pepper, cinnamon and paprika, while nuts and seeds are also added, especially pine nuts, almonds, walnuts, and sesame and caraway seeds.

The first course in Lebanese restaurants is the *mezze*, which consists of a vast range of small hors-d'oeuvres. In many restaurants, the waiters keep bringing *mezze* dishes until you ask them to stop. In fact, some people start and finish their meal with the *mezze*, not having sufficient room for a main course! Therefore, it's best to stipulate the dishes that you want. The following is a list of some of the more popular ones. (In view of the flexible nature of Arabic/English transliteration, spellings of the dishes often vary.)

- *Baba Ghanouj* – a paste of aubergine (eggplant), onion and tomato, sometimes also including pomegranate;
- *Borek* – small pastries filled with cheese, mince or spinach;
- *Fattoush* – bulgur wheat, often mixed with lemon, garlic, parsley and fried bread;
- *Humous* – a paste of cooked chickpeas, garlic, lemon and tahini;
- *Kibbeh* – a small burger or patty of minced lamb and wheat and pine seeds, deep fried;
- *Kibbeh Nayeh* – raw minced lamb and cracked wheat: the *mezze* equivalent of steak tartare;
- *Kibda* – liver, steeped in garlic and lemon;
- *Labneh* – a varying blend of yoghurt, cheese, garlic and mint;
- *Loubieh* – a salad of French beans, tomatoes, onion and garlic;
- *Mashi* – courgettes, peppers or aubergines stuffed with mince, rice, parsley and other herbs, and baked;
- *Muttabel* – a paste of aubergine, tahini, yoghurt and olive oil;
- *Shinklish* – a salad of strong cheese, onion and tomato;

- **Tabbouleh** – a salad of bulgur wheat, tomato, parsley, sesame seeds, lemon and garlic;
- **Tahina** – a sesame-seed paste.

Main courses often include fish, favourites being *hammour*, red snapper and mullet. Fresh prawns are also a local delicacy. Meat dishes are predominantly lamb and chicken, including stews and casseroles. (Australia, New Zealand and the USA supply much of the region's meat.) All meals are accompanied by bottled water and hot pitta bread. Menus are usually written in Arabic and English, occasionally also in French.

In addition to food from Lebanon, restaurants in the region serve similar cuisine from Egypt, Iran, Iraq and Syria. There are also restaurants offering food from Italy, France, Germany, America, Britain and Ireland (in pubs), Mexico, Spain, China (various cuisines), Thailand, India, Pakistan and others. Some of the Indian and Pakistani restaurants at the lower end of the price range are excellent and many expatriates use them.

Desserts include a variety of sticky and sickly concoctions made from pastry, nuts, milk, sugar and other ingredients (see **Bread & Cakes** on page 315).

Fast-food outlets are everywhere, and the local population has taken to this type of food enthusiastically. The internationally known chains are well represented, including Burger King, Dominos Pizza, Hardees, Kentucky Fried Chicken, McDonald's, Pizza Hut, Pizzaland, Wimpy and many Arab versions of these. But many lesser-known outlets have also sprung up, mostly selling doughnuts and biscuits. An increasing number of large modern shopping malls have 'food halls', where busy shoppers can buy take-aways of every kind of food imaginable, including American, Italian, Chinese, Korean, Japanese, Thai, Indian, Egyptian and Lebanese. There are also many ice-cream parlours, including well-known operations such as Baskin-Robbins, as well as upmarket shops selling hand-made Belgian and Austrian chocolates and other sweets.

Don't turn your nose up at the Gulf's plentiful supply of snack bar counters, usually found on the pavements (sidewalks). They often sell kebabs or shawarmas, which consist of roast chicken or lamb, sliced directly from the grill, wrapped in pitta bread and served with a mixed salad. This type of fast food can be delicious and is usually fresh, although it's wise to make sure that the counter you intend to use has a rapid turnover of food.

During the holy month of Ramadan (see page 354), the daily fast is broken at sunset, when the special meal of *iftar* is served. Restaurant buffets, which are usually spectacular anyway, excel themselves on these occasions. Incidentally, while Muslims are observing the strict rules of fasting in the hours between sunrise and sunset, hotels provide meals but no alcoholic drinks for their non-Muslim guests. Muslims who are travellers, expectant mothers or sick may eat during daylight hours.

Restaurants in Saudi Arabia must observe strict rules, including having separate sections for men on their own and men accompanied by their wives and families. The segregation is commonly men only on the ground floor, families upstairs, and separate entrances are also used. Like shops (see page 312), restaurants in Saudi Arabia close at prayer times (see page 354). You won't be admitted to a restaurant if you arrive ten minutes or less before the start of prayers. If you're already inside when prayers start, you may usually continue your meal, and if you finish your meal during prayers, you might be allowed to leave or you might have to wait until they're finished.

In other states, most restaurants are open at 'western' hours, although Arabs tend to eat later than expatriates. Lunchtimes are generally between 12.30 and 2.30 or 3pm. Most restaurants are closed between 3 and 7pm, but some fast food outlets remain open all day. In the evenings, restaurants open at between 6.30 and 7.30pm but are quiet before 7.30, if there are any customers at all, and they remain open until around midnight, although orders aren't taken after 11.30. Most restaurants serving Arab food stay open later than those serving western food, but fast food outlets also keep late hours.

Restaurants in the region are strictly and regularly inspected for cleanliness, for the condition of their food and the facilities inside the premises. You need therefore have little fear about the quality and hygiene of the food served in restaurants in the Gulf. Indeed, newcomers are often pleasantly surprised by the standard and range of food on offer. In some restaurants, particularly hotel restaurants, there's a non-smoking section.

There's a range of establishments and prices to suit everyone. An inexpensive Lebanese or Indian restaurant can serve you a respectable meal for the equivalent of $4.50 (£3). Making a booking at popular restaurants is strongly recommended, but many lower-priced establishments and pubs don't accept bookings. Many restaurants offer a dish of the day or special dishes at attractive prices. A 'special' can apply to a main dish or to a two or three-course meal, but at lunchtime (particularly during the working week) it's usually just a main course. Some pubs offer a free or reduced price breakfast at weekends to encourage custom.

Wine in those restaurants that serve alcohol tends to be expensive, but most serve drinkable house wines at reasonable prices. During the working week, however, most people avoid drinking a lot of alcohol at lunchtime, as the hot climate is soporific enough already, without further assistance. See also **Alcohol** below.

At fast food outlets, you pay for your food as you receive it, while in restaurants and bars it's usual to run a tab and pay when you leave. In pubs, you must usually pay each time you're served a round of drinks. The western habit of leaving a credit card behind a pub bar has caught on, but can be regarded as ostentatious. Most establishments include in their prices any tax to be paid as well as a service charge, so tipping is unnecessary, unless you feel that you've had exceptional service. Tips aren't expected in pubs and bars.

ALCOHOL

Different states have different views about the sale and consumption of alcohol. The commonly agreed rule, however, is that Muslims must not consume it. (Some religious scholars maintain that there's no reference to alcohol's prohibition in the Koran, but the general interpretation is that it's forbidden.) The possession and consumption of alcohol are strictly forbidden in Saudi Arabia and Kuwait. If convicted of consuming alcohol, you can expect to be jailed for weeks or months, depending on the circumstances. For bringing alcohol into the country or manufacturing and selling alcohol, particularly to Muslims, the sentence can be several years and might include flogging.

Expatriates in Saudi Arabia and Kuwait invariably live in housing compounds, which are to some extent closed communities. Those housing western expatriates usually have alcoholic drinks available, and making these is a popular pastime. A distillation of sugar and water, known as 'sid' (short for siddiqi meaning 'friend') in Saudi Arabia and 'flash' in Kuwait, and 'Jeddah gin' (a fermentation of fruit, vegetables, sugar and yeast) are powerful (and sometimes toxic) drinks requiring dilution by at least 50 per cent with water before they can be drunk.

Note that some of these products are inexpertly made and can be lethal. 'Wine' is also made, from non-alcoholic grape juice, sugar and yeast (Ribena can be turned into something resembling a Merlot, according to some expatriates – who presumably haven't tasted the real thing for quite a while), and is also quite powerful. Beer is made from non-alcoholic beer by a similar fermentation process.

Although the authorities often know that illicit alcohol is being made in certain compounds and might turn a blind eye, you shouldn't count on this. You're breaking the law and risk severe punishment.

The production and sale of these drinks is sometimes cleverly organised, boxes marked with the name of a bottled water being delivered to homes. Any connection with this trade is particularly dangerous.

Some other states allow the sale to and consumption of alcohol by non-Muslims, with strict regulations applying to the outlets where it's sold and the individuals permitted to use them. The legal age for drinking is 18 or 21, depending on the state or perhaps on the ownership of the establishment. But be warned that drunken behaviour (e.g. aggression, swearing and blasphemy) and drunk-driving (see page 188) bring severe penalties throughout the region. Should such behaviour occur in states where alcohol is banned, you will automatically be found guilty, irrespective of the circumstances. Committing this type of offence will almost certainly put you in breach of contract with your employer and he might fire you. It should be understood that your sponsor, who is usually your employer, is responsible for your being in the country, and your behaviour is seen as a reflection of his judgement. Should you bring any serious dishonour to his reputation, he might wish to end the working relationship immediately.

Beer

Pubs and bars serve a wide variety of alcoholic and non-alcoholic beer. Beers come in bottles and on draft, and most of the favourite UK brands and some European and American beers are available. Non-alcoholic beer is widely available throughout the region and if 'doctored' with yeast and sugar can approximate 'real' beer, although some drinkers find it repulsive. In the non-alcoholic parts of the Gulf, such recipes are a common topic of conversation at expatriate parties.

Wine

Wines from Europe (notably France and Spain) and New World wines, whose popularity has recently grown enormously, are available in hotels and, occasionally, licensed restaurants in Bahrain, Oman, Qatar and most of the Emirates of the UAE, as well as from licensed retailers in certain states (see page 318). Wines tend to be slightly more expensive than in Europe and North America, and some wines don't travel well, although cooled transporters have now made this less of a problem.

Cocktails & Spirits

Younger drinkers in the livelier states are keen on B52s, Long Island cocktails and other such noxious concoctions. For more conservative tipplers, all the well known brands of spirits are available, Johnny Walker Black Label being the preferred choice in the region, with John Jamieson catching up, probably as a result of the Irish 'mafia' at work in the UAE. There's a black market in alcohol in the 'dry' states, where branded bottles of spirits are very expensive — and of course illegal.

BARS & CAFES

Bars are found in most hotels in states that permit the consumption of alcohol. Occasionally, a bar can be found outside a hotel complex, but generally this is prohibited. In hotels, there are many different types of bar, some with a popular theme (e.g. 'Irish pub'), others ranging from ultra-expensive cocktail bars to laddish sports bars where international sporting events are broadcast on satellite television. There are also piano bars, disco bars, live music bars, bar restaurants and beach bars on hotels' private beaches (which aren't always adjacent to the hotel, although transport is provided).

Hotel bars can open 24 hours a day, but like restaurants tend to operate two shifts: usually from 11am until 3pm and from 5.30 until 11pm or later, depending on the type of premises and the number of customers. Early evening 'happy hours' are popular in the region's bars, when cheaper drinks are sold for an hour or so to boost custom. You normally pay for your drinks as they're served, with no tips expected. Other bar bills (e.g. food) are paid when you leave and a service charge is usually included.

Cafes are often found in hotels but also in shopping areas and malls. They sell soft drinks, various kinds of coffee and tea. There's usually also an extensive range of snacks, salads, pastries and cakes. The style of these cafes tends to be French, possibly because of the Lebanese ownership of some of them. In the cooler months, pavement cafes come into their own and remain open until quite late in the evening.

Arab-style cafes sell Arabic coffee, tea, soft drinks and fabulous liquidised fresh fruit drinks, which are both nutritious and delicious. These cafes are traditionally meeting places for the older generation, especially in the morning, where they sit and talk, play backgammon and watch the world go by. Smoking hookahs (water pipes) is banned in some places, probably for hygiene reasons, but it's common to see a 'hubble-bubble' being enjoyed by both old and young.

Even in entertainment-starved Saudi Arabia, the outdoor cafes in the old market area of Jeddah are popular and normally crowded, except at prayer times, when everything stops. There are also coffee shops with a Brazilian theme in many shopping malls in Saudi Arabia.

Coffee

The Arab world has a long association with the production of high-quality coffee. Indeed, the world's most widely grown cofee tree, which also yields the best beans, is called Coffea Arabica and the town of Al-Mukha (usually 'translated' as Moka or Mocha) in Yemen has given its name to the mixture of chocolate and coffee. Arabic coffee is always freshly ground and usually flavoured with cardamom, giving it a distinctive taste, which isn't enjoyed by everyone.

Wherever you go and meet Arabs, be it at home, in the office or even if you visit a state ruler at his palace (many businessmen do this and are warmly received), you will be served coffee. The traditions attached to the offering and taking of coffee, both at home and in the office, can be quite formal – indeed, almost ceremonial – in Arab culture. One should never refuse an offer of coffee (or a similar drink) when the invitation is made either formally or informally. Obviously, if your host is an old and well known friend it's different, but an offer of coffee in all other circumstances indicates a gesture of hospitality and one should accept or run the risk of offending the host.

Coffee is served from a *dallah*, the traditional Arab coffee pot with a long pouring spout, which is seen everywhere and holds a special significance in Arab culture. Coffee is served in very small cups without handles, which should be held in the right hand and it's usual to accept two or three cupfuls. It's important to know how to call a halt to your cup being refilled, which otherwise continues indefinitely. You must shake the empty cup from side to side, in a horizontal, semi-circular motion, rather like turning a knob on a radio. Then hand it back to the server or place it on the pile of cups which he is holding in his hand. On certain formal occasions, saying no politely in a non-Arabic language will not do, as servants might not understand you.

Tea

Tea is widely available in cafes, restaurants and bars. There are also tea shops, invariably with 'Liptons' tea signs on their fascias, and these are especially popular with older male Arabs and Asians. On many occasions, Arabs offer tea as well as coffee, particularly at office meetings where the coffee making facilities are limited (thermos flasks are often used for coffee), usually served with lemon or milk. The tea is most likely to be *suleiman*, which is ordinary tea with sugar added. Alternatively, you might be given mint tea, which is normally served with neither lemon nor milk (although the addition of either to suit western tastes is magnanimously tolerated). Tea is always served in tiny glasses, which might have a small handle. It tends to be raging hot and it's common to exchange introductory pleasantries while suffering second-degree burns to the fingers.

Soft Drinks

Soft drinks are available everywhere, which isn't surprising given the region's hot climate and the ban on alcohol. International brands such as Pepsi-Cola, Coca Cola and Seven Up are popular, as are non-carbonated drinks, squashes and cordials. Vimto is popular with Muslims when they break their fast between sunset and sunrise during Ramadan, as its high fruit and sugar content are believed to give energy for the fasting period. Fruit juices are widely available and are sold in small and one-litre cartons. Those taking up residence in a 'dry' state might be interested to know that Ribena, given the right treatment, can apparently be made to taste remarkably like a red wine made from the Merlot grape (see **Alcohol** on page 287)!

LIBRARIES

There are public libraries in the Gulf states, but they cater mainly for the indigenous population, most books being in Arabic. Some of them, however, have English-language books. The British Council runs its own libraries, and there are private libraries in many places, run by expatriate organisations and social clubs. These are well patronised, as books are quite expensive in the region, even at airport shops. Book 'swap shops', where you can buy second-hand books at low prices and sell books that you've finished with, are also increasing in popularity.

16.

SPORTS

The provision of a wide range of sports facilities is high on the agenda of all Gulf states governments, who regard sport as a way of developing links with the rest of the world. With young populations (in many states, half the population is aged under 20), there's a need to offer diversion and entertainment – and young people are better educated than their parents and their expectations are higher. The great influx of foreign workers to the region has brought new ideas and lifestyles, and local demand for sports facilities has grown.

Today, the Gulf states can boast some of the best sports stadia and complexes in the world. There are sports clubs for indoor and outdoor sports, multi-sport and social complexes, private country clubs, golf clubs, tennis clubs, gymnasia and health centres. There's also a considerable duplication of facilities, mainly because the local and expatriate populations don't often mix in the sporting arena, tending to have their own clubs and leagues. Even western and eastern expatriates, the latter making up the majority of the working population, rarely mix.

All the main sports are played in the region, including soccer, rugby, cricket, tennis, golf, basketball, squash, volleyball, handball (and beach handball), softball, ten-pin bowling, bowls, snooker, darts, ice-skating, go-karting and horse riding. Athletics, both track and field, in indoor and outdoor stadia, has become popular with young locals, and the Gulf countries are sending more representatives to the Olympic Games than ever before. But the local population's first love is soccer, with basketball next in popularity.

With long coastlines and fine beaches, there are plenty of marinas and sailing clubs, and watersports are tremendously popular. There's a great deal of sailing in boats of all classes, waterskiing, windsurfing, swimming and parascending. The beaches themselves are generally well-maintained, the sea is safe for swimming, and there's year-round sunshine. The summer months of May to September are excessively hot during the day, but the period from October to April enjoys ideal weather for outdoor pursuits, invariably with cloudless skies and warm sunshine.

SOCCER

Soccer (or association football) is the national sport in all Gulf states and is without doubt the sport that draws the most fervent support.

There are football clubs and excellent pitches in most cities and towns, and each state has its own leagues, which are as competitive as any in the world. There are also inter-Gulf tournaments, the Gulf Cup being a source of great competition. The Asian Cup is an important event, but the World Cup is the pinnacle each state aims for.

The arrival of foreign football managers has contributed a great deal to the development of the game in the region, and their expertise and rigorous training methods have brought more success to many teams, at both club and national level. Managers tend to come from Europe and Brazil, but also from other Arab nations, such as Egypt, that are increasingly enjoying international success. Some states, such as the United Arab Emirates (UAE), have lifted the prohibition on foreign players in their club sides, to encourage skills and raise standards.

There's a considerable amount of soccer on television in the region, with commentary in either Arabic and English. The English FA Cup is keenly followed, especially the final, while BBC Worldwide features games from the English Premier and Scottish Leagues, and viewers can also enjoy games from Italy's Serie 'A'.

RUGBY

Rugby union is played in the region by western expatriates, many of them British. They've been joined by players from Australia and New Zealand and recently by an increasing number from the other major southern hemisphere rugby nation, South Africa. Other European nationalities are also joining in, as are some local Arabs and players from the USA. The American Eagles are a mainly Saudi-based rugby team.

The major event on rugby's calendar is the Rugby Sevens Tournament held in Dubai in November or early December. The tournament, which is linked to the notable Hong Kong Sevens, draws national teams from both the northern and southern hemispheres, including the winner of the Gulf's own sevens tournament. There are usually some world-class players taking part and the event is a sell-out, supporters coming from all over the Gulf. This is an important social as well as sporting occasion, when old friends from around the region get together.

CRICKET

Cricket is an important sport in the region but, although the various expatriate communities sometimes meet on the cricket pitch, the game is predominantly played by Asian sides. The usual rivalry between India and Pakistan is very much in evidence and, when their national teams visit the area, they're given a vociferous reception. Cricket is played in most Gulf states, but rarely in Saudi Arabia. The driving force behind attracting international teams to play in the region is, perhaps surprisingly, a United Arab Emirates Sheikh, and Sharjah in the UAE hosts the most important matches. Sharjah has welcomed visiting teams from India, Pakistan, Sri Lanka, Australia, England, Zimbabwe and the West Indies, competing for the Coca Cola Cup and the Champions Cup.

There are numerous cricket clubs in the region participating in competitions, notably in Bahrain and the UAE, where Sharjah is the centre of activity. Many social clubs field a reasonable cricket team, and there are inter-state as well as intra-state matches.

WATERSPORTS

Watersports are one of the most popular participant sports in the Gulf. Sailing is excellent on the region's waters, which are calm for most of the year, although when strong winds blow the seas can become rough. There's a wide variety of boats, from dinghies and catamarans to larger, ocean-going vessels, and there are marinas of all sizes and prices, making the region ideal for both experienced sailors and novices. The region's marinas are also home to large motor cruisers or 'floating gin palaces', mainly owned by local Arabs. At weekends, invariably with a complement of bikini-clad girls, they can be seen making short trips along the coast.

With a constantly changing expatriate population, there's an active boat resale market in all states, so finding one at a reasonable price isn't difficult. Less straightforward is joining a sailing club, as there's invariably a waiting list. It's usually quite easy to obtain entry to the social side of these clubs, however, and there are frequent calls for people to crew yachts, which is the quickest way to ease yourself in. Membership fees and berthing and mooring charges vary considerably between clubs, depending on their location, facilities and snob value.

Similarly, charges for slipway use, cranage and cleaning follow the same pattern. Most states require that all boats are registered with the marine authorities, usually the coastguard service.

Diving is also popular in the Gulf, where many people take advantage of the warm water to learn. (It's common to see sub-aqua classes in the large swimming pools at the region's social clubs.) For the experienced diver, the region's waters provide exciting underwater scenery, the Red Sea being a magnet for serious divers.

Equipment for jet-skiing, waterskiing and windsurfing can be rented from the many coastal hotels, to residents and non-residents alike. A number of jet-skiing accidents, particularly in the UAE, has prompted the authorities to restrict the areas where jet-skis can be used, however, with limits on how close they can come to the beach and to bathers.

Powerboat racing at world class level has recently become popular in the region, Dubai leading the way. Backed by Dubai's ruling family, the 'Victory' racing team is a leader in this rich man's game. Competitive boats and their crews from around the world regularly come to the region to race.

FISHING

Sea fishing trips are popular in the Gulf. (The only fishing to be had in the region is sea fishing, the Gulf being short of rivers.) Many choose to fish from small Arab dhows, manned by a captain and one or two crew. If required, the captain can organise food, often provided by one of the hotels, as well as alcohol, if permitted. The fishing part of the trip often comes a poor second to drinking cold beer and swimming off the dhow. Dhow fishing is particularly popular in Bahrain.

More serious fishing, for sharks and sailfish, is also popular, and day and half-day trips into the deeper waters of the Gulf, where large catches have been reported, can be arranged with local owners of suitable boats. Licences aren't needed for any type of fishing, but the coastguard service requires you to register your trip with them, including the number of people on board (and in most cases their names), the general direction that you intend to take, and your expected time of departure and return to port, in case you experience difficulties.

SWIMMING

Not surprisingly, given the Gulf's climate and extensive beaches, swimming is popular in the region. The warm waters of the Gulf are inviting all year, although in the summer months (between May and September) the water can actually be too warm if the purpose of the swim is to cool off. The many miles of beaches are generally deserted in the hot months of June, July and August, although swimmers can be seen from around 6am, before the sun becomes too fierce.

Beaches are kept very clean in those countries that have embarked on the serious development of their tourist trade. Others are more lax about clearing up the litter left over from weekend beach barbecues. The main municipal beaches in the region usually have showers, toilets and perhaps a cafe or restaurant, or at least an ice-cream kiosk. On crowded weekends, there are lifeguards to watch for swimmers in difficulty. The international safety system of flags (green denoting safe conditions, yellow for the exercise of caution and red for when it's too dangerous to enter the water) is widely in use. The beaches of the Gulf shelve gently. This is usually an advantage for children and nervous swimmers, but it can also cause large waves, which are particularly dangerous for non-swimmers. Despite the presence of lifeguards and regular patrols by the coastguard and police, accidents occur quite frequently.

There are also periods when hordes of jellyfish invade swimming areas, usually as a result of high winds blowing them onshore. Their sting can be painful, causing an irritating rash. Sea snakes are also encountered occasionally, some of them being highly venomous. Most dangerous of all are stonefish, which are found (albeit rarely) in the shallows — often buried in the sand or under stones — and swimmers are recommended to wear plastic shoes to protect their feet from a potentially deadly sting. Splashing the water with your feet sometimes frightens them away, but it's no guarantee. Sharks are regularly spotted in Gulf waters but don't often come inshore, and attacks on humans in the region are rare.

Most of the many social clubs in the Gulf have good swimming pools, usually with a separate children's pool and a paddling pool for toddlers. These can become crowded, when it isn't possible actually to swim in them but merely to cool off. Schools normally also have swimming pools and generally provide instruction for beginners.

Men are expected to wear modest swimming trunks or shorts, and foreign women generally feel more comfortable if they avoid skimpy swimwear because some Arab men visit beaches to ogle expatriate women. (Cruising the beaches in four-wheel drives is a favourite pastime among young Arab men). But there are severe penalties for harrassment, and women are invariably safe. **Topless and nude bathing aren't allowed in public anywhere in the region and this rule is strictly enforced.** Breaking it will invite arrest. In many countries, there are women's gardens and beaches, strictly reserved for females and boys under the age of ten, where some of the more liberal Arab women wear swimming costumes and swim.

TENNIS

Most social clubs that cater for the foreign community and the many hotels in the region have tennis courts. Hotels usually offer professional tuition for reasonable fees. Wealthy Arabs also enjoy tennis and many have courts at home. Tennis has a strong social element, leading to the mixing of locals and expatriates, which isn't the case with some other sports. Dubai can claim to be the tennis centre of the Gulf, the Dubai Duty-Free Open, held every February at the Dubai Tennis Stadium, being a major event on the international professional circuit.

GOLF

As leaders in the development of the region's tourist trade, Dubai and Bahrain are the main destinations for golf. (It's said that when the Dubai government first sought to attract foreign investment and commerce to the country, a leading Japanese businessman was asked what social aspects of life there would interest prospective companies and their senior management. His reply was, 'Golf.') The first world-class, professional, championship golf course in the Gulf, with two superb 18-hole courses, was built in Dubai in 1988 and named the Emirates Golf Club. It was the first in the Middle East to host the European PGA Tour and gained international acceptance with the $1 million Dubai Desert Classic, which has become the opening tournament on the European fixture list every spring and attracts top players from all over the world. The fairways and greens are maintained by a complex 24-hour recycling system, and the superb clubhouse is built to resemble a group of traditional Arab tents (*majlis*).

The success of the Emirates Golf Club led to the construction of other courses in Dubai, including the Dubai Creek Golf and Yacht Club and the Dubai Golf and Racing Club at Nadd Al-Shiba, and there are plans to build another four or five golf courses between Abu Dhabi and Dubai, including two championship courses at Umm Al-Nar, designed to attract top players and tournaments.

Even before the construction of the Gulf's championship-quality courses, golfers had been playing in the region since the discovery of oil in the 1920s, and Abu Dhabi had a proper course by the late 1950s. The Jeddah Golf Club in Saudi Arabia was formed by enthusiastic amateurs who set up a course in the desert and remains a 'rough' course, with 'water' hazards marked by posts and signs, and 'trees' with piles of sand. The 'rough' consists of ungraded desert and fairways are graded to create a smoother surface. Instead of greens, there are 'browns', a mixture of heavy oil and sand rolled flat. Each player has a piece of 'turf' (usually a mat or piece of Astroturf) from which to tee off. Rough courses can also be found in other states (and they make possible interesting ricochet shots off rocky surfaces), but most courses are of the traditional green variety, and most states have some fine courses.

Green fees vary considerably. Among the most expensive courses is the Majlis at the Emirates Golf Club, where a round costs AED365 ($90) and a golf buggy AED45 ($10). Many of the region's other courses are up to 50 per cent cheaper. Top hotels invariably offer their guests membership of the major local golf clubs.

Most courses operate all year, but during the hottest months of June, July and August, golfers must start soon after dawn (around 5am) and aim to complete their round before the extreme heat begins at around 10am. Some courses are floodlit, to allow play at night. Newer courses have rest areas where you can obtain a drink from a dispenser and sit at a table in the shade (there's usually also a toilet), but on the older, rough courses you must take your own drinks, which are important to prevent dehydration.

HORSE RACING

With the Arab love of horses and the famous Arab lineage of bloodstock, it's little wonder that horse racing holds is so important in the region. Much has been written about the swiftness of Arab horses, which according to one poet "leave no footprints in the sand". The UAE and Bahrain are the leading horse racing states, the former having five race tracks. (The UAE's ruling family, the Al-Maktoums, own the highly successful Godolphin stable and have the largest collection of racehorses in the world.) The most famous event in the Gulf is the Dubai World Cup, which started in 1996 and now has prize money of some $10 million ($4 million for the race winner!). Most racing takes place at night on dirt tracks, but some surfaces are treated with a combination of oil and sand for a smoother run. Entrance to horse races is usually free, and the major cup events are also stylish social occasions. Betting isn't officially allowed, so prize money derives from sponsorship or is provided by the racecourse. What happens off-course, however, is another matter and betting does take place, certainly among expatriates.

CAMEL RACING

This specifically Arab sport is widely enjoyed at racecourses across the Gulf, where owners and enthusiasts can be seen following the races from the comfort of their pursuing Range Rovers. Races are often televised. Some racing camels are highly prized and worth a small fortune. The jockeys are very young boys, usually from Pakistan, the belief being that their childish cries spur the camels to greater speed. The jockeys' pants are allegedly fitted with Velcro fastenings to stick them to the saddle. Unfortunately, however, injuries do occur, although the rewards for the boys and/or their parents can be substantial and there's no shortage of recruits, despite occasional calls to stop the exploitation of small children.

FALCONRY

This is the sport of rich Arabs. The falcon holds a special place in the heart of the Gulf Arab, being seen as an icon symbolising the values and virtues of the people. Renowned for its hunting abilities, the falcon is beautiful, fast, intelligent and ruthless in the pursuit of its quarry. The most serious hunters take their birds to the mountains of Pakistan for their sport. (In the early days of the oil boom, it wasn't uncommon to see the whole of the first class section of an Arab airliner taken over by the birds, their owners and handlers.) Expatriates are unlikely to be involved with the sport, unless they're well connected to an Arab enthusiast. There are, however, many training establishments where birds can be seen, but you should make an appointment.

WADI BASHING

'Wadi bashing' is the regional term for desert driving and is a popular pastime for many (Arabs and expatriates alike) in all the Gulf states, but especially in the UAE. It's less common in Bahrain and Kuwait, and in fact you're advised against wadi bashing in Kuwait. While the main residential areas have been cleared of the many landmines left from the Gulf War, much of the desert hasn't. And because sand moves – especially dunes – buried mines move with it and are therefore difficult or impossible to map.

Wadi bashing tests your driving skills at travelling up and over massive sand dunes, without slipping back or overturning. You need a four-wheel drive vehicle and must observe certain precautions and master various techniques (see **Off-road Driving** on page 182). It isn't for the inexperienced or faint-hearted. If you don't have your own vehicle or prefer to let an expert do the driving, there are several companies offering desert tours for tourists and resident expatriates. Equipment and food are supplied, and the trip might include a desert barbecue, which is usually a feast accompanied by belly-dancing or other entertainment. In Saudi Arabia, there are few tour companies, but similar trips are often organised by groups of friends.

Despite the dangers, wadi bashing is a unique way of experiencing the desert landscape and seeing its flora and fauna, of which there's much more than might be expected.

ATHLETICS

The region has no shortage of athletics stadia and athletics clubs, although these are mostly used by locals. There are also amateur road races, including marathons, half-marathons and 'mini-marathons', which you can enter for a small fee. These are invariably charitable events, and many of the competitors are 'sponsored'. Needless to say, you need to be extremely fit to undertake even a mini-marathon in the region's hot climate.

A less formal (and less demanding) athletic event is offered in Dubai and Oman by the Hash House Harriers, an informal group of 'athletes' who organise short runs over a desert course. You don't need to be particularly fit to join them, and you can walk if you prefer! The course is marked by 'hares' (actually human beings) holding signs and clues – some of them designed to mislead. The aim is to complete the course (optional) and enjoy a party or barbecue afterwards (compulsory). There are prizes and penalties, the latter invariably involving a hapless person being drenched in foul-looking liquid. Those who enjoy such activities can contact the Hounds on the telephone numbers below or via the Internet (💻 www.gthhh.com).

Dubai

Barbie Hash House Harriers (☎ 971-4-337 0380)

Creek Hash House Harriers (☎ 971-4-451 5847)

Desert Hash House Harriers (☎ 971-4-457 1941)

Moonshine Hash House Harriers (☎ 971-4-774 1580)

Oman

Jebel Hash House Harriers (☎ 968-516370)

Muscat Hash House Harriers (☎ 968 513556)

Wudham Hash House Harriers (☎ 968-316709)

HEALTH CLUBS

Many of the region's hotels have a well-equipped health centre and gymnasium. People over a certain age (usually around 45 or 50) might need a doctor's certificate to confirm that they're fit enough to use them. As in many other countries, it's standard practice for the staff to discuss your needs and capabilities in order to recommend a beneficial and safe exercise regime. Centres usually also offer a games room, with table tennis and snooker, and massage and aromatherapy might also be available. The facilities are usually free for hotel guests; others must normally pay a membership fee. Costs vary in line with the status and ranking of the hotel.

OTHER SPORTS

● **Billiard** and **snooker** tables are found in hotel bars or games rooms and in almost every social club throughout the region.

- **Bungee jumping** is available in Dubai, invariably operated by New Zealanders or Australians.
- **Darts** is popular throughout the region, and in some states there are competitive leagues.
- **Go-karting** can be found in Dubai and Oman (e.g. at the Oman Automobile Club in Muscat, ☎ 968-510239).
- **Softball** is popular among Americans in the Gulf, who organise leagues, and games are social as well as sporting occasions.
- **Ten-pin bowling** is available at a number of centres and is popular among both locals and expatriates, so booking is usually necessary.

Finally, there have been attempts to bring Formula One racing to the Gulf, particularly Dubai, but so far they've come to nothing. Bahrain is currently reported to be assessing the possibility of staging a Grand Prix event on the island.

17.

SHOPPING

Shopping in the Gulf isn't only big business, it's also a major leisure pursuit, in the absence of other diversions. There's a wide choice of shops in the region, ranging from those selling luxury goods in the world's most exclusive shopping malls to small grocery stores in souks (see page 319), supplying the needs of ordinary people. There's a selection of supermarkets, hypermarkets (i.e. large supermarkets) and large department stores in all major towns (see page 320). The variety of goods on offer is extensive and prices are generally competitive, particularly for electrical goods, household appliances and high-cost items such as cars, owing to low import taxes. Imported food, however, tends to be expensive, although there are plenty of reasonably priced local alternatives and the price of certain basic foodstuffs is government-controlled (See also **Cost of Living** on page 246.)

Haggling over prices is still a treasured part of life in the Gulf and enjoyed in many outlets, but not in supermarkets or in many of the shops in new shopping centres and malls, which work on a fixed price basis (although even in some of the most impressive looking stores you will be forgiven for trying to barter!). On the other hand, the vast majority of goods sold in the souks and older shopping centres of the region are subject to haggling, including clothing, footwear, household goods, furniture and furnishings, electrical appliances and white goods of all kinds, carpets, curtains, hi-fi equipment, televisions and radios. You will have no joy bargaining for food in shops, as the only deals are likely to be for Arab families buying in bulk at their favourite shops, although in markets it's expected.

Haggling becomes serious with major purchases such as cars and expensive jewellery. When buying a major item, it's useful to take a local Arab along so that you get an idea of the going rate, or send him in on his own first to enquire. (An alternative for men is to take an attractive woman, or send her in on her own, as she will often be able to secure a bigger discount than you!) The question 'Is this your last (or best) price?' is the usual start of some good-natured bargaining. There's usually a price below which the trader won't go, and the aim is to get as close to that price as you can. Your demeanour is very important when haggling: it must never be aggressive or insulting to the trader, but rather should be good-humoured at all times. Many traders adopt a slow pace when doing business and you will invariably be offered some refreshment (i.e. tea or a soft drink) while the price is negotiated. You should accept this offer and take your time.

The variation in prices among different retailers can be significant, so it's worth having a look around before opening negotiations. In many cases, however, a dealer has the sole concession for the sale of particular items and there's little room for manoeuvre, although you can always try.

Note that haggling is invariably based on the assumption that the transaction will be in cash, and using a credit card invalidates any reduction you've negotiated. In fact, if you haven't told the trader that you want to pay with a card, the price often rises, especially if a charge card such as American Express is proffered. Some establishments don't accept charge cards at all. Personal cheques are rarely accepted either, except perhaps for a major purchase where a long delivery time allows the cheque to clear before the goods are delivered. Some traders only accept cash, and you should always check in advance if you are intending to pay by card or cheque.

Many cities and major towns have a souk area which specialises in cheaper clothes and counterfeit 'designer' goods, including major clothing and sportswear brands and jewellery such as 'Rolex' and 'Cartier' watches, at knock-down prices. Although customs are unlikely to show interest in one or two counterfeit items, Gulf administrations are beginning to prohibit the import of such goods, as well as of pirated CDs and audio tapes. The United Arab Emirates (UAE) and Bahrain in particular have introduced legislation to this effect.

In most Gulf states, there are fixed sales periods, set by the Chamber of Commerce, when prices are reduced considerably. These are normally twice a year, in spring and autumn, but sales also occur at other times, such as at the start of school terms, when children's clothes and school items are reduced in price. Sales aren't merely an excuse for shops to get rid of junk, and many locals and expatriates purchase major items in sales. Dubai is famous for its duty-free shopping and hosts several shopping festivals (see **Festivals** on page 279).

The region's spice markets are of special interest (see **Markets** on page 319), as are its 'gold souks', with street upon street of shops selling gold jewellery and other goods. Some jewellery is made locally, but much is imported from Italy. Shopping around and haggling is more important in these souks than in most of the region's other retail outlets. Occasionally, jewellers will buy your old jewellery in part-exchange for a new item. But don't offer them any nine-carat gold items: no self-respecting Arab jeweller will handle what he considers to be low-quality gold. In fact, this grade of 'gold', widely sold throughout Europe, is considered something of a joke in the region, where 18, 22 and 24-four carat gold is standard.

A traditional regional shop is a perfumery, where Arab women have exotic perfumes made up to their own recipes. Fragrances are bought by both men and women, as cleanliness and smelling fresh are regarded as important. Literally tons of perfume is imported into the region every year, and perfumeries have thousands of bottles on display.

Other traditional purchases in the region are intricately designed wooden room screens, chests, nests of coffee tables, ornamental doors, camel saddles made of leather and other colourful fabrics, dress fabrics in all designs and colours imported from India and Egypt, carpets imported from Iran (i.e. Persian carpets) and Pakistan, prayer mats and wall tapestries. The natural pearl trade almost died out with the arrival of Japanese cultured pearls, but you can still buy the genuine article in the Gulf, where traders have stockpiles from earlier times.

Shopping etiquette in the Gulf is reasonably straightforward and there's some semblance of queueing. Occasionally, a local Arab will deem himself important enough to jump the queue, but if you try doing so, you're likely to face opposition. At airports in the region, on the other hand, queueing is at best hazy, and a degree of self-assertion is taken for granted. Note that in Saudi Arabia, where it's rare for women to shop without a male family escort, there are separate entrances for single males and females. Note also, that women aren't allowed to drive cars, so expatriate women, in common with their Arab counterparts, must go shopping by bus.

Most of the region's shops are manned by Indian or Pakistani staff, who, like hotel staff, are invariably friendly and helpful, as they appreciate the value of having a job in the Gulf. Shoppers can therefore expect courtesy and attentive service. There's little shoplifting or theft from shops or people. In some states, the penalties for theft are severe, persistent offenders risking limb amputation.

SHOPPING HOURS

Shopping hours vary across the region. With the exception of Saudi Arabia, where shops must close during prayer times (see page 354), there are no statutory trading times imposed on the retail trade.

Nevertheless, a general pattern of opening hours has become established, and most shops and supermarkets open at between 9 and 10am, although smaller shops might open at 8.30am, particularly in industrial areas. Some shopping malls don't open until 10am because of their late closing times. Shops usually close at between 12.30 and 1pm for lunch and reopen at 3.30 or 4pm, remaining open until around 10pm. Supermarkets and hypermarkets usually open all day without a lunch break and some of the large establishments stay open for 24 hours, particularly in the UAE.

It's important to note that the trading days of the week are Saturdays to Thursdays, Friday being the Muslim day of rest. On Fridays, most shops remain closed for the important Friday prayers, but in the late afternoon many of them open, including most food shops, bakers' and supermarkets. Many of the small clothing shops in the souks also open on Friday evenings.

In Saudi Arabia, the opening and closing time of shops tends to be rather later than in the other states and prayer times (see page 354) must be strictly observed. The dawn prayer is unlikely to affect shoppers, but the others mean that you must plan your shopping trips to avoid interruption. Shops must close ten minutes before each prayer time, to allow the shop to be cleared, and remain closed until the prayer time is over. Some of the large stores allow customers to remain inside during prayer time, but this is frowned upon and trading stops anyway. Most shops are closed all day on Fridays, although some supermarkets open on Friday mornings and many in the afternoon and evening.

During Ramadan, the holy month of fasting (see page 354), shopping hours in all states are usually reduced, some shops opening much later than usual in the morning but remaining open later in the evening. Working hours are legally restricted to six hours for Muslims (and for non-Muslims, although this isn't always observed by those employing non-Muslims), because of the need to fast during the day. In Saudi Arabia during Ramadan, night in effect becomes day for shopping.

SHOPPING FOR FOOD

Until recently, shopping for food was done at small shops. They carried essential lines of general dry goods, tinned meat and fish, fresh fish and meat, vegetables, milk, yogurt, flour and bread. Rice was (and is still) a staple, with fresh vegetables and dates grown locally, and goats providing meat and milk for yogurt. Most of the produce was local and the close connection between the shopkeeper and his customers was as much a social contact as it was a necessary service.

Today, while small shops trading in the old way still exist and will continue to, food shopping is centred on supermarkets, large and small. Expatriates have influenced shopping trends in the region, and the local Arab population is increasingly attracted to the one-stop shopping that supermarkets offer as well as to the range of new imported food items they stock. With a diverse range of expatriates, the choice of food on offer is enormous. Some shops serve particular ethnic tastes and needs, e.g. Indian.

You can often purchase either locally produced or imported varieties of many foods. The locally produced version is likely to be considerably cheaper and is usually equal in quality to the import. Food items are strictly inspected in the region and there are extensive safeguards to protect public health. All foods must be date-stamped with their production and expiry date, and food imports are stringently inspected to ensure that there's no dumping of poor quality or out-dated food.

Meat

Meat is traditionally sold at small butchers' shops in the older parts of towns and cities, and at some fish and meat markets. The most popular meats are lamb and goat, as well as chicken, which is inexpensive compared to other meats. Veal is widely available, but beef is less common. With no beef herds in the region, it must be imported, mainly from Australia, the United States and Holland, and is therefore expensive. There's little or no game meat for sale.

Muslims are prohibited from eating the meat, blood or any other matter derived from pigs, which are prohibited in Kuwait, Qatar and Saudi Arabia. In the other states, the import and sale of pork, ham and bacon are carefully handled to avoid offence to Muslims. (For example, different utensils and containers are used for pork and other meats to avoid 'contamination'.) Even in states where they're permitted, however, some supermarkets refuse to stock pig meat products, although many do. These display them on separate counters from other meats and clearly label them in Arabic and English. This applies to both fresh and tinned products. Pork and ham are most widely available, and bacon and pork sausages can also be bought at some stores.

All meat, whether locally produced or imported, must have been killed expressly for consumption and according to the ritualistic *halal* method; no stunning or other mechanical means of slaughter are allowed. Much meat is imported 'on the hoof' and slaughtered locally. New Zealand exports much of its famous lamb and mutton to the region and it can be bought fresh, semi-chilled or frozen. The meat sold in small shops bears little resemblance to the cuts usually found in Europe and North America, and westerners may be taken aback by displays of whole sheep's heads. Supermarkets, on the other hand, tend to offer cuts that westerners are familiar with. Offal is available in larger stores, but little horse meat is imported.

Fish

Arabs have long enjoyed fresh fish, their fishing fleets ensuring a constant supply from the waters of the Gulf. Shellfish — especially prawns — are commonly available and range from the giant Gulf prawn (one or two of which are sufficient for a main course) to much smaller species. These are sorted and sold by size and frequently by origin. Lobster and crab are also popular. The most favoured fish in the region is the succulent *hammour*, a fleshy, fairly dense, tasty fish, usually plain grilled and served with lemon. Tinned fish is available everywhere, including tuna, salmon, mackerel, herrings, sardines, anchovies and kipper fillets, and smoked kippers are usually also available at larger supermarkets.

Bread & Cakes

The standard Arab bread is the flat, unleavened pitta, which can be found everywhere, fresh from the bakers or packaged in plastic and usually also quite fresh. The many large bakeries also produce and distribute western-style white and brown loaves baked with different types of flour, both sliced and uncut, in fairly standard shapes. The widest choice of bread and cakes is usually found at the fresh bread counters of supermarkets, most of which have in-house bakeries. You can buy fresh baguettes, rolls and breads of varying flour content, shapes and sizes, and the big stores bake at least two batches of bread every day.

If you're lucky enough to live close to a Lebanese bakery, you can enjoy the combined flair of French, Lebanese and Arab baking. Turnover is rapid at these popular establishments, with bread, cakes and pastries fresh from the oven, as well as various savoury breads, with roasted poppy-seeds and other toppings.

Arabs generally have a sweet tooth, and the region's shops (as well as cafés and restaurants) serve a wide variety of desserts originating from North Africa and the eastern Mediterranean as well as the Middle East. Favourites include *om ali*, a spicy bread and butter pudding, *um ali* (not to be confused), made from puff pastry, raisins, nuts, cream, milk and sugar, and *muhallibia*, a milk mousse flavoured with cinnamon and cardamom. The Greek dessert *baklava*, a filo pastry cake with nuts, cinnamon and syrup made from honey and lemon juice, is also widely enjoyed, as is *halvah*, a sort of nougat made with flour, sugar, saffron and rose water.

Fruit & Vegetables

The freshest fruit and vegetables can be bought at the large central markets found in all Gulf states (see page 319). If it isn't convenient to visit the central market, the large supermarkets are the next best places in terms of range and freshness. This sometimes leaves the smaller stores with poorer produce. Fresh food deteriorates quickly in the hot climate, so all fruit and vegetables need to be kept refrigerated.

Locally produced vegetables are of good quality and invariably cheaper than imports, although local tomatoes and lettuce are of a coarser variety than is usual in the USA and northern Europe – similar in texture to Mediterranean varieties. Potatoes from Egypt are excellent, clean and firm, and they're also inexpensive and have little wastage. Fruit of many kinds is imported from Europe, South Africa, the United States and other countries. Dates are popular and locally grown, and you may be surprised by the variety of dates available. Shops in luxurious shopping malls have beautiful displays entirely devoted to dates, some varieties retailing at unusually high prices.

Note that the organic food phenomenon has yet to reach the Gulf.

Cheese

The cheese counters of the big supermarkets have extensive ranges of cheeses from around the world, including New Zealand, Dutch and

Australian cheddar-type cheeses and more expensive varieties from France, although there are few British cheeses. Arab cheeses, which lack a strong flavour, include *halloumi*, a semi-hard mint-flavoured cheese usually made from sheep's milk but sometimes goat's milk, and various other soft and hard goat's milk cheeses. Processed cheese (Arabs call it 'boiled cheese') is everywhere and is sold in large blocks as well as packaged slices. The Saudis produce several brands, notably 'Al Marai'.

Milk

Arab companies have a first class reputation for dairy produce, which is date-stamped and quality-controlled. Perhaps surprisingly, there are large dairy herds throughout the region. (For example, a large farm outside Riyadh in Saudi Arabia keeps 17,000 dairy cattle, and there are many similar operations elsewhere.) Local fresh milk is available in full-cream, semi-skimmed (half-cream) and skimmed varieties. It's sold in both plastic and treated-cardboard containers, in sizes up to 2.5 litres. Other milk products include single and double cream, plain and fruit flavoured yoghurts, and *labneh* – the Arab version of buttermilk. UHT milk is also available.

Oils

Olive oil plays a significant role in the cuisines of the region, as does ghee (clarified butter). Many brands of olive oil are available, mainly from Italy, Greece and Spain. Spanish oils are normally the cheapest, but also of reasonable quality. The finest olive oils come from the first pressing of the olives, labelled 'extra virgin', which has a distinctive green colour. Refined olive oil, which is light yellow, is a mixture of virgin oil (from the second pressing) and non-virgin oils (from subsequent pressings). The acidity of the oil is also significant and, if you're looking for flavour, choose one with an acidity of 1 per cent or less.

The large Asian community, predominantly from the sub-continent, has had an impact on the region's cuisine, and ghee is an important ingredient in their cooking. Dairy fats such as butter and margarine are widely available, the butter tending to come from New Zealand, Ireland, Denmark and France. Cooking oils are mainly vegetable oil, corn oil, sunflower oil and sesame oil, including well-known international brands. (Until recently, Arabs had a low incidence of heart disease, probably as a result of using olive oils and vegetable oils rather than dairy fats, but this is changing, partly due to their new-found liking for fast foods.)

Spices

As throughout the Arab world, there are shops devoted entirely to spices, which tend to be in the older parts of towns, as well as spice stalls in the markets. Their colourful displays and pungent odours are an experience not to be missed. The range of spices is too wide to be described here; suffice it to say that you can to find just about every spice known to man, and traders are more than happy to help with queries on this extensive subject.

BUYING ALCOHOL

Resident expatriates of Bahrain, Oman, Qatar and the UAE (except Sharjah) are allowed to purchase alcohol from selected retail outlets provided they've been issued with the appropriate liquor licence. Alcohol is strictly forbidden in Kuwait and Saudi Arabia and cannot be bought anywhere; the penalties for possession of alcohol in these states are severe (see page 287).

Even in those states and Emirates where alcohol is permitted, if you don't have a licence and are found in possession of alcohol outside licensed premises, you're liable to be prosecuted.

Penalties include fines, jail sentences and expulsion, depending on the circumstances. Note also that, although duty-free shops at the airports of countries that allow the sale of alcohol have a wide range of branded drinks available to outgoing travellers, incoming passengers are advised not to bring alcohol with them, even to countries that allow it (see page 85).

To obtain a liquor licence, you must complete an application form, which is obtainable from police stations, have it signed by your sponsor (who effectively takes responsibility for your capacity to behave properly when under the influence of alcohol) and take it back to a police station. Your sponsor (who is usually your employer) must state your salary on the form, and your monthly alcohol 'allowance' is usually 10 per cent of your monthly salary. In some cases, there's a cost or quantity limit to the amount of alcohol you may purchase in any month, but don't despair: it's usually more than the average family can drink! Licences take the form of a book containing the holder's photograph in which a record of all alcohol purchases is kept.

Once you've obtained a licence, you're permitted to make purchases at designated shops. There are usually several shops in a city. They have neutral exteriors but can be identified by the company logo (usually 'Gray Mackenzie' or 'African & Eastern'). They carry an extensive stock and often run promotions and special offers. Prices vary but are comparable with average European prices and in many cases slightly lower.

MARKETS

There are regular markets in fixed locations throughout the region. They're usually housed in large, covered, air-conditioned, warehouse-like structures, as the region's climate isn't conducive to open-air shopping for much of the year. The main markets tend to specialise in certain commodities; for example, there will be a fish market, a fruit and vegetable market and another for meat, although sometimes the meat and fish markets are combined. The fruit and vegetable markets sell fresh, locally produced as well as imported produce. The region's spice markets are of special interest, being a riot of colour and smells. Fans of curry should try baharat, a favourite of Bahrainis.

As well as food markets, there are many 'markets' selling clothing, sporting goods and footwear – usually in the poorer parts of a town. These tend to be rows of shops rather than markets, although there are usually racks of clothing on the pavements. Much of the stock is imported from Hong Kong, Taiwan and India. Jeans of all types and brands are everywhere, as are T-shirts and footwear, particularly trainers and football boots, including a good deal of fake and counterfeit 'brands' (see page 311).

A kind of market peculiar to the Arab world is the souk, which is either a group of small shops packed tightly together in a town or city or a similarly tightly packed group of market stalls, either temporary or permanent.

Prices in the markets are generally considerably lower than in shops but vary from stall to stall, so it's worth shopping around. Although the price per kilo of produce is always clearly marked, haggling is expected, and you can usually drive a fairly hard bargain, particularly if business is poor that day. Markets usually start early in the morning (at dawn in many cases) and continue until around noon.

SUPERMARKETS & HYPERMARKETS

The opening of the first American supermarket in eastern Saudi Arabia a quarter of a century ago caused some amusement when an elderly Arab lady filled her shopping trolley and proceeded to attempt to bargain the price of each item at the checkout. Needless to say, things have changed a great deal since then, and there are now western-style supermarkets throughout the region, although hypermarkets (i.e. large supermarkets – there's no official definition of a hypermarket in the Gulf) are less common, having only recently arrived in the region. Many supermarkets are owned by foreign chains such as France's Continente (a division of Carrefour) and Prisunic, India's Lal's and Choitram's, and the UK's British Home Stores and Safeway. Continente was responsible for bringing the first real hypermarket to the Gulf, a massive store in Dubai. There are also major Arab operations, such as Spinneys in the UAE and Jeddah International Markets in Saudi Arabia.

Supermarkets and hypermarkets are manned by multi-lingual staff, usually Indians and Filipinos, so there are few communication problems. Opening hours are usually from 10am to 10pm, although some stores open at 8.30 or 9am and a few of the bigger stores remain open 24 hours a day. These hours apply on Saturdays to Thursdays, Friday trading starting at noon, after prayers. Smaller stores may close at around 12.30 or 1pm and open again at around 4pm, as do all Saudi Arabian stores, which also close at prayer times (see page 354). Opening hours change in all states during the month of Ramadan (see page 354), stores remaining open much later in the day, particularly in Saudi Arabia.

Supermarkets and hypermarkets are air-conditioned and provide ample parking, and there are usually plenty of available taxis nearby. Many are located next to other outlets, including cafes, restaurants, book shops, stationers, key cutters and film-developers, and there's usually a row of ATMs nearby. Many stores have toilet facilities and phone boxes, although in most Gulf countries you can ask to use any telephone, as local calls are free.

Smaller supermarkets, with fewer customers and a slower turnover of fruit and vegetables, aren't usually the best places to shop for fresh produce, and in all stores fruit often suffers from poor handling, so you should inspect it before buying. Frozen food is readily available but can be expensive. Government controls ensure that all packaged items are date-stamped with production and expiry dates. (Stores incur large fines and the offending stock is removed if they're found to be in default.)

The bigger supermarkets and the new hypermarkets carry a tremendous range of products in addition to foodstuffs, including garden furniture, camping and sports equipment, clothing, perfumes and toiletries, jewellery, books, magazines, children's toys, bedding, pillows, duvets and rugs. Hypermarkets sell electronic goods including television sets, video cassette recorders, radios, hi-fis, mobile phones, cameras, photographic equipment, washing machines, refrigerators and freezers. In fact, some electronic goods can be purchased more cheaply than in specialist shops (even after haggling!). Arabs being natural bargain-hunters, Gulf supermarkets have a mania for promotional and special offers, including two-for-one and money-off offers, competitions and give-aways.

Even at supermarkets, the preferred payment method is cash. Some of the large supermarkets and hypermarkets accept debit cards, but it's wise to have enough cash with you. Many supermarkets insist on your checking-in any other shopping bags you have with you before entering the store. There's usually a counter where you're issued with a numbered receipt for your items, which you can reclaim as you leave.

Shopping trolleys are free, the coin-operated versions not having arrived in the region. At most large supermarkets and hypermarkets, your purchases are bagged for you at the checkout, and many stores have staff to carry bags to your car. You can even order your shopping by telephone and have it delivered to your home (free for goods worth over $37/£25 or so). Payment is made in cash on delivery or, if you're a regular customer and have an account with the store, you can pay for all your purchases at the end of each month.

DEPARTMENT & CHAIN STORES

The nearest thing in the region to a department store (i.e. one that stocks a wide range of goods) is a hypermarket or large supermarket. Apart from these, the concept of department store shopping doesn't exist in the Gulf. On the other hand, there are many chain stores, including international chains such as Benetton, Body Shop, British Home Stores, Debenhams, Lacoste, Mothercare, JC Penney, Prisunic, Toys 'R' Us, Woolworths (South Africa). There's also a limited number of locally-owned chain stores in each state.

TOBACCONISTS

Although the Gulf governments periodically run advertising campaigns warning people of the dangers of smoking, cigarettes are widely smoked throughout the region, and tobacco products are sold everywhere, in stores ranging from small corner grocery shops to hypermarkets. All the major international cigarette brands are available: American, British, French, Greek, Indian, Indonesian and Turkish. Bars, pubs and some restaurants also have dispenser machines that carry supplies of the better known brands. Cigars are available in a wide variety of brands in the higher-class hotels and restaurants. Duty-free shops at airports stock the better-known brands of cigarettes and cigars, and shopping malls usually contain a tobacconist which, in addition to cigarettes, cigars and pipe tobaccos, carries a range of smoking accessories. Many tobacconists have 'humidor areas', which are enclosed rooms maintained at a constant temperature and humidity to keep expensive cigars in perfect condition! Cigarette prices are low in the region, and Indian-made cigarettes are particularly cheap.

CLOTHING

Foreigners aren't expected to wear Arab garments, and western dress is the norm for expatriates. There are numerous stores selling western-style clothes, shoes and accessories, including well-known 'designer' labels (some of which may be fake – see page 311). Major fashion chains provide good quality clothes at reasonable prices. Some of the locally manufactured clothing is also of good quality and inexpensive. The region's hot climate and customs call for informal but smart dressing. Suits are rarely worn in the Gulf, except for important business meetings and related social events, and you won't find tailors offering made-to-measure suits at ridiculous prices as in parts of the Far East. Standard wear in the office is a shirt (usually long-sleeved), tie and lightweight trousers.

It's important to note that women should generally dress conservatively in the region, especially in Saudi Arabia, where all women are required to wear an *abaya* (see page 357).

Many expatriates buy clothes in their home countries or when on holiday in other countries, where prices are often lower.

NEWSPAPERS, MAGAZINES & BOOKS

The Gulf states are saturated with newspapers and magazines, dailies, weeklies and Sunday editions. Each state has several national newspapers, some of which are available in other states: Bahrain has four, Oman five, Qatar six, Kuwait seven, the UAE eight, and Saudi Arabia no fewer than 18. Newspapers can be bought in shops, supermarkets, book shops and in some states from newsboys at traffic lights at busy junctions. Newspapers cost the equivalent of around 50¢ (30p), and it's usual to tip newsboys. Some of the larger circulation papers have a home delivery service.

Newspapers cover a wide range of subjects, including national and international news, business and financial news, human interest stories, sports reports, some political coverage and invariably news about the region's ruling families and details of administrative legislation. In the UAE, Official Gazettes are published containing decrees by the rulers and other legislation affecting citizens and residents.

Unlike most western countries, the Gulf doesn't have an entirely free press, and both news coverage and editorial opinion are subject to 'discussion' between editors and Ministries of Information. Some Ministries have weekly briefings with national press editors and issue guidelines as to how controversial stories should be handled. Locals don't regard this government censorship as sinister or restrictive.

Each state has at least one English-language newspaper. In Bahrain, there's the **Bahrain Tribune** and the **Gulf Daily News**, which includes a useful 'What's On' section. Kuwait's most prominent English-language newspapers are **The Arab Times** and the **Kuwait Times**. In Oman there's the **Oman Daily Observer** and the **Times of Oman**, in Qatar the **Gulf Times** and **The Peninsula**, in Saudi Arabia the **Arab News**, **Riyadh Daily** and **Saudi Gazette**, and in the UAE **Emirates News**, **Gulf News**, **Gulf Today** and **Khaleej Times**. All these papers include international news, European news (predominantly UK coverage) and US news as well as stories from the sub-continent. Sport of all kinds is covered, particularly football and cricket. All papers also provide daily exchange rates for the world's major currencies, which is useful if you're trying to judge the best time to convert your savings to send home or overseas. Television listings for both local and satellite stations are included, and some papers also publish a weekly schedule.

The world's national dailies and Sunday papers are also available in the region, usually a day or two after publication. The majority are English and Indian, with some French, German and Philippines newspapers. **The International Herald Tribune** and **US News Today** are also available.

It's estimated that around 150 magazines are in circulation in the region. Well-known international titles such as **Time**, **Newsweek**, **Business Week** and **The Economist** are available, as well as a variety of magazines covering fashion, sports and a wide range of special interests. Needless to say, 'adult' magazines aren't available, and even titles like **Cosmopolitan** are subject to censorship. Not surprisingly, Saudi Arabia imposes the strictest rules: any photographs of over-exposed bodies have the offending parts blacked out. (See page 87 for restrictions on the import of magazines and other publications.)

There are also several local English-language magazines: in Bahrain the monthly **Bahrain This Month** for BD1 ($2.65), the free, bi-monthly **What's On in Bahrain** and the annual **Visitor's Complete Guide to Bahrain** for BD1.5 ($4); in Oman **Oman Today**, published every two months for 500 baiza ($1.30), and **Adventure Oman**, which contains articles about caving, mountain biking and rock climbing; and in the UAE **What's On**, a monthly magazine aimed at expatriates, costing AED12 ($3.25). Certain titles are available in all states, e.g. the popular **Emirates Woman** and **This is Bahrain**, as well as glossy magazines published by the various governments for tourists and foreign residents, whose content is mainly details of forthcoming events, fashion stories, sports coverage, film reviews, recipes, restaurant guides and other items of local or regional interest.

There are a few book shops in most Gulf cities and they usually stock Arabic, English, French and German-language books. The foreign books are mainly of the 'pulp' variety, with the usual complement of crime, romance and science-fiction, although the latest bestsellers are usually slow to arrive in the Gulf. Serious literature can also be found, however, as can some reference works and self-teaching publications on numerous subjects. Books generally aren't cheap in the region, although book-lovers have recently benefited from an increase in the number of second-hand book 'swap shops' in the Gulf, where you can sell your old books and buy others at low prices. There are also public libraries, run by the authorities and private organisations (see page 292). As with magazines, any book whose content is deemed to be offensive, sexually explicit or politically sensitive (e.g. containing criticism of any of the Gulf states or of Islam) is banned.

FURNITURE & HOUSEHOLD GOODS

Few people who come to work in the region bring their furniture with them, unless they're moving from another Gulf state, where they've purchased furniture and furnishings (in which case shipment is usually at company expense). Most other expatriates arriving in the Gulf must buy furniture and furnishings locally, as the majority of apartments and villas are rented unfurnished, although most have built-in wardrobes and many include kitchen appliances such as cookers, fridge-freezers and washing machines. If your work contract is short, e.g. a few months, and you don't want to buy new furniture and soon afterwards have to sell it or ship it home, you may be able to buy from the outgoing tenants of the property. If you're moving into a brand new property, as is often the case, however, you will have little option but to buy new furniture and furnishings.

Fortunately, there's a wide choice of furniture and furnishings, in all designs and at all prices, in the Gulf states. Some furniture stores stock international designs and others Arab styles. Arab furniture tends to be ornate, with very large beds, lounge suites and dining tables (designed for large families). International companies like IKEA and Habitat have outlets in most Gulf countries, and these and other large stores offer complete household furnishing packages, including not only main items such as three-piece suites and beds but also curtains, crockery and household utensils.

Furniture tends to be more expensive in the Gulf than in Europe and North America, although heavy curtains and bedclothes, for example, aren't required in the hot climate. Another saving comes from the fact that most property has tiled floors, obviating the need to buy carpets. There are at least two official sales periods each year in the Gulf (see page 311), which are the best times to buy expensive items of furniture. In any case, you should never buy at the advertised price but always barter. The more items you're buying, the stronger your bargaining position. Take your time, be polite, smile and start at around half the advertised price.

Most household appliances are imported from Italy, Greece, France, Germany, Great Britain and Scandinavia. Some Arabs with large families prefer the much larger American appliances, which are also widely available. You should check, however, that they've been adapted to operate on the 240 volts used in the Gulf, although 110v appliances can usually be used in Saudi Arabia (see page 103). Small appliances such as vacuum cleaners, irons, hair-dryers and toasters are inexpensive, with a wide range of brands to choose from. If you're bringing a television set or VCR to the region, check that it's of a specification that can be used in the Gulf. Similarly, if you buy equipment in the region with the intention of taking it home when you leave the Gulf, check its compatibility. For example, although some televisions can be used anywhere, others have audio filters that must be changed in different regions to be able to receive sound, even if you can receive a picture.

SHOPPING ABROAD

With the Gulf states centrally positioned between east and west, access to many of the world's tourist and shopping centres is relatively quick and easy. The Gulf's national airlines regularly fly to Europe and on to the USA, and in the other direction to cities in the Far East and Australasia. Promotional deals make foreign shopping trips inexpensive, particularly to Bangkok, Singapore and Hong Kong. Electronic goods are sold at bargain prices there, although Gulf shops can often match them (depending on your bartering skills), and – particularly in Japan – you may have access to the very latest technology and to items that aren't exported. London and Paris are also popular shopping destinations, particularly for clothes, although inveterate shoppers tend to head to New York.

Within the region itself, intra-Gulf travel is relatively simple provided that you hold a residence visa for one of the states. Each state has something different to offer the shopper. Cars tend to be cheaper in Saudi Arabia, for example, while in Oman you can buy wonderful wooden furniture such as dowry chests and carved room screens, some of which are 'antiqued' but are nevertheless sound purchases, and Oman's famous *kanjar*, the curved ceremonial dagger, can be found in many designs. Go to Bahrain for pottery and old carved wooden doors, which, when covered with glass, make decorative coffee tables. Although there are gold souks in all six states, Dubai probably has the largest number of jewellers.

On overseas excursions, particularly when visiting the Far East, make sure that your luggage is securely locked and that it hasn't been tampered with. Similarly, never accept a parcel from someone to deliver to a 'friend' in the Gulf, because it could contain drugs and the penalties for trafficking are horrific.

Duty-free Shopping

There's little advantage in bringing duty-free items into the region, as only small amounts of duty are levied on imports. Should you wish to do so, however, duty-free allowances for goods imported into the region for personal consumption are as follows:

Item	Duty-free Allowance
Cigarettes	2,000
Cigars	400
Loose tobacco	2kg
Alcohol in the countries that permit its import	2 litres of spirits and 2 litres of wine

You're also allowed a 'reasonable' amount of perfume, which is ill-defined but must not be a quantity that could be used for commercial purposes.

Duty-free shops at Gulf airports are internationally famous and, although tax savings are minimal, offer a wider choice of the latest goods than most other shops, particularly cameras, computers, jewellery and designer clothes. Many of them are open to inbound as well as outbound travellers.

Dubai Duty Free is generally recognised as the best in the world, for its quality, range and prices. It was the first to introduce the controlled raffle, where 1,000 tickets are sold for AED500 (around $120) each, the prize being a luxury car such as a Rolls Royce, Bentley, Mercedes or BMW, delivered anywhere in the world (or the equivalent cash value). Other Gulf airports followed suit after its success; Sharjah in particular attempts to match the superb duty-free facilities of Dubai.

INTERNET SHOPPING

Shopping on the Internet has yet to become common in the region. Access to the net is widely available, particularly for business applications, but its use is still low among the indigenous population. Shopping is one of the region's main forms of entertainment, particularly in Saudi Arabia, where it's one of the few pleasures open to everybody, so ordering from a computer at home is unlikely to become popular.

If you decide to buy goods via the Internet, make sure that you're dealing with reputable companies, particularly when it comes to disclosing your credit card details. Credit card payment is recommended, however, as it offers extended protection: in most cases, the consumer and credit card issuer can jointly seek compensation from the vendor or supplier if necessary, but you should check this with your credit card issuer. It's always wise to insure significant purchases from overseas sources against loss or damage in transit. There might be a small duty charge on certain imports, e.g. clothing. There are no VAT charges.

RECEIPTS & CONSUMER RIGHTS

It's wise to insist on a receipt for any purchases you make, as they're required if you need to return or exchange an item. Shop security systems are also frequently used in the region, and a receipt avoids misunderstandings if alarms sound as you exit a store. With no personal tax in the region, there's no need to keep receipts for tax claims. There are few consumer protection laws in the Gulf, although many items are covered by a manufacturer's warranty.

If you have a complaint about a product or service, you should make it to the relevant dealer or retailer. Local traders are generally reasonable and, if you buy faulty goods, the vast majority will exchange them immediately. If this doesn't resolve it, approach the manufacturer or the importer. If you have a serious complaint, you might find someone at the local Chamber of Commerce who is willing to help. Chambers of Commerce are invariably led by the most important local businessmen, and traders take note of their opinions. Gulf society is tribal, and personal appeals are a way of life, meaning that personal influence and pressure are often effective. If the Chanmbers cannot help, you must approach the civil courts, but this is very much a last resort.

18.

ODDS & ENDS

This chapter covers miscellaneous information. Although all topics aren't of vital importance, most are of general interest to anyone planning to live or work in the Gulf, including everything you ever wanted to know (but were afraid to ask) about Ramadan and Shariah law.

BUSINESS HOURS

Office hours are fairly standard throughout the region, i.e. from 9am to 1pm and from 2 until 5.30 or 6pm. There are, however, variations in these times, particularly when dealing with traditional Arab businesses, whose midday break can extend until 3pm, the business remaining open until 7pm. Arab owners used to have a tendency to be unreasonable about time-keeping, arriving late in the morning, staying a short time and reappearing just before closing time in the evening, obliging staff to stay until he decided to leave. Fortunately, this practice is dying out. However, certain 'cultural' differences persist with regard to time-keeping, western staff tending to arrive and start on time and leave at the appointed hour, whereas some Arab staff might start late but continue working later in the evening.

The working week is usually from Saturday to Thursday, with Friday the rest day for those working a six-day week. A five-day working week is becoming the standard for offices, however, although some businesses take Thursdays off (on the basis that schools are closed on that day), others Saturdays (in line with most of the rest of the world).

During the month of Ramadan (see **National Holidays** on page 348 and **Religion** on page 352), the working day is reduced to six hours, with a later start in the morning and earlier closing. In Saudi Arabia, there can be dramatic changes to the working week during Ramadan, some offices working more at night than during the day.

Government working hours tend to be different from those in the private sector. Not surprisingly, they're shorter and are fairly strictly adhered to – especially closing times! Government staff also enjoy longer periods of official public holidays (see **National Holidays** on page 348).

CALENDAR

Although the world standard Gregorian calendar is in general use throughout the region, the Islamic calendar is also referred to, and diaries and calendars show both sets of dates. In Saudi Arabia, all official documents adhere to the Islamic calendar, which can make it difficult to calculate important dates, such as visa expiry dates. Conversion tables are available and are useful to have to hand, as there may be a range of unofficial 'interpretations'.

The Islamic calendar began in the Gregorian calendar year 622AD, which was the year of the Prophet Mohammed's move from Mecca (*Makkah* in Arabic) to Medina, referred to as the *Hijra*, or *Hegira*. When referring to the Islamic calendar, dates are known as the *Hijri* year and denoted 'AH' (after *Hijra*). The complications arise from the fact that there are just 354 days in the Islamic year and that leap years (with 355 days) occur at different intervals from Gregorian leap years (in the 2nd, 3rd, 5th, 7th, 10th, 13th, 16th, 18th, 21st, 24th, 26th and 29th years in each 30-year cycle, for those who are interested in such things). The Islamic calendar is based on lunar months (around 29.5 days) and has 12 months to the year, as follows:

Islamic Month	No. of Days
Muharram	30
Safar	29
Rabi I (or Rabi'Al-Awal)	30
Rabi II (or Rabi'Al-Thani)	29
Jumada I	30
Jumada II	29
Rajab	30
Shaaban	29
Ramadan	30
Shawwal	29
Dhul-Qa'da	30
Dhul-Hijah	29 (30 in a leap year)

Currently (2003), the beginning of the Islamic year falls during the Gregorian month of March and 1st January 2003 was the 28th day of Shawwal according to the Islamic calendar (see **National Holidays** on page 348). The ninth Islamic month, Ramadan, is a time of fasting (see page 354), and the great pilgrimage (Haj) takes place during the twelfth month, Dhul-Hijah (see page 355).

CITIZENSHIP

As a foreigner, you won't be granted rights of citizenship in any of the Gulf states. The region's governments are keen to protect the status quo and don't want to compromise their cultural values or standard of living by allowing foreigners to become a permanent part of society. Your only route to becoming a naturalised citizen is by marriage to a national; even this, however, doesn't guarantee citizenship, particularly for non-Muslims. In exceptional circumstances only, a Gulf state's ruler might grant citizenship to a foreigner who has provided outstanding service to the state over a number of years. A generous employer might reward a loyal worker who has made a major contribution to the company over many years by providing him with a work and residence permit of indefinite duration. After your retirement, however, the employer would have to be a figure of considerable influence to maintain this gift and satisfy the labour authorities. In this case, you wouldn't be a citizen, but merely be allowed to remain in the country indefinitely.

Children of foreigners born in any of the Gulf countries don't have rights of local citizenship and automatically assume the nationality of the parents. If one of the parents is a national of the Gulf country, the child will usually be granted local nationality (although in Saudi Arabia the Islamic faith is a prerequisite for citizenship) and may later become a national of that state and obtain a local passport.

It's recommended that you fully acquaint yourself with the implications of giving birth in one of the Gulf states.

In many cases, the child isn't affected, but any children that he has might not enjoy the same rights of nationality, citizenship, abode, etc. as his parents and grandparents (see **Births & Deaths** on page 209).

CLIMATE

The countries of the Gulf are among the driest on earth, and the four defined seasons found in much of Europe and the United States are generally lacking. The 'summer' months (May to September) are excessively hot during the day, but the period from October to April enjoys beautiful weather, invariably with cloudless skies and warm sunshine. There might be an occasional day of rain in January (which makes a pleasant change for locals), but the region's 'winter' climate is generally regarded as one of the world's best. The climate varies somewhat from state to state, and even within states in some cases, as follows:

Bahrain

Bahrain is surrounded by the warm waters of the Arabian Gulf, making it humid in the hot summer months, but mild and pleasant in winter. October to March has average daytime temperatures of between 15°C (59°F) and 32°C (90°F), while summer averages 35°C (95°F), with a peak of 40°C (104°F) in July and August. Fortunately, summer is freshened by the *shamal*, a cool wind from the north. Bahrain averages around eight days of rain per year.

Kuwait

Kuwait experiences extreme heat in the summer, with daytime temperatures reaching between 40°C (104°F) and 50°C (122°F), although the average is a more bearable 33°C (91°F). Dust storms are a problem throughout the year, especially during the spring. Kuwait's position at the north of the Gulf means that winter can be cool, temperatures sometimes dropping below 10°C (50°F), although 16°C (61°F) to 20°C (68°F) is more usual. Humidity at the northern end of the Arabian Gulf isn't as high as it is further south, although when winds blow from the south-east humidity can rise to uncomfortable levels. Rainfall is concentrated between October and April, with annual rainfall of between 25 to 175mm (1 to 7in) and around 12 wet days per year.

Oman

Oman has a variety of climates. Between April and October, the daytime temperature in Muscat averages 34°C (93°F), although it can soar to 50°C (122°F). The winter season often brings beautiful weather, with temperatures between 19°C (66°F) and 30°C (86°F). Salalah is hotter, averaging around 30°C (86°F) throughout the year. Average rainfall in much of the country is 100mm (4in) per year and occurs predominantly in December, January and February. The south of the country around Salalah sometimes experiences a 'monsoon' between June and September, when around 30mm (12in) of light rain can fall. Humidity in Oman is at its highest between July and September, and can reach 90 per cent, although inland areas are less humid than the coast. Average hours of sunshine are ten per day and the Sultanate has around eight days of rain per year.

Qatar

Average daytime temperatures between October and April range between 20°C (68°F) and 30°C (86°F), although it can drop to 10°C (50°F). In summer, the mercury rises to just over 40°C (104°F). Rainfall is mainly in November, December, February and March, averaging nine days per year, and humidity is highest between November and February. Average hours of sunshine are ten per day, and sandstorms are common throughout the year.

Saudi Arabia

The largest country on the peninsula averages less than 125mm (5in) of rain per year and in the driest part – 'The Empty Quarter' in the south-east – a decade can pass without rain. The central region and southern highlands have more rainfall, particularly in winter, while Jeddah, in the west, averages eight days of rain per year. The Asir mountains in the south-west attract a good deal of rain and generally enjoy more equable temperatures than most of the rest of Saudi Arabia, where summer is excessively hot.

Daytime temperatures reach 50°C (122°F) and average around 40°C (104°F), and coastal regions are humid. Winter can be quite cold, however, particularly in northern and central areas, where temperatures occasionally fall below freezing, with snow and frost on high ground. Winter temperatures average 14°C (57°F) in the central province and 23°C (73°F) in the west. October to May is the most pleasant period of the year in most parts, with daytime sunshine and cool nights.

United Arab Emirates

Average winter temperatures in the UAE are very pleasant, between 20°C (68°F) and 25°C (77°F), while in summer temperatures reach between 40°C (104°F) and 50°C (122°F). Humidity can be unpleasantly high, reaching 100 per cent, particularly on the coast, and hot shamal winds can bring strong dust storms at the end of summer. October to April, however, enjoy excellent weather, with occasional clouds and a little rain, averaging about six days per year.

CRIME

The region has traditionally been largely free of crime, making the Arabian peninsula a safe place to live and work relative to most European countries and the USA. Among the indigenous population, the strict codes of behaviour provided by the Islamic faith, as well as family and tribal loyalties and the region's general affluence and lack of unemployment ensure that criminal behaviour is rare.

However, the situation has changed with the enormous influx of foreigners to the region that has taken place since the 1970s. Although the change was initially slight, 'undesirable elements' have recently begun to arrive, particularly from the former eastern bloc countries. Some 'tourists' have brought with them prostitution, never previously countenanced in the region, despite prohibitions on the issue of entry visas to young single females.

This has generated mafia-like activity, resulting in an increase in crime, including a minor drug market, which the authorities are increasingly clamping down on. Today, in a few Gulf states, prostitutes are obviously active in some low-class hotels.

There have recently been some terrorist attacks in Saudi Arabia, where a few foreigners (notably Britons) have been jailed for mysterious reasons and 'persuaded' to confess to misdemeanours (see **Embassy, Consular & Legal Assistance** on page 338). Bahrain has also experienced some political unrest in recent years, largely because a significant proportion of the population are Shia Muslims, who have affiliations with Iran and seek change.

It should be remembered that the possession or consumption of alcohol is a criminal offence in Kuwait and Saudi Arabia and strictly regulated in other states (see **Alcohol** on page 287), and that 'recreational' drugs are illegal in all states (see page 85). Any altercation or offence in the street is likely to be dealt with rapidly, law enforcement is generally strict and punishments can be severe (see **Legal System** on page 341).

CULTURE SHOCK

Although there are many differences between the cultures of the Gulf and those of eastern and western countries, culture shock is rare among incoming workers and their families. The many expatriate clubs and associations ease a newcomer's transition to the region and its culture. In addition, the Gulf's attractive climate — except at the height of summer — encourages outdoor gatherings and sports, although some people miss the cultural activities that they enjoyed at home, such as the theatre, ballet and opera.

Culture shock, if it does strike, comes in three stages. The first is a feeling of disorientation caused by the unfamiliarity of your environment and dislocation from relatives and friends. This sometimes develops into a form of aggression owing to the frustrations of setting up a new home. Finally, some expatriates adopt a superior attitude, as if they know better than the locals. But this is unusual, mainly because of the welcoming nature of the Gulf Arabs, the affluent lifestyle and the comfort provided by the large expatriate community. The vast majority of expatriates thoroughly enjoy their stay and consider themselves privileged to live and work in the Gulf.

EMBASSY, CONSULAR & LEGAL ASSISTANCE

The embassy or consulate of your home country can provide legal information and other assistance and it's wise to register with it on arrival in the Gulf — so that it has a record of your presence, if nothing else (see page 88). If you fall foul of the law while in the region, you must notify your embassy or consulate as soon as possible. If you're held by the police, a representative of the embassy or consulate will visit you and liaise with your relatives, although he will be unable to provide or pay for legal advice or assistance and you shouldn't expect to be 'bailed out', as your individual plight might be considered of little importance. Note also that embassies and consulates won't intervene in any dispute between an employee and his employer.

In the event of a serious accident or illness, the embassy or consulate will contact your doctor in your home country and help to arrange repatriation if necessary, although again it won't pay for this or other medical assistance, except perhaps in extreme circumstances; even then, you will be asked for security against the 'loan' and will have to pay a stiff surcharge in addition to repaying the loan itself. In extreme situations (such as that which arose in Kuwait when it was invaded by Iraq), the embassy or consulate might be called upon to evacuate its citizens. (When Turkey invaded Cyprus, however, the British embassy infamously had a 'Closed' sign on its door!)

GEOGRAPHY

The Arabian Peninsula, on which the Gulf states (and Yemen) are situated, is bounded by the Red Sea to the west, the Gulf of Aden to the south-west and Arabian Sea to the south-east, and the Arabian Gulf to the east. Jordan and Iraq lie to the north (see map on page 6).

Bahrain

Bahrain is the Arab world's only island state. It's also the smallest Gulf state and consists of a group of 33 islands, with a total land area of around 700km² (270mi²) – slightly larger than Singapore. although constant dredging is reclaiming land from the surrounding Gulf. The archipelago lies half way down the west shore of the Arabian Gulf, 22kms (14 miles) off the east coast of Saudi Arabia, to which it was linked in 1986 by the King Fahad Causeway. The name Bahrain is derived from two Arabic words, thnain Bahr, meaning 'two seas'; this is in reference to Bahrain's spring water mixing with sea water. Bahrain island is the largest in the archipelago, accounting for around 85 per cent of the country's area, and the site of the capital city of Manama. Bahrain is connected by causeway to Muharraq, where the international airport is situated. The main island is largely flat, peaking at just 134m (442ft) above sea level at Jabel Dukhan. Much of the terrain is limestone, sometimes with a sparse covering of soil, sand or salt, the last creating salt flats (sabkha). A small area of fertile ground in the north sustains some agriculture.

Kuwait

Kuwait lies at the north-west end of the Arabian Gulf and has an area of around 17,800km² (6,870mi²) – just over half the size of Belgium.

Iraq lies to the north and west, and Saudi Arabia to the south. The terrain is largely flat and the main feature is the Zor Ridge, which peaks at 145m (445ft) above sea level. Kuwait is an arid land, the only oasis being Sebihiya, to the south of the capital, Kuwait City. Much of the country is covered by scrub, and less than 10 per cent of the land is devoted to agriculture.

Oman

Oman occupies the south-east of the Arabian peninsula, with over 2,000km (mi) of coastline on the Arabian Gulf and Indian Ocean. The UAE sits to the north-west, Saudi Arabia to the west and Yemen to the south-west. It covers an area of 212,457km^2 (82,030mi^2) – slightly less than that of the UK – with a mixed topography of flat desert land, fertile valleys and a few mountains, the highest peak Jabal ash Sham reaching 2,980m (9,780ft) above sea level. Part of the state is on the Musandam Peninsula on the Straits of Hormuz, an area strategically important to Gulf shipping which is separated from the rest of the country by UAE territory.

Qatar

Qatar lies to the south of Bahrain, a large peninsula half way down the west coast of the Arabian Gulf, with a 60km (37mi) border with Saudi Arabia. It's around 160km (100mi) long, 80km (50mi) wide, covers 11,440km^2 (4,417mi^2) – slightly larger than Cyprus – and has around 700km (435mi) of coastline. Qatar is primarily flat desert, the highest point being only 110m (360ft) above sea level. Most of its coast consists of salt flats (sabkha), although there are some impressive sand dunes in the south. Qatar has several islands off its coast, notably Halul and the Hawar Islands; ownership of the latter is disputed with Bahrain.

Saudi Arabia

Saudi Arabia is by far the largest country on the Arabian peninsula, its territory accounting for around 80 per cent of the area. Saudi covers around 2.33 million km^2 (900,000mi^2) – over two-thirds the size of India – which makes it the world's 13th-largest country.

(Saudi's exact area is unknown, as border demarcations in some places have traditionally been indistinct. In fact, only its borders to the north, with Qatar and part of that with Yemen are exact.) Saudi has borders with Iraq, Jordan and Kuwait to the north, with Oman and Yemen to the south, and Bahrain, Qatar and the UAE to the east (along with the waters of the Arabian Gulf), while to the west lie the Red Sea and Africa.

The country is largely barren and boasts the world's largest expanse of uninterrupted desert, known as Rub Al-Khali ('The Empty Quarter'), which covers most of the south, joining the Nafud desert in the north. Other landscape features include the Tihama plain along the Red Sea coast, the Najd Plateau in the centre of the country, and two mountain ranges: the Sarawat mountains inland of the Tihama plain, and the Asir mountains in the south-west, both of which rise to around 2,740m (3,000ft) above sea level.

United Arab Emirates

The UAE lies on the south-west coast of the Arabian Gulf. Six of the seven Emirates have Arabian Gulf coastlines, while Fujairah has its coastline on the Gulf of Oman, and there are around 200 offshore islands. The overall land area is approximately 84,000km^2 (32,430mi^2) – the same size as Austria – with Abu Dhabi by far the largest Emirate, accounting for around 85 per cent of the total area – 67,000km^2 (25,870mi^2). Dubai is the second-largest, covering a mere 3,885km^2 (1,500mi^2) – around one-and-a-half times the size of Luxembourg. The UAE's terrain is largely flat desert and salt plains, the Hajar mountains providing a natural barrier between Fujairah and the other Emirates.

LEGAL SYSTEM

In general, Gulf states operate as largely patriarchal societies, headed and administered by ruling families, whose aim is to maintain the status quo while moving towards increased democracy (although in many cases the authorities seem to follow the old adage: 'If it ain't broke, don't fix it'). The Islamic system of law, known as Sharia (or Shari'a or Shariah), derives from four sources: the Holy Koran (Qu'ran), Sunnah, Ijma and Qiyas. The Holy Koran, being the word of God (Allah), is the principal source. The *Sunnah* comprises the accepted deeds and statements of the Prophet Mohammed, accepted by the whole Islamic world (the *Ummah*). *Ijma* is a consensus among religious scholars (the *Ulema*) regarding solutions to matters not specifically covered in either the Koran or the *Sunnah*. In difficult cases, where there's no information to provide the basis for a clear decision, 'analogous consideration' (*Qiyas*) is applied in conjunction with the three other sources of the law.

In *Sharia* law, as in other legal systems, a person is presumed innocent until proven guilty. The plaintiff and defendant are equal before the law – i.e. in a court of law – and it's incumbent upon the former to provide proof of guilt. This involves producing two or four eyewitnesses, depending on the seriousness of the crime. If a plaintiff isn't able to produce eyewitnesses, he can insist on the defendant swearing an oath as to his innocence. If the defendant refuses to take this oath, he's judged to be guilty, as perjurers suffer hellfire and eternal damnation according to Muslim belief. Jews and Christians swear a different oath, but it has equal validity. A judge (*qadi*) presides over the court and can put questions to all parties at will. There are no juries and often no lawyers to present the case for their clients. There are systems of appeal, which can be used in cases of serious crime and punishment.

According to ancient law, the payment of 'blood money' (*diya*) for injury or death can be requested by the victim's family as compensation. The amount of blood money required varies between the states (it's most likely to be exacted in Kuwait, Saudi Arabia and the UAE) and according to the circumstances of the death and to the extent of the hardship that the death will cause. For example, the death of a father of 12 would attract a larger payment than that of a child. A local Muslim's life will be assessed for a larger financial benefit than people of other religions, faiths or nationalities. For example, in Saudi Arabia, a male Muslim's life is worth SR100,000 (around $24,000), but Christians are worth only around half as much. And if the incident occurs in the Holy month of Ramadan, the penalty is usually doubled.

Under Islamic law, the crimes that carry defined penalties are murder, apostasy (rejection or desertion of Islam), adultery, fornication, homosexuality and theft. Interpretations of the law and punishments vary from state to state. Lesser offences might include debt, usury, alcohol and drug abuse, and use of pornography.

As an expatriate, you're subject, of course, to the laws of the country you're in. If you're thought to have broken a law, you're taken under arrest to a police station, questioned and instructed to make a statement. Up to this point, it's highly unlikely that you will be allowed access to outside help, either legal or consular. If the offence is deemed serious enough to warrant your detention, you might have to wait some time before your case comes up. You will be allowed legal representation, but everything will be conducted in Arabic. Your statement will be translated into Arabic, and it's important to insist that an appropriate official, e.g. a member of staff from your consulate, checks the accuracy of the translation and the content of anything you're required to sign. If no one is available to do this, you should refuse to sign, or sign with an endorsement to the effect that you don't have a clear understanding of the document.

In court, an interpreter will be present to assist you and an official from your embassy or consulate is likely to be present, although only as an observer. If you're found guilty, the judge will sentence you and ask for your written acceptance of the sentence, unless you want to appeal. Appeals obviously go to higher courts, depend a great deal on the severity of the accusation and sentencing, and can take time. In very serious cases, political influence might be brought to bear on your behalf, provided that your country has sufficient influence, but this is rare. Having influence with a person in authority can be of help to you, although expatriates rarely have such influence. Locals, on the other hand, may be able to petition their ruler to seek his guidance and help. In minor cases, your employer might intervene to help, particularly if you're valuable to him, as long as he won't lose face.

If you're unfortunate enough to be given a custodial sentence, this is intended as a punishment rather than rehabilitation. If you're found guilty of a serious crime, you may find yourself in a hot, overcrowded prison, where treatment is often harsh and you might have to witness the punishment of others, including their flogging.

Ignorance of the law isn't accepted as an excuse before the law, so it's as well to acquaint yourself with the laws of the country that you choose to live in.

Non-Muslim expatriates sometimes regard *Sharia* law as unbending and overly punitive, which it often is by western standards – and for good reason. Expatriates are largely expendable commodities and, if you've engaged in criminal activity, you're sent home after punishment.

Although the legal system is similar throughout the Gulf, there are variations from state to state, as outlined below.

Bahrain

The legal system in Bahrain is based on several threads of *Sharia* law and some components of British civil law, largely introduced by advisers in the 1920s during the British 'protectorate' period, before complete independence in 1971. The Bahrain Constitution directed that the judiciary be an independent and separate branch of the administration, headed by the Minister of Justice and Islamic Affairs, who is appointed by the Prime Minister. The Emir is the ultimate authority over the legal system and the right of pardon.

The civil court, which operates a system of summary courts and a supreme court, deals with both civil and criminal actions. The *Sharia* court handles divorce, matrimonial disputes, jurisdictional cases, inheritance judgements and cases concerning private material matters. The Supreme Court of Appeal is the highest authority for appealing against judgements, although the Emir might become involved in certain instances.

Kuwait

Kuwait's legal system is based on *Sharia* law, Egyptian practice, English law and elements from the Ottoman system. *Sharia* courts deal mainly with personal and family issues. An appeal system is in place, culminating with the Emir.

Oman

Sharia law applies in conjunction with elements of English common law. There are appeal courts, and the Sultan is the supreme authority (and last resort). Civil cases of a commercial nature are dealt with in a similar way to cases in western countries.

Qatar

Sharia law is the predominant feature of Qatar's legal system, although there are also civil courts. Sharia law is applied to criminal matters and, although no executions or amputations have been carried out for some years, floggings do take place. The Emir is the country's supreme authority.

Saudi Arabia

Sharia law applies throughout the Kindgom, although there have also been some secular decrees introduced as supplements to the law. Shariah law is strictly enforced through over 300 courts, which also act as courts of appeal. Both civil and criminal cases are presided over by a judge (qadi) in the normal way. In more serious cases, such as murder, immorality and major theft, three judges are involved. The Ministry of Commerce appoints and supervises committees to hear and adjudicate commercial actions, and the Chief Justice of the country, supported by a committee of judges, sits in Riyadh and Mecca to hear appeals. The King, who is the representative of God and responsible for the enforcement of his laws, has the final authority over appeals, and crimes calling for capital punishment are automatically referred to him.

Saudi Arabia imposes the strictest punishments in the region on those convicted of breaking Sharia law and has religious police in addition to general police (see **Police** on page 351).

It's vital that foreigners make themselves aware of the conduct required while living in Saudi Arabia, and particularly the following offences:

- Men being in the company of women who aren't close relatives.

- Women being with men other than close relatives, who are treated as prostitutes and can be deported with a 'persona non grata' endorsement in their passports, forbidding them from returning to any Gulf state.

- Women driving cars. See also **Rules of the Road** on page 177.

- 'Indiscreet' dress (e.g. shorts or short-sleeved shirts for men, and uncovered hair, short dresses, exposed arms and shoulders for women).

- Practising a religion other than Islam, carrying a Bible, wearing a cross.

- Blasphemy, particularly if you swear at a Muslim, making derogatory remarks about Islam, taking the name of *Allah* or the Prophet Mohammed in vain, and any form of behaviour that's deemed to be 'immoral'.

- Homosexual acts, which are illegal throughout the region, but for which punishments in Saudi Arabia range from imprisonment to flogging to deportation; there have even been instances of capital punishment.

- Drug dealing and possession. (Note that, although most Gulf states decree capital punishment for those caught dealing in drugs, in Saudi Arabia this is invariably carried out.)

United Arab Emirates

As in other Gulf states, the legal system is a mixture of *Sharia*, civil and criminal law, implemented by the Federal Judiciary, which comprises courts of first instance and supreme courts. The Supreme Council of Rulers, the highest ruling body in the UAE, appoints the five members representing the Federal Supreme Court, who preside over matters concerning constitutional law and rule on cases affecting disputes between any of the Emirates and the Federation as a whole. Local government plays an important part in legislation within each Emirate.

MARRIAGE & DIVORCE

Although Gulf Arabs are entitled to marry as soon as they reach puberty, the average age at which people marry has increased considerably in recent years, to around 20. Traditionally, the ideal marriage was tribal, related families encouraging their offspring to marry cousins or other relatives in order to increase and strengthen the tribe, or occasionally to marry into another tribe in order to heal rifts between families. Another reason for such marriages was that families knew the background of the partner.

As is the case in some Latin countries, young couples in the region are allowed to meet under the watchful eye of a chaperon. In some of the stricter Gulf societies, however, the marriage is arranged without any part of the female partner's body (including her face) having been seen by the prospective groom, who must rely on the reports of his female relatives as to his wife's appearance.

There are three main elements in an Arab marriage. First, the groom must discuss and agree the dowry with the bride's father. This might include gold, jewellery and clothing and is usually of considerable value. After the dowry settlement comes the actual marriage contract, which is conducted by a legal or religious representative. The bride is asked in the absence of the prospective groom if she agrees to the marriage and this question is then put to the groom. After agreement, the groom joins hands with his future father-in-law and, with two witnesses present, the marriage becomes official. However, there's another stage before the couple actually meet as man and wife: the wedding party. Celebrations are segregated, with the women in one section of the house and the men in another. Finally, on the last night of celebrations, the couple meet, accompanied by all their friends, and eventually leave on their honeymoon. On their return, they either set up home with the groom's parents and become members of the extended family or – as is increasingly the case – set up home by themselves.

According to Sharia law, a Muslim man may have four wives, provided that he can look after them materially and treats them equally. This practice is now dying out, however, not only because only a few can afford it, but also because women are becoming more independent and assertive and many refuse accept it. In fact, a Muslim woman can insert a clause in the marriage contract that restricts her husband from marrying another woman for as long as the contract is valid. The wife also retains her own name after marriage. Although gender roles have always been clearly defined in the Islamic world, with the man as 'provider' and the woman as 'nurturer', both man and wife are increasingly going out to work, although this is much less common in Saudi Arabia, where there are restrictions on women working, except in culturally 'acceptable' occupations such as medicine and teaching. However, many Saudi men are reluctant to marry doctors and nurses, who have been exposed to male bodies.

A man can divorce his wife simply by saying 'I divorce you' three times. He can rescind the divorce if this was done in the heat of the moment, but only if the wife agrees (and only on three occasions!). On the other hand, even if a wife has good reason to seek a divorce (e.g. if her husband has been unfaithful, abused or deserted her, or engaged in criminal activity), she must go to a court for the case to be heard. The husband must maintain a divorced wife and any children from the marriage if the wife is unable to support herself. He can claim custody of any sons when they reach the age of ten. A female divorcee usually returns to her family, and few remarry.

Although a Muslim woman may not marry a non-Muslim man unless he converts to Islam, the reverse isn't the case. However, non-Muslim women are often pressurised into converting, and there have been many cases of foreign women marrying Arabs and then discovering that the local culture and lifestyle are unacceptably restrictive. It should also be noted that, in the event of the breakdown of such a union, the children are usually kept by the husband in his home country.

Expatriate workers can usually be married in the Gulf, provided that they meet the civil and religious requirements of their home country. Embassy and consulate staff sometimes perform civil marriage ceremonies, again provided that certain requirements are met. Religious ceremonies can be arranged, but only in countries that allow churches or similar non-Muslim places of worship. This isn't the case in Saudi Arabia. If people of different nationalities marry, the authorities sometimes scrutinise the circumstances to ensure that marriages of convenience aren't taking place in order to circumvent immigration requirements.

NATIONAL HOLIDAYS

Important dates in the Islamic calendar are the Prophet's ascension (*Al Isr'a Wal Mairaj*) and the Prophet's birthday (*Maulid Al-Nabi*), the start of Ramadan and the two 'festival' (*eid*) holidays, *Eid Al-Fitr* and *Eid Al-Adha* (see **Religion** on page 352), which are observed as holidays in all the Gulf states except Saudi Arabia, where the two *Eid* holidays are the only official holidays, although some of the others might be observed by private institutions. *Eid Al-Adha* normally lasts two or three days and *Eid Al-Fitr* four or five days, except in Saudi Arabia, where each holiday usually lasts around a week. However, there's generally a difference between the duration of holidays in the public and private sectors, government workers generally enjoying longer breaks than those in private enterprise (some things are the same in the Gulf as in the west!). Another holiday called Ashura, which commemorates the death in battle of the Prophet's grandson, Imam Husain, is observed in Bahrain, Oman, Qatar and the UAE.

Islamic holidays are determined by lunar sightings but, whereas some Muslim countries use information derived from observatories, unaided observations are preferred in the Gulf, which makes exact dates difficult to predict, as the moon may be obscured by cloud, for example. There's also a complicated conversion to be made from the Islamic to the Gregorian calendar (see **Calendar** on page 332). The dates shown below are therefore approximate, and the only way to be sure that a holiday has begun is to hear the gun that's traditionally fired on such occasions, to hear an announcement on the local radio or to wake to hear less than usual traffic noise!

Holiday	Date (Islamic Calendar)	Approx. Date (Gregorian Calendar)		
		2003	2004	2005
Eid Al-Adha	10 Dhul-Hijah	12/2	2/2	21/1
Muslim New Year	1 Muharram	5/3	22/2	10/2
Ashura	10 Muharram	14/3	2/3	19/2
Prophet's birthday	12 Rabi II	14/5	2/5	21/4
Prophet's ascension	27 Rajab	24/9	12/9	1/9
Ramadan	1 Ramadan	27/10	15/10	4/10
Eid Al-Fitr	1 Shawaal	26/11	14/11	3/11

In addition to the above, the following holidays are observed in the different states:

State	Holiday	Date (Gregorian Calendar)
Bahrain	New Year's Day	1st January
	National Day/Independence Day	16th December
Kuwait	New Year's Day	1st January
	National Day	25th February
	Liberation Day	26th February

Oman	National Day	18th November
	Sultan Qaboos' Birthday	19th November
Qatar	Emir's Accession	22nd February
	National Day/Independence Day	3rd September
UAE	New Year's Day	1st January
	Ruler's Accession (Abu Dhabi only)	6th August
	National Day	2nd December
	Christmas Day	25th December

Note that a National 'Day' usually lasts two or three days!

PETS

Pets aren't common in the Gulf, where wild dogs and cats roam the streets. In fact, in some states, when the wild dog population grows too large, it's culled by the police. Wild dogs and cats are sometimes dangerous and spread disease, although some foreign animal-lovers provide homes for them.

You can usually import your pet but must provide up-to-date medical reports showing the absence of rabies, with a valid vaccination certificate, and similar clearance for other diseases. However, the import of cats into Saudi Arabia isn't allowed and the import of any pet is likely to be difficult. Consular officials at the various Gulf embassies might help you with the paperwork for the import of pets but are unlikely to see this as an important part of their work. There's a British Veterinary Centre in the UAE (✉ britvet@emirates.net.ae), which can provide relevant details, and there's no shortage of vets in the region, although most of them are more used to caring for livestock than for domestic animals. Once in the region, animals must be given annual vaccinations and are usually banned from parks and beaches.

If you import or 'adopt' a dog, don't imagine that your much-loved pet will to be well received in the region. Dog are seen as unclean (haram), and according to superstition favour ill-fortune. And if any pet makes a nuisance of itself, you might be obliged to have it put down. The concept of animal welfare is, unfortunately, alien to the Gulf states.

POLICE

Although there are variations in the organisation of policing across the region, the Gulf states' police forces are usually divided into two main sections: security police (concerned with public order and internal and external security) and traffic police, who deal with traffic infringements, accidents and registrations. In Saudi Arabia, there are also religious police (*Matawa, Mutawa* or *Mutawwa'iin*), who patrol public places alongside the general police, their role being to ensure that the public adheres to Islamic rules of behaviour and appearance. The religious police are 'enthusiastic' about their work, and even minor infringements can provoke confrontation, harassment and arrest. In some cases, the police strike offenders with small canes.

This mainly applies to Muslims who are thought not to be observing the calls to prayer at prayer times, although foreigners and non-Muslims aren't immune from such punishment. In general, however, although there appear to be police everywhere in the Gulf, they maintain a low profile and are helpful, cheerful and respectful.

POPULATION

The Population figures for the Gulf states in many cases are estimates, although organised census-taking is now becoming more common.

Bahrain

The population of Bahrain was estimated in 1997 at 616,342, including 224,640 foreign nationals, with an anticipated annual growth rate of around 2 per cent. Of the total population 10 per cent are nationals of other Arab countries, 8 per cent are Iranian (not considered to be Arabs), 13 per cent are Asian and 6 per cent come from a variety of other countries. Shi'a (or Shi'ite) Muslims account for 75 per cent of the local population, Sunnis 25 per cent.

Kuwait

The population in 1998 was registered as 2.3 million, with a forecast annual growth rate of 2.7 per cent. Foreigners account for approximately 60 per cent of the population. Sunni Muslims make up 45 per cent of the local population, Shi'a Muslims 40 per cent, and the rest are a variety of faiths. Almost half the population is under 15 years of age, and 56 per cent are female.

Oman

In 1999 the population was 2.45 million, with a forecast of 3.3 million by the year 2010, with 74 per cent nationals and 26 per cent foreigners. Ibadi Muslims account for around 75 per cent of the local population; the rest are made up of other faiths. The male to female ratio is 51 to 49, with around 46 per cent of the population under the age of 15.

Qatar

In the early 21st century, the population was around 640,000, with a forecast annual growth rate of 3.5 per cent. Only 25 per cent of the population is indigenous, just 32 per cent are female, and almost 50 per cent are under 15 years of age. Doha is home to around 80 per cent of the country's population.

Saudi Arabia

The population was estimated at 21.5 million in 1999, with a forecast of 29.7 million by 2010, given an estimated annual growth rate of 3.4 per cent. Nationals account for 73 per cent, males for 56 per cent and children under 15 for almost 50 per cent of the population.

United Arab Emirates

The population in 1998 was 2.8 million, 70 per cent of them expatriates. It's expected to drop to 2.7 million by 2010. Roughly 70 per cent of the population is male and almost half of the total population is under the age of 15.

RELIGION

Needless to say, Islam is the main religion in the Gulf, although the practice of other religions is permitted in Bahrain, Oman and the UAE.

Learning something about Islam and respecting its traditions and practices is important for all expatriates.

Note that followers of the Islamic faith are Muslims or Moslems, depending on the chosen spelling of the word. They aren't to be called Mohammedans. For Muslims, Islam isn't just a religion but a way of life that governs and guides their path through this world and the next. It's an integral and pervasive part of all aspects of life. Public worship is viewed as more important than almost anything else, religious books and writings are found everywhere, and the phrase 'In the name of God, the Compassionate, the Merciful' is found at the top of most correspondence.

Islam means 'active submission to the will of God'. The religion teaches that Allah controls absolutely everything and, when making plans, you often hear the response 'in sha Allah' ('God willing'). You will also hear 'La ilaha illa Allah, Mohammadun rasulu Allah' ('There's no God but God, and Mohammed is his Prophet'). Mohammed was born in Mecca in around 571AD and began to receive revelations at the age of 40. Three years later, he started to preach and to challenge the local pagan religions. As a result, Mohammed and his followers — Muslims — had to flee to the town of Medina in 622AD. This exodus (hejira) is regarded as the beginning of the Muslim age and is therefore year zero, the beginning of the Islamic calendar (see **Calendar** on page 332), in the same way as the date given for Christ's birth is the beginning of the Christian calendar.

The Holy Koran (Qu'ran) is God's word as revealed by the angel Gabriel to the Prophet Mohammed in Mecca and, along with other writings, it sets out rules for every aspect of life. Whereas the Christian Bible and the Jewish Torah consist of later writings of a number of individuals, the Koran is seen as the direct word of God. The God of Abraham is the one true God for all Christians and Jews, but Mohammed claimed that they altered their books and that the message of the Koran is the final truth.

The main point of disagreement with Christianity is that, while Muslims perceive and venerate Jesus as a prophet (second in stature only to Mohammed), they dispute his divinity. In the words of the Koran, 'Neither was God born, nor did he give birth'. The Muslim believes that all people are born to Islam but are diverted to other religions, usually by their parents.

There are five 'pillars' of Islam:

Faith (shahada): The first pillar is the profession of faith, which is the belief that 'there is no God but Allah and Mohammed is the Prophet of God'.

Prayer (salah or salat): The second pillar lays out the obligatory prayers to be performed by devout Muslims five times a day. As the sun rises for each new day, the faithful are called to prayer by a muezzin (or nowadays often by a tape recording) with the following declaration of faith, known as the 'Shahadah': 'God is most great. I testify that there is no God but Allah and that Mohammed is the Prophet of God. Come to the prayer. Come to the salvation. Prayer is better than sleep. God is most great. There is no God but God.' Each phrase is repeated. (The reference to sleep is used only in the first call to prayer.)

Prayer times are at dawn (fajr), noon (dhuhr), mid-afternoon (asir), sunset (maghreb) and nightfall (isha). The times of the dawn and sunset prayers are traditionally the earliest and latest times at which you can see the difference between a black thread and a white thread, using only natural light. All newspapers publish the prayer times to be observed on that day. The duration of prayers varies with the prayer leader (Imam) but is usually between ten minutes and half an hour. You can pray anywhere, but Friday noon prayers must be performed in a mosque. Muslims wash before praying to show a willingness to be purified.

Non-Muslims aren't expected to do anything in particular during prayer times, although you shouldn't watch or pass close in front of anyone who is praying or step on his prayer mat.

Charity (zakat): The third pillar of the Muslim faith involves the (obligatory) donation of a 40th (i.e. 2.5 per cent) of the value of your assets annually – a sort of 'alms tax'. Fortunately, this doesn't apply to non-Muslims.

Fasting (sawm): The fourth pillar concerns the Ramadan Fast, when Muslims must fast during the hours of daylight for the whole of this Holy month (see **Calendar** on page 332). The fast is an act of self-purification and a test of strength, patience and inner knowledge. Muslims must refrain from drinking, eating, smoking and all other physical pleasures, including sexual activity. Eid Al-Fitr ('the big festival'), is the festival of the breaking of the fast, when the whole community celebrates, families visiting each other and children wearing new clothes (see **National Holidays** on page 348). Non-Muslims usually join in and enjoy the fun. This is also an occasion for people to pay their respects to the ruler and any notable families that they do business with or are in regular contact with. Coffee and sweets are served, and the host and his family and friends are wished 'Eid mubarraq' ('congratulations on the occasion of the festival). The Eid Al-Fitr is also a time when people pay money or donate food to a charity called Sadaqah Al-Fitr, which provides food for the needy.

Pilgrimage (Hajj or Haj): The fifth and final pillar of Islam declares that it's incumbent on every Muslim who can afford it to make a pilgrimage to Mecca, at least once in his life. The reward for doing so is impressive: forgiveness for all sins. The Haj is an annual event, which takes place in the 12th month (Dhul-Hijah) of the Muslim calendar (see **Calendar** on page 332). It's a well-organised event, although such is the demand to make the pilgrimage that quotas have had to be enforced on each country.

Some branches of Islam insist that men shave their heads for the pilgrimage, and on arrival at Mecca all pilgrims must wear the ihram, a seamless white garment wrapped around the body and making the wearer indistinguishable as to class or status: all are equal before God. There are also many complex rituals to be observed. At the end of the Haj, the Eid Al-Adha (Festival of Sacrifice) is celebrated (see **National Holidays** on page 348).

According to Islam, the 'sabbath' or holy day is Friday (Al-Juma), when shops and businesses are normally closed.

Muslim Sects

When Islam arrived in the seventh century, Christianity and Judaism had become riven by factions and disagreements. The new religion seemed to offer a pure alternative to both of them, without hierarchies and rituals and offering a direct relationship with God. This didn't last for long, however. When the prophet died in 632AD with no sons, the succession was disputed by Abu Bakr (the father of Mohammed's second wife, Aisha) and Ali (Mohammed's cousin and the husband of his daughter, Fatima). Power was initially given to Abu Bakr, who became Mohammed's successor. Ali agreed, albeit reluctantly. This fragile harmony was short-lived, ending when one of Abu Bakr's successors was murdered. Ali reignited his claim to power and won the struggle for it, but he was assassinated in 661AD. Ali's successor Hussein was defeated in 680 by the Umayyad dynasty, which came to prominence throughout most of the Muslim world and created the Sunni sect. Those who remained loyal to Ali's descendents were called Shi'ites (or Shi'a Muslims).

The two sects still exist today, Sunnis being the more orhodox group and accounting for around 90 per cent of the world's approximately 1 billion Muslims. Except in Bahrain, Iraq, Lebanon and Yemen, Sunnis are the majority in all Arab countries. They regard the Shi'ites as giving excessive importance to prayer leaders (*Imams*), whom they regarded as a kind of divine intermediary of God — to an extent that's almost sacriligious. Shi'a representation is also strong in Kuwait, the eastern province of Saudi Arabia, and Iran (which lays claim to Bahrain), and Shi'ites have gained notoriety because of the unrest caused by some of their followers, although the vast majority are peaceful and reasonable people. There are also sub-groups of each sect, further complicating matters. For example, two important Sunni sub-groups are the Wahhabis, who follow the the teaching of 18th century 'reformer' Ibn Abd Al-Wahhab and who have strong influence in Saudi Arabia, and the Ibadis, who are prevalent in Oman (as well as Algeria). Shi'a sub-groups include the Ithna-Asharis, the Ismailis and the Zeidis.

RULING FAMILIES

Of the six Gulf states, four are ruled by emirs (in fact, there are seven emirs in the UAE), one (Saudi Arabia) by a king, and one (Oman) by a sultan, although in effect all have similar status. He (they're all men) is the supreme authority in the nation, and many members of his family are given important portfolios to administer and generally do so competently. (This is partly because they're experienced at this type of work and partly because they have sound advisers.) The ruling families are viewed as benevolent patriarchies, looking after the country's progress and the well-being of the people.

Arabs, being traditionally tribal, find nothing unusual at all about non-elected administrations, and the ruling family system works smoothly, although things are now beginning to change. The Gulf states have been broadening their administrations for some time, moving from hereditary compositions to the inclusion of Councils of Ministers and other advisory and administrative bodies. An aspect of Arab government that comes as a surprise to many foreigners is the ease with which the local people can approach high officials,

Ministers and even the ruler himself, who's available to discuss and resolve their problems.

SOCIAL CUSTOMS

Needless to say, many Arab customs are very different from those in the west, and you should be aware of what you're expected to do and not to do. Although Arabs are understanding and unlikely to take offence at social blunders, provided they arise from ignorance rather than malice, you will be made far more welcome if you acquaint yourself with local ways of doing things. It's important to remember that you're a foreigner and you must therefore adapt to the customs and social behaviour of the region – not the other way round. In addition to actions and behaviour which are regarded as criminal (see **Legal System** on page 341), there are certain unwritten rules that you must observe in order not to offend local sensibilities.

Dress: There are two distinct types of women's clothing in the region: one for locals, the other for expatriates. Outside the home, most Arab women dress according to religious custom, which means that they must cover most of the body, from head to foot. The traditional black overgarment (*abaya*) is ankle length with long sleeves and a high neckline, and the hair is covered. Some Arab women are totally covered, including their face and hands, especially Saudis and those with strictly religious husbands. This is meant to protect women protection from unwanted attention, and in Saudi Arabia even foreign women must wear an *abaya* outside the home; the relgious police will stop any woman who has her head uncovered and direct her to cover her hair immediately. In the other states, foreign women may wear western clothes but should always dress conservatively. The region's hot climate and customs call for informal but smart dressing. Arabs frown on clothes which reveal the shoulders, arms and legs, and any woman dressing provocatively will be regarded as being of 'easy virtue' or perhaps even as a prostitute. In the home, however, when not entertaining close friends or relatives, Arab women often adopt western dress, particularly younger women, and there are no restrictions on the way foreign women may dress in private.

Arab men wear the *thobe*, a loose, ankle-length robe made from fine white cotton (or heavier woollen material in winter). There are different styles of thobe, both in the cut of the cloth and in the fastenings at the neck and front. Perhaps the most distinctive are those worn by the Omanis, which sport a tassel. The *thobe* can be worn for all occasions, either social or business. An outer cloak, the *bisht*, is worn on formal occasions and can be very costly, with border embroidery in gold thread and the material itself of the finest quality.

The traditional, distinctive head covering is the *guthra*, a white or red and white checkered cloth held in place by the *agal*, a black 'rope' which was originally a camel tether. There are different types of *agal*: for example, Qataris normally wear a more African-style headdress, with two long 'tails' reaching down the back. Arab men sometimes wear casual dress on very informal occasions or at the beach, but Saudi men are strongly encouraged to wear national dress at all times.

Obviously, foreign men aren't expected to wear Arab garments, and western dress is the norm. Men should avoid wearing shorts and sleeveless shirts in the street, as is these are regarded as excessively casual, although with the development of tourism, this attitude is softening. However, suits are rarely worn in the Gulf, except for important business meetings and related social events. Standard wear in the office is a shirt (usually long-sleeved), tie and lightweight trousers.

Terms of Address: Arabs generally value civility highly, and it's important that you greet (and part from) local people in the correct way. The use of Arab names can be confusing for newcomers to the region. For example, a man might be called Abdullah bin Abdul Aziz Al-Jishi. Abdullah is his given name and he's the son or grandson of (bin) Abdul Aziz; Al-Jishi is the family or tribal name. To make matters even more complicated, given names are often abbreviated: for example, Mohammed can be shortened to Mohd, Hamad or Hamed. It's important to use the full name, however, particularly on formal occasions and in correspondence. Abdullah bin Abdul Aziz Al-Jishi should never be called Abdullah (let alone the diminutive Abdul), although the patronymic may be omitted and he can be addressed as Abdullah Al-Jishi.

The general formal address is 'Sayyed' ('Sir') for a man or 'Sayeeda' (or 'Sayedity') for a woman, followed by the person's full name. Arab women can be addressed as 'Madame'.

Rulers are usually addressed as 'Your Highness' ('Your Majesty' in the case of the King of Saudi Arabia). Senior members of ruling families are called 'Your Excellency' followed by 'Sheikh' (pronounced 'shake' and not 'sheek') and their full name. Government ministers of the ruling line are 'Your Excellency, Minister of . . .' and other ministers simply 'Your Excellency' followed by the full name. Lesser members of ruling families and those in religious authority are addressed as 'Sheikh' followed by their full name. In Saudi Arabia, the title has somewhat less significance and is also being used by powerful members of the business community. The conventions for addressing rulers and members of ruling families are complex, and you should always check locally before being introduced to any dignitaries.

Greetings: The most common greeting in the Gulf is *Salam alaykum* ('Peace be upon you'), to which the correct reply is *Wa alaykum as-salam* ('And upon you be peace'). Other common greetings and the accepted replies are:

Greeting	Meaning	Reply
Ahlan wa sahlan	Hello	Ahlan bik
Sabah al-khayr	Good morning/afternoon	Sabah an-nur
Masa al-khayr	Good evening	Masa an-nur

Note that *tisbah ala-khayr*, meaning 'good night', is said on parting, as in English, and the reply is *wa inta min ahlu*. You should always shake hands when greeting and parting from Arab men. In the case of Arab women, you should be guided by the woman's behaviour: many Arab women won't shake hands with non-Arab men, although educated women might. This is normal even with close friends whom you meet frequently. If the handshake you receive when leaving somebody is longer than the one you received when meeting him, it indicates that you've made a good impression. Incidentally, newcomers should note that refusals or protracted reluctance to meet people are frowned upon. Note also that you shouldn't approach Arab women, look at them or talk to them unless you've been properly introduced.

After handshaking, it's customary to enquire after the other person's health and other matters, and you should expect similar enquiries to be directed at you. (Don't enquire after the health of the female members of an Arab's family, however, but restrict your questions to those regarding the family in general or the sons.) This can take a long time, as neither party wishes to be the one to draw matters to a close. Foreigners aren't expected to know or use all the subtleties this ritual involves, but you will make a good impression if you learn at least some of the standard expressions and use them in the correct way. Whether in face-to-face conversation or speaking to people on the telephone, don't talk business straight away; if you do so, Arabs will assume that you're impatient or not interested in them personally.

Hands & Feet: You should accept refreshment whenever it's offered, but note that you should always use your right hand for drinking and eating, as the left hand is regarded as unclean (as it's used for 'toilet purposes'). Similarly, you should avoid showing the soles of your shoes or feet, which implies that you think the other person is 'dirt', which is obviously highly offensive. You should therefore keep your feet flat on the ground and not cross your legs.

Invitations: If you're invited to the home of an Arab, you should always accept. You should generally take every opportunity to become acquainted with local people and avoid the natural tendency to stay within the social and physical confines of your foreign 'ghetto'. Your Arab host will be interested in you and your views. However, you should avoid politics and religion as subjects for discussion; your opinions might be regarded as ill-informed or even offensive, even if they seem acceptable to you from a western perspective.

When you enter the majlis, the reception room for visitors, you should always remove your footwear, unless the host indicates otherwise (you should therefore ensure that there are no holes in your socks!). If you're with a female companion, she will be whisked off to join the women. You will almost certainly be offered something to drink and perhaps eat; accept the offer. Arabs are almost always polite and expect the same from those they meet, and believe that sharing a meal with a person positively affects the relationship.

The standard greeting is Ahlan wa sahlan – which means welcome - and this will become familiar to all who visit the Gulf States. It's certainly worth learning enough Arabic to communicate the pleasantries, greetings and responses of the country you're living in. You will enjoy people's reaction and your hosts invariably offer encouragement to those who attempt to speak their language. It's important to note, however, that the Arabic language has a special significance, having been designed to carry the word of God, so it's important to use it respectfully.

You should also never call at an Arab's house without warning him that you're coming. If the women of the family are present, this won't be appreciated, particularly in Saudi Arabia. You should also avoid expressing admiration for any of your host's possessions, as tradition dictates that he must then offer it to you. Although this tradition isn't followed by everybody, it can nevertheless cause embarrassment. What's more, the correct response is for the recipient to give an even more valued gift in return, so think twice before admiring an Arab's Rolls Royce!

Other Dos and Don'ts: You should also heed the following warnings:

● Don't offer alcoholic drinks to an Arab, unless you're certain that he drinks alcohol. This can cause great offence.

● Don't walk on a prayer mat or in front of any person at prayer and try not to stare at people who are praying.

● Don't try to enter a mosque without first asking permission. It's unlikely that you will be allowed in.

● In Saudi Arabia, don't try to enter the Holy sites of the areas surrounding Mecca and Medina. The roads are well signposted to notify everybody of this restriction. If a non-Muslim is found within the prohibited areas, he's likely to be assaulted and will be afforded no protection against the assailants.

● Avoid blasphemy, particularly in the presence of Muslims and particularly in Saudi Arabia (see page 345). Remember that there are many non-Gulf Arabs working in the region, who aren't always as relaxed or tolerant as locals are.

● Avoid putting an Arab in a position where he might suffer a 'loss of face' in front of other Arabs. He will appreciate this, if he notices your action.

● Don't beckon to people with a finger, as this is considered particularly impolite. Arabs might use such a gesture to summon a dog.

● Avoid shouting and displays of aggression or drunkenness at all times, as such behaviour is rarely tolerated.

● During Ramadan (see page 354), don't eat, drink or smoke anywhere where you can be seen by Muslims during the hours of daylight (especially in Saudi Arabia) and don't engage in any noisy behaviour or embrace or kiss anyone in public.

TIME DIFFERENCE

There are two time zones in the region, measured against the international standard of Greenwich Mean Time. Bahrain, Kuwait, Qatar and Saudi Arabia are on GMT plus three hours, Oman and the UAE are on GMT plus four hours. Gulf time is constant throughout the year, which means that from the end of March to the end of October Bahrain, Kuwait, Qatar and Saudi Arabia are only two hours ahead of the UK and Oman and the UAE three hours ahead. Both the 12-hour and the 24-hour systems of reporting time are used.

The time difference between the different states (at noon in January) and some major foreign cities is shown below:

	Noon in Bahrain/Kuwait Qatar/Saudi Arabia	Noon in Oman/UAE
Sydney	8pm	7pm
London	9am	8am
Cape Town	11am	10am
Tokyo	6pm	5pm
Los Angeles	1am	Midnight
New York	4am	3am

19.

THE GULF ARABS

Who are the Gulf Arabs? What are they like? Let's take a candid look at them, tongue firmly in cheek, and hope they forgive our flippancy or that they don't read this bit (which is why it's hidden away at the back of the book). The typical Gulf Arab is wealthy, formal, good-humoured, tribal, respectful, proud, a procrastinator, well-dressed, rude, a devout Muslim, courteous, argumentative, tolerant, hard-nosed, hygienic, lazy, superior, a born haggler, generous, serious, loyal, multilingual, patient, intolerant, apolitical, hospitable, inscrutable, leisurely, honourable, informal, frustrating, kind, fatalistic, and has two camels, four wives, eight children and a dozen cars!

You may have noticed that the above list contains a 'few' contradictions (as does life in the Gulf), which is hardly surprising as there's no such thing as a typical Gulf Arab and few people conform to the popular stereotype (whatever that is). The Arab world is huge, stretching from the waters of the Arabian Gulf (originally known as the Persian Gulf) through the North African countries bordering the southern shores of the Mediterranean to the Atlantic coast. Gulf Arabs are relatively few but, thanks to their oil reserves, enjoy some of the highest incomes in the world. Indeed, they've enjoyed relative affluence for centuries thanks to their success as seafarers and traders, and the foreign workers who arrived in the 1970s to take part in the oil boom were by no means the first to form links with the inhabitants of the Arabian Gulf.

In ancient times, merchants traded goods from India and China and sent them via caravan routes to the Mediterranean, providing an important link between east and west. The Portuguese arrived in the region in the 16th century, when the sphere of influence of the flourishing Kingdom of Hormuz in Oman extended to the southern coast of Iran. The Portuguese had their eyes on the Arab's trading success and established themselves by force, taking over the lucrative trade to the east. The region went into decline over the following decades, when the populace migrated inland from their traditional seaports and trading bases.

The British, through the East India Company, brought change in the 17th and 18th centuries, establishing a strong presence in both India and the Gulf, although not in Saudi Arabia. Meanwhile, the Arab tribes that had moved inland following the Portuguese invasion re-established themselves along the Gulf coast, which was the beginning of the Gulf states as they are today. An agreement in 1820 cemented British control of both political and military matters in the region, which became known as the Trucial Coast. In the late 19th century, the British signed a defence agreement with the states in return for trade concessions, which lasted until the 1970s, when the Gulf states became independent (although Britain still has a pact of 'eternal friendship').

Today's Gulf Arabs are the descendants of the Bedouin tribes that populated the coastline centuries ago, and their sense of tradition and close tribal links and family connections remain strong. Most Gulf Arabs have relatives and friends in other Gulf states, and when visiting on business or holiday usually have people to visit or stay with. Nevertheless, their new-found affluence and outside influences – introduced by foreigners or the media – are slowly changing the way that Gulf families live. Couples used to have as many as seven or eight children, several generations of a family living under the same roof or in adjacent dwellings, while wealthier families had their own small compound of houses. Today, the average number of children born to Arab families has fallen to three or four – or even to two among more educated people. Newly-weds tend to want independence from their parents and to live in their own homes, although family ties remain very strong.

Wide-ranging educational programmes have resulted in increasing numbers of men and women being educated to tertiary level. Women, who could previously expect to live most of their life in the home, now find that the world of commerce and industry is open to them and they're increasingly found in fields such as banking, the medical profession, teaching or even run their own businesses. Men have had to face the challenge of earning their living in an environment very different from that which their fathers encountered. The traditional rural, agricultural way of life is increasingly rare, and today's Arab lives either in excellent, low-cost housing with all mod cons, including 100-channel satellite TV, or (for the fortunate few) in luxury palaces.

Arabs are noted for their warm hospitality – a characteristic often claimed but rarely much in evidence. In the Gulf, it's a way of life and part of the heritage of the Bedouin, whose hospitality, loyalty and strict code of conduct (dating back to the days when survival was constantly threatened by the elements and outsiders) are portrayed as models of good behaviour. A guest of the Bedouin, when offered food or drink or upon kissing the hem of a tent, comes under the total protection of his host for three days. You're unlikely to come into contact with the few remaining desert Bedouin, except perhaps when 'wadi bashing', although you may encounter those who have chosen to combine tradition with the advantages of the modern world and who live in black tents near to villages or towns, with jeeps as well as camels, goats and sheep. To a certain extent, however, all Gulf Arabs are Bedouin, and most are kind and good-humoured, greeting people with genuine pleasure (in the lonely open spaces of the desert, encounters were few and far between), and the elderly are treated with respect, age being equated with wisdom.

Arabs tend to be patient to the point of being leisurely. This can be frustrating to the western mind, which invariably equates speed with efficiency. You will often encounter a *mañana* attitude – or rather an *in sha Allah* ('God willing') attitude – particularly with some tradesmen. On the other hand, some types of business (e.g. alterations to a suit at a tailor's) are carried out while you wait, which can be surprising. You may even find yourself discussing your affairs with a traditional Arab businessman in the presence of others, which is entirely acceptable to locals, as all conversations are deemed to be confidential (although it may be unwise to discuss the new oil field you've just discovered!).

Arabs are essentially fatalistic – a characteristic they derive from their religion and upbringing. For example, if an apparently insoluble problem arises in business, instead of persistently trying to find a solution, an Arab will often simply walk away from it. Whereas the western businessman generally sees quick, positive decision-making as a sign of good management, Arabs tend to take their time and regard the option of doing nothing as an attractive one. (You will be delighted to hear, however, that this doesn't apply to the region's airline pilots – particularly in a crisis!)

The Gulf Arab doesn't like to say 'no', being too polite to reject an offer outright. In business, this can lead to unfortunate misunderstandings with foreigners and it's therefore important to be aware of what's being implied, and also to take account of body language. If, following your sales pitch, an Arab says 'let me think about it' or 'leave it with me', you can usually kiss the deal goodbye. If he's enthusiastic about a proposition, he will leave little room for doubt about his intentions. As for finalising an agreement, be prepared for some hard bargaining before a deal is concluded. However, once a contract is signed, Arabs will stick to the letter of the agreement and will expect you to do the same. Woe betide you if the contract has gaps or loopholes in it, as Arabs are masters at finding and exploiting them to their advantage (and they will expect you to do likewise).

Not only do Arabs sometimes find it difficult to reach agreement with foreigners, but they often have difficulty agreeing with one another – at the highest political level as well as when discussing minor matters. There's also an element of the 'blame culture' in the Arab make-up. If a mistake is made, Arabs tend to try to avoid blame being attached to them (even if they share the responsibility), as this involves a 'loss of face'. Disputes are therefore best resolved in private.

Although many Arabs appear to be westernised or at least to have a reasonable understanding of western ways, at heart and in character they aren't at all. Indeed, some Arab employers see foreign workers as commodities rather than individuals, believing that 'there's plenty more where he came from'. Nevertheless, this is very much the exception rather than the rule.

If you're willing to meet the locals half way (and perhaps learn a few words of their language) and respect their traditions, religion and way of life, you will invariably be warmly received and will find that people go out of their way to welcome and help you. The vast majority of the millions of foreigners who work in the Gulf develop great affection for the locals, often remaining in the region for many years or visiting regularly long after they've returned home.

Ahlan wa sahlan! (Welcome to the Gulf!)

20.

MOVING HOUSE
OR
LEAVING THE GULF STATES

If you decide to change your accommodation within the Gulf, move to another state or leave the Gulf altogether, there are numerous matters to consider and people to notify. The checklists in this chapter will help to make the process easier and help prevent an ulcer of nervous breakdown – provided you don't leave everything to the last minute!

Moving is usually fairly straightforward, as all expatriate accommodation is rented. And if the rental contract is in your employer's name, as it often is, you avoid direct responsibility if there are any problems, although your employer will, of course, hold you liable for any disputes that might be passed on to him. If your employer is an important, regular client of the landlord, this may be to your advantage. If, on the other hand, the contract is in your name, you must deal with any difficulties yourself.

If you want or need to move before the termination date of the rental contract, the owner of the property might insist on retaining the deposit you paid on moving in, as well as any overpaid rent (rent being paid in advance), or he might require you to find a replacement tenant before giving you a refund. There might, however, be a clause in the contract covering a situation where you're obliged to leave the country earlier than expected. In any case, the termination of leases isn't usually a cause for concern and can invariably be successfully negotiated.

If the contract has run its course, there should be no problems of this kind, although in it there might be a clause requiring notice of intent not to renew the contract, and you should be careful to abide by this.

MOVING HOUSE

If you're moving house *within* the Gulf, you should consider the following matters:

- Inform the following, as appropriate:
  - Your employer and/or sponsor, who must be notified of any change in your accommodation, as he's responsible for you while you're in the country.
  - Your electricity/water, telephone and gas suppliers, who will obviously require any outstanding bills to be paid and disconnect supplies when necessary. However, you should talk to your

landlord before agreeing to the disconnection of any supplies, as these might be in his name and he might not wish them to be disconnected.

- Any relevant insurance companies, e.g. if you have insurance for your household contents or a car. You might be entitled to a refund.

- Your bank and other relevant financial institutions, although your employer's work address is used on your behalf for most transactions.

- Your medical practitioners.

- Regular correspondents, friends and relatives.

- Your consulate or embassy.

● If you're going to take up employment in another Gulf state, you should at least have a letter of contract and a clear indication from your new employer that he will be able to obtain the necessary legal documentation to allow you to work and reside in your new country.

● If the move involves a change of school for your children, ensure that places are available at the prospective new school.

● Arrange the move with a removal company or hire a small utility vehicle with a driver and helpers, according to how many possessions you have, or ask friends to help you move.

LEAVING THE GULF

If you decide to leave the region, either on completion of your contract or for any other reason, there are matters to consider in addition to the above:

● First, consider whether leaving is the best option. You might be able to find other employment with new challenges and perhaps a different lifestyle in another Gulf state. It's likely that you will have become accustomed to an affluent, tax-free lifestyle in a region where the sun usually shines and the expatriate social scene is lively. You may have experienced lower bills, less administrative hassle, less competitiveness and more positive attitudes than in your home country. So think at least twice about the decision to leave.

- Make sure you definitely have a job to take up in the country you're moving to.

- If you're returning home and you've been renting your house, check that there's a clause allowing you re-possession of it on your return.

- Your employer/sponsor must cancel your work and residence visas in order to replace you. An exit visa might be necessary in Qatar and will certainly be required in Saudi Arabia (see page 73).

- In most cases, the Ministry of Labour will want to see you to ensure that you're leaving without any outstanding disputes or owing any money. Indemnity (bonus) payments usually form part of your remuneration package at the conclusion of your contract, and the Ministry will help to arrange this for you. The Ministries are generally fair to expatriate employees and protect their interests.

- In the unlikely event that you've participated in a company pension scheme, make the appropriate claim or transfer of credits.

- If you've bought a car in the region, note that you cannot sell it for a year after importing it into an EU country. You must also go through the process of de-registration (see page 173) and obtain export plates for the vehicle. You must provide proof of ownership and proof of your identity.

- If you're shipping your personal possessions home, you have the choice of whether to use international removal companies or local Arab shipping companies. The former tend be much more expensive but, if choosing a local firm, it's best to use one that has been recommended, and you should check that the agreement is comprehensive. **Always insist on delivery to your home address**, or you might find yourself trying to clear your goods at a seaport or airport and probably incurring the cost of a clearing agent and transport company.

- If you've acquired pets in the Gulf, check the requirements for importing them into the country you're travelling to, including any quarantine regulations (and costs).

- Cancel all outstanding agreements and pay all bills. (It has been known for people who are trying to avoid paying a large utility bill to find themselves stopped at the airport.)

- Notify your home tax authorities, who will no doubt be pleased to welcome you back. If possible, work out the best time to return, from the point of view of the tax year. If you've been away for less than a certain time (usually a year), you might be liable for tax on your overseas earnings.

Good luck!

Appendices

APPENDIX A: USEFUL ADDRESSES

Gulf State Embassies & Consulates Abroad

Bahrain

Canada: Consulate, Rene, Levesque West Montreal, Quebec H3H IR4, ☎ 450-931 7444.

France: Embassy, 3bis, Place des Etat-Unis, 75116 Paris, ☎ 01.47.23.48.68.

Germany: Consulate, Klingelhoeferstr 7, 10785 Berlin, ☎ 0308-6877 777.

UK: Embassy, 98 Gloucester Road, London SW74 AU, ☎ 020-7370 5132.

USA: Embassy, 3502 International Drive, NW, Washington, DC 20008, ☎ 202-342 0741.

Kuwait

Bahrain: Embassy, King Faisal Highway, Manama, ☎ 534 040.

Canada: Embassy, 80 Elgin Street, Ottawa ON, KIP IC6, ☎ 613-780 9999.

Oman: Embassy, Jameat A'Duwal Al-Arabiya Street, Medinat Qaboos Diplomatic Area, Muscat, ☎ 699 626.

Qatar: Embassy, Diplomatic Area, beyond Doha Sheraton Hotel, Doha, ☎ 832 111.

Saudi Arabia: Embassy, Diplomatic Quarter, Riyadh, ☎ 01-488 3500.

UAE: Embassy, Diplomatic Area, Airport Road, Abu Dhabi, ☎ 02-446 888. Consulate-General, Beniyas Road, Deira, Dubai, ☎ 04-284 111.

UK: Embassy, 2 Albert Gate, Knightsbridge, London SW1X 7JU, ☎ 020-7590 3400.

USA: Embassy, 2940 Tilden Street, NW, Washington, DC 20008, ☎ 202-966 0702.

Oman

France: Embassy, 50 ave d'Iena, 75116 Paris, ☎ 01.47.23. 01.63.

Germany: Embassy, Lindenallee 11, 53173 Bonn, ☎ 228-357031.

Netherlands: Embassy, Koninginnegracht 27, 2514 AB Den Haag, ☎ 70-361 5800.

UK: Embassy, 167 Queen's Gate, London SW7 5HE, ☎ 020-7225 0001.

USA: Embassy, 2535 Belmont Rd, NW, Washington, DC 20008, ☎ 202-387 1980.

Qatar

France: Embassy, 57 Quai D'Orsay, 75007 Paris, ☎ 01.45.51. 90.71.

Germany: Embassy, Brunnenallee 6, 53177 Bonn, ☎ 228-957520.

UK: Embassy, 1 South Audley Street, London W1Y 5DQ, ☎ 020-7370 6871.

USA: Embassy, 4200 Wisconsin Ave, NW, Suite 200, Washington, DC 20016, ☎ 202-274 1600.

Consulate, 747, 3rd Ave, 22nd Floor, New York, NY 10017, ☎ 212-486 9355.

Saudi Arabia

Australia: 12 Culgoa Circuit, O'Malley, Canberra 2606 ACT, ☎ 06-286 2099.

Bahrain: Embassy, King Faisal Highway, ☎ 537 722.

Kuwait: Embassy, Sharq district, Arabian Gulf Street, ☎ 240 0250.

Oman: Embassy, Jameat A'Duwal Al-Arabiya St, Al-Khuwair, ☎ 601 744.

Qatar: Embassy, Diplomatic Area, ☎ 832 722.

UAE: Embassy, Diplomatic Area, Airport Road, ☎ 445 700.

UK: 30 Belgrave Square, London SW1X, ☎ 020-7235 0303.

USA: 601 New Hampshire Ave, NW, Washington, DC 20037, ☎ 202-342 3800.

UAE

Australia: Embassy, 36 Culgoa Circuit, O'Malley ACT 2606, ☎ 02-6286 8802.

Bahrain: Embassy, Juffair, ☎ 723 737.

France: Embassy, 3 rue de Lota, 75116 Paris, ☎ 01.45.53. 94.04.

Germany: Embassy, Erste Fahrgasse, 54113, Bonn, ☎ 228-267070.

Kuwait: Embassy, Istiglal St, Diplomatic Area, ☎ 252 7693.

Oman: Embassy, Jameat A'Duwal Al-Arabiya St, Al-Khuwair, ☎ 600 302.

Qatar: Embassy, off Al-Khor St, Khalifa Town district, ☎ 885 111.

Saudi Arabia: Diplomatic Quarter, Riyadh, ☎ 482 6803.

UK: Embassy, 30 Princes Gate, London SW1, ☎ 020-7581 1281.

USA: Embassy, 3000 K Street, NW, Suite 600, Washington, DC 20007, ☎ 202-338 6500.

Foreign Embassies & Consulates in the Gulf

Bahrain

France: Embassy, Al-Fatih Highway, ☎ 291 734.

Germany: Embassy, Al-Hassaa Building, Sheikh Hamad Causeway, ☎ 530 210.

Kuwait: Embassy, King Faisal Highway, ☎ 534 040.

Netherlands (also covers Belgium & Luxembourg): Consulate, ABN Building, ☎ 713 162.

Oman: Embassy, Al-Fatih Highway, ☎ 293 663.

Saudi Arabia: Embassy, King Faisal Highway, ☎ 537 722.

UAE: Embassy, Juffair, ☎ 723 737.

UK: Embassy, Government Avenue, ☎ 534 404.

USA: Embassy, off Sheikh Isa bin Sulman Highway, Al-Zinj, ☎ 273 300.

Kuwait

Bahrain: Embassy, Surra district, St 1, Block 1, Bldg 24, ☎ 531 8530.

Canada: Embassy, Da'iya district, El-Mutawakil Street, Area 4, House 24, ☎ 256 3025.

France: Embassy, Mansouria district, St 13, Block 1, Villa 24, ☎ 257 1061.

Germany: Embassy, Bahiya district, St 14, Block 1, Villa 13, ☎ 252 0857.

Netherlands: Embassy, Jabriah district, St 1, Block 9, House 76, ☎ 531 2650.

Oman: Embassy, Udailia district, St 3, Block 3, House 25, ☎ 256 1962.

Qatar: Embassy, Istiglal St, Diplomatic Area, ☎ 251 3606.

Saudi Arabia: Embassy, Sharq district, Arabian Gulf St, ☎ 240 0250.

UAE: Embassy, Istiglal St, Diplomatic Area, ☎ 252 7693.

UK: Embassy, Arabian Gulf St, ☎ 240 3334.

USA: Embassy, Al-Masjid Al-Asqa St, Plot 14, Block 14, ☎ 539 5307.

Oman

Bahrain: Embassy, Al-Kharjiyah St, Shatti Al-Qurm, ☎ 605 074.

France: Embassy, Jameat A'Duwal Al-Arabiya St, Al-Khuwair, ☎ 681 800.

Germany: Embassy, Al-Nahdha St, Ruwi, ☎ 702 164.

Kuwait: Embassy, Jamat A'Duwal Al-Arabiya St, Al-Khuwair, ☎ 699 626.

Netherlands: Embassy, Villa 1366, Way 3017, Shatti Al-Qurm, ☎ 603 706.

New Zealand: Consulate, Mutrah High St, Mutrah, ☎ 794 932.

Qatar: Embassy, Jameat A'Duwal Al-Arabiya St, Al-Khuwair, ☎ 691 152.

Saudi Arabia: Embassy, Jameat A'Duwal Al-Arabiya St, Al-Khuwair, ☎ 601 744.

UAE: Embassy, Jameat A'Duwal Al-Arabiya St, Al-Khuwair, ☎ 600 302.

UK: Embassy, Jameat A'Duwal Al-Arabiya St, Al-Khuwair, ☎ 693 077.

USA: Embassy, Jameat A'Duwal Al-Arabiya St, Al-Khuwair, ☎ 698 989.

Qatar

France: Embassy, Diplomatic Area, ☎ 832 283.

Germany: Embassy, Al-Jezira Al-Arabiyya St, ☎ 876 959.

Kuwait: Embassy, Diplomatic Area, ☎ 832 111.

Oman: Embassy, 41 Ibn Al-Qassem St, Villa 7, Hilal district, ☎ 670 744.

Saudi Arabia: Embassy, Diplomatic Area, ☎ 832 722.

UAE: Embassy, Off Al-Khor St, Khalifa Town district, ☎ 885 111.

UK: Embassy, Al-Istiqlal St, Rumailiah district, ☎ 421 991.

USA: Embassy, 149 Ahmed bin Ali St, ☎ 864 701.

Yemen: Embassy, Al-Jezira district, ☎ 432 555.

Saudi Arabia

The following embassies are all located in Riyadh's Diplomatic Quarter, except the Omani embassy:

Australia: ☎ 488 7788.

Bahrain: ☎ 488 0044.

Canada: ☎ 488 2288.

France: ☎ 488 1255.

Germany: ☎ 488 0700.

Ireland: ☎ 488 2300.

Kuwait: ☎ 488 3500.

New Zealand: ☎ 488 7988.

Oman: Al-Ra'id district, ☎ 482 3120.

Qatar: ☎ 482 5544.

UAE: ☎ 482 6803.

UK: ☎ 488 0077.

USA: ☎ 488 3800.

The following consulates are in Jeddah:

UK (also handles matters for Australian, Canadian & New Zealand citizens in Jeddah): a-Andalus Street, a-Shate'e district, ☎ 654 1811.

USA: Falasteen Street, ☎ 667 0080.

UAE

The following embassies are in Abu Dhabi:

Australia: Gulf Business Centre, ☎ 789 946.

Bahrain: Al-Najda St, behind Abu Dhabi Islamic Bank, ☎ 312 200.

Canada: Al-Nahayan Street, ☎ 456 969.

France: Al-Nahayan Street, ☎ 435 100.

Germany: Al-Nahayan Street, ☎ 435 630.

Kuwait: Diplomatic Area, ☎ 446 888.

Netherlands: Al-Masaood Tower, 6th Floor, Shaikh Hamdan bin Mohammed Street, ☎ 321 920.

Oman: Airport Road, ☎ 463 333.

Qatar: Diplomatic Area, ☎ 493 300.

Saudi Arabia: Diplomatic Area, ☎ 445 700.

UK: Khalid bin Al-Walid Street, ☎ 326 600.

USA: Sudan Street, ☎ 436 691.

APPENDIX B: FURTHER READING

The lists contained in this appendix are only a selection of the many books written about the Gulf states and Saudi Arabia. The publication title is followed by the name(s) of the author(s). Note that some titles may be out of print but may still be obtainable from book shops and libraries.

History & Politics

Arabia Without Sultans, Fred Halliday. This covers the development of the Gulf over the last few decades.

The Arabs, Peter Mansfield. A good history of the wider Middle East region, from pre-Islamic times.

The Arab World: Forty Years of Change, Elizabeth Fernea and Robert Warnock. One of the best books on the subject.

A History of the Arab Peoples, Albert Hourani. A heavyweight study, packed with information.

The New Arabians, Peter Mansfield. A rather uncritical study of Gulf history and life, focusing on Saudi Arabia but with good coverage also of Kuwait.

Travel

Arabia Through the Looking Glass, Jonathan Raban. A fascinating account of the Gulf oil boom, including musings on expatriate life.

Expats, Christopher Dickey. A study of expatriate life in various Middle East countries, including the Gulf.

Sandstorms, Peter Theroux. An account of the author's seven years as a journalist in Riyadh.

Middle East, (Lonely Planet). Lonely Planet is one of the best travel guide series and this is a useful, well-written and researched guide to the entire region.

Religion & Society

Islam, Alfred Guillaume. A good source of information, but a heavy read.

Living Islam, Akbar Ahmed. A well-researched and written introduction to the religion.

Nine Parts of Desire, Geraldine Brooks. A fairly sympathetic consideration of Islam's attitude to women.

Price of Honour, Jan Goodwin. Also about women and Islam but, unlike the above, critical of the religion's treatment of women.

Art

Calligraphy and Islamic Culture, Annemarie Schimmel. A comprehensive consideration of the subject.

Islamic Art, David Talbot Rice. A comprehensive study.

Islamic Arts, Jonathan Bloom and Sheila Blair. Well-written and illustrated.

Bahrain

Bahrain: A Heritage Explored, Angela Clark. A comprehensive guide to Bahrain's history and heritage.

Bahrain: A MEED Practical Guide. Plenty of detail, some of it out-of-date.

Bahrain Island Heritage, Shirley Kay. An impressive study.

Bahrain Through the Ages: The Archaeology, Sheikh Haya Ali Al-Khalifa & Michael Rice.

Bahrain Through the Ages: The History, Sheikh Haya Ali Al-Khalifa & Micheal Rice.

Looking for Dilmun, Geoffrey Bibby. An interesting account of, among other things, Bahrain in the mid-20th century.

Resident in Bahrain, Parween Abdul Rahman & Charles Walsham. Recommended for those living and working in Bahrain.

Kuwait

Looking for Dilmun, Geoffrey Bibby. Describes Kuwait in the mid-20th century and the archaeological digs on Failaka Island.

The Modern History of Kuwait 1750-1965, Ahmad Mustafa Abu-Hakima. A comprehensive consideration of the subject, including some interesting old photographs.

Tides of War: Eco-Disaster in the Gulf, Michael McKinnon & Peter Vine.

Oman

Arabian Sands, Wilfred Thesiger. One of the region's travel writing classics; includes accounts of Thesiger's journeys in various parts of Oman.

The Maverick Guide to Oman, Peter Ochs. Recommended for those wanting to get off the beaten track in Oman.

The Merchants, Michael Field. Includes an interesting consideration of the development of modern Oman.

Off-Road in Oman, Heiner Klein & Rebecca Brickson.

Oman – A Comprehensive Guide to the Sultanate of Oman (Directorate of General Tourism). Comprehensive but understandably lacking in objectivity.

Oman and its Renaissance, Sir Donald Hawly. A history of Oman.

Travels in Oman: On the Track of the Early Explorers, Philip Ward. An interesting blend of tales by early travellers to Oman with a consideration of the country now.

Qatar

Arabian Time Machine, Helga Graham. An interesting set of interviews with Qataris about their lives before and after the oil boom.

Qatar: A MEED Practical Guide. A useful guide, albeit uncontroversial and non-critical.

Welcome to Qatar, American Women's Association of Qatar. Aimed at American residents.

Saudi Arabia

Arabian Sands, Wilfred Thesiger. This 1959 classic includes an account of Thesiger's journeys in The Empty Quarter of Saudi Arabia.

At the Drop of a Veil, Marianne Alireza. The story of an American woman who married into a Saudi family in the 1940s.

The Kingdom, Robert Lacey. A good history of the country, up to the 1980s.

Personal Narrative of a Pilgrimage to Al-Madinah and Meccah, Richard Burton. One of the very few accounts (from 1955) of these holy cities by a non-Muslim.

UAE

Arabian Sands, Wilfred Thesiger. This regional classic describes, among other things, life in the United Arab Emirates (then known as the Trucial Coast) before oil.

Father of Dubai: Sheikh Rashid bin Said Al-Maktoum, Graeme Wilson. A study of the founder of modern Dubai.

Mother Without a Mask, Patricia Holton. A woman's perspective on local life.

The Myth of Arab Piracy in the Gulf, Sultan Muhammad Al-Qasimi, Emir of Sharjah. A local account of the region's history.

Off Road in the Emirates I and II, Dariush Zandi. Recommended for wadi bashers.

Appendix C: USEFUL WEBSITES

General

Arabia.com (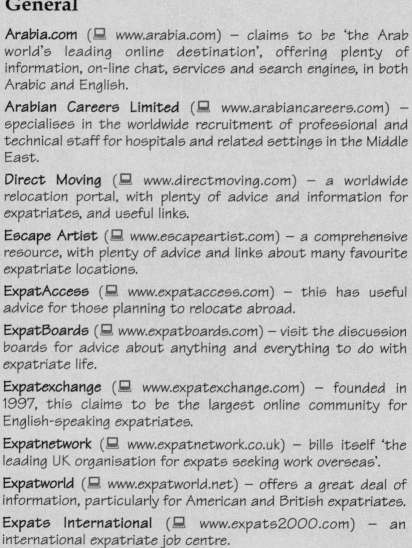 www.arabia.com) – claims to be 'the Arab world's leading online destination', offering plenty of information, on-line chat, services and search engines, in both Arabic and English.

Arabian Careers Limited (www.arabiancareers.com) – specialises in the worldwide recruitment of professional and technical staff for hospitals and related settings in the Middle East.

Direct Moving (www.directmoving.com) – a worldwide relocation portal, with plenty of advice and information for expatriates, and useful links.

Escape Artist (www.escapeartist.com) – a comprehensive resource, with plenty of advice and links about many favourite expatriate locations.

ExpatAccess (www.expataccess.com) – this has useful advice for those planning to relocate abroad.

ExpatBoards (www.expatboards.com) – visit the discussion boards for advice about anything and everything to do with expatriate life.

Expatexchange (www.expatexchange.com) – founded in 1997, this claims to be the largest online community for English-speaking expatriates.

Expatnetwork (www.expatnetwork.co.uk) – bills itself 'the leading UK organisation for expats seeking work overseas'.

Expatworld (www.expatworld.net) – offers a great deal of information, particularly for American and British expatriates.

Expats International (www.expats2000.com) – an international expatriate job centre.

Gulfdirectory (www.gulfdirectory.com) – a business-to-business directory of the Gulf, with over 91,000 addresses.

Living Abroad (💻 www.livingabroad.com) – has informative country profiles (payment required).

Real Post Reports (💻 www.realpostreports.com) – relocation services, reading lists and accounts written by expatriates about many places in the world.

World Travel Guide (💻 www.wtgonline.com) – aimed at expatriates and travellers.

Bahrain

Albahrain (💻 www.albahrain.net) – covers news, local events, what's new, shopping, sports, clubs and much else.

Bahrain Airport (💻 www.bahrainairport.com) – tells you all you could wish to know about the airport and also has useful, up-to-date information about visa requirements and costs.

Bahrain Arts Society (💻 www.bahartsociety.org.bh) – the Bahrain Arts Society describes itself as 'one of the most prestigious Arabic cultural foundations'.

Bahrain Government (💻 www.bahrain.gov.bh/english) – the Bahrain government site, offering plenty of information about all aspects of the island, obviously with a flattering slant.

Bahrain Tourism (💻 www.bahraintourism.com) – sponsored by the Bahrain Ministry of Information Tourism Affairs, the site is obviously official and therefore tends towards the uncritical, but it's full of information about many subjects, including tourist attractions, hotels, restaurants, banks, car hire firms, travel agencies, what's on and much else.

Bahrain Traders (💻 www.bahraintraders.com) – offers an extensive list of all types of trades and businesses in Bahrain.

Bahrain Tribune (💻 www.bahraintribune.com) – the site of the *Bahrain Tribune*, which bills itself 'the leading English newspaper in Bahrain', with extensive coverage of local, regional and international news, sports, features and much else.

Bahrain Yacht Club ( www.bahrainyachtclub.com) – the obvious site for those of a nautical bent.

British Council (www.britishcouncil.org/bahrain) – has plenty of useful information about what the Council offers, ranging from courses to a video library.

Embassies (www.embassyworld.com/embassy/bahrain.htm) – has useful lists of Bahrain embassies around the world and of other nations' embassies in Bahrain.

Gulf Daily News (www.gulf-daily-news.com) – the *Gulf Daily News* calls itself 'the voice of Bahrain' and, while this site doesn't boast the most sophisticated graphics or layout, it has lots of useful information concerning local and world news, business, sport and many other subjects.

Gulfing (www.homestead.com/Gulfing) – aimed at South African residents in Bahrain but useful for all expatriates.

Yellow Pages (www.bahrainyellowpages.com) – lists over 8,500 business addresses.

Kuwait

British Council (www.britishcouncil.org/kuwait) – details the Council's services and facilities.

Kuwait Airport (www.kuwait-airport.com) – tells you everything about the airport.

Kuwait Airways (www.kuwait-airways.com) – the site of the country's national airline.

Kuwait Daily (www.kuwaitdaily.com) – as well as extensive news coverage, the *Kuwait Daily* site offers lots of useful information about many things, from jobs to travel and restaurants to visas.

Kuwait Information Office (www.kuwait-info.org) – contains a great deal of information about the country's history, culture, attractions and much else, from the official point of view.

Kuwait Internet Pages (🖥 www.kuwait-pages.com) – a glossary covering sites and organisations concerned with everything from the arts to employment and health.

Kuwait Online (🖥 www.kuwaitonline.com) – this site offers plenty of information about Kuwait's history, geography, government, culture and much else.

Kuwait Times (🖥 www.kuwaittimes.net) – the *Kuwait Times* calls itself 'the leading independent daily in the Gulf' and has reasonable coverage of local, regional and international news, business, sport and other issues.

Kuwait's Top List (www.kuwait-toplist.com) – a handbook of Kuwait's largest corporations.

Yellow Pages (🖥 www.kuwaityellowpages.com) – local business directory.

Oman

British Council (🖥 www.britishcouncil.org/oman) – the site of the ever-useful British Council.

Destination Oman (🖥 www.destinationoman.com) – endorsed by the Directorate General of Tourism, Ministry of Commerce and Industry, Sultanate of Oman, and therefore an official site.

Ministry of Information (🖥 www.omanet.com) – the site of the Ministry of Information, with a good deal of information about Oman, from a government point of view.

Oman Information Center (🖥 www.omaninfo.com) – a directory of everything from arts to travel and science to shopping. Also has plenty of information for residents and visitors about most aspects of life in Oman.

Oman News Agency (🖥 www.omannews.com) – has a daily news and pictures bulletin covering items of Omani and regional interest.

Oman Observer (💻 www.omanobserver.com) – claims to be 'Oman's largest circulated English daily', with reasonable coverage of local, regional and international news, sports, business and other issues.

Oman Studies Centre (💻 www.oman.org) – a site for those interested in taking courses.

Oman Times (💻 www.omantimes.com or www.timesof oman.com) – the site of the oldest English-language newspaper in the Sultanate, with plenty of local, regional and international news, and information about many matters, including weather, films, TV and radio, duty pharmacies and much else.

Oman Web Directory (💻 http://directory-oman.com/index.htm) – describes itself as 'Oman's premium online directory service'.

Yellow Pages (💻 www.omanyellowpages.com) – local business directory.

Qatar

British Council (💻 www.britishcouncil.org/qatar) – the site of the British Council.

British in Qatar (💻 www.british-in-qatar.com) – has plenty of information and links for the newcomer and established resident alike.

Destination Qatar (💻 www.www.destinationqatar.com) – the site of the official magazine of Qatar National Hotels Company, with plenty of information and features and an extensive links page.

Gulf Times (💻 www.gulf-times.com) – the site of Qatar's oldest English-language newspaper, this has plenty of news, sports, classifieds and articles.

Qatar Airways (💻 www.qatarairways.com) – tells you all about the airline as well as offering general information about the country.

Qatar Globe (🖥 www.qatarglobe.com) – as well as reasonable news coverage, this site has plenty of visitor and resident information.

Qatar Net (🖥 www.qatarnet.com) – offers plenty of information about Qatar and services in the country.

Qatar Petroleum (🖥 www.qp.com.qa/qp.nsf/web/living) – the site of Qatar Petroleum, this also has a section about all aspects of living in Qatar.

QAPCO (🖥 www.qapco.com/about/qatar.htm) – QAPCO is a joint venture company set up to use the ethane gas associated with petroleum production. This part of its site provides information about Qatar.

Yellow Pages (🖥 www.qataryellowpages.com) – self-explanatory.

Saudi Arabia

Arab News (🖥 www.arabnews.com) – plenty of news and features from 'Saudi Arabia's first English daily'.

British Council (🖥 www.britishcouncil.org/saudiarabia) – the site of the British Council.

Saudi Airlines (🖥 www.saudiairlines.com) – the site of the country's airline.

Saudi Arabia Internet Guide (🖥 www.argji.com/saudi) – has plenty of news, information, services and, apparently, humour.

Saudi Arabia.net (🖥 www.saudiarabia.net) – provides links to plenty of goods and services outlets.

Saudi Arabian Internet Pages (🖥 www.saudi-pages.com) – has plenty of links to information about all aspects of the country and its services.

Saudi Embassy (🖥 www.saudiembassy.net) – the site of the Royal Embassy of Saudi Arabia, Washington DC, containing lots of information about the country.

Saudi Times (💻 www.sauditimes.com) – has extensive news coverage as well as features.

Saudi Ministry of Information (💻 www.saudinf.com) – contains over 2,000 pages of information on every aspect of Saudi.

US-Saudi Arabian Business Council (💻 www.us-saudi-business.org) – as well as describing the services of the business council (designed to foster US-Saudi business) offers useful general information about the country.

Yellow Pages (💻 www.saudiarabiayellowpages.com) – local business directory.

UAE

British Council (💻 www.britishcouncil.org/uae) – the site of the British Council.

Dubai City Guide (💻 www.dubaicityguide.com) – 'complete information on Dubai City', concerning tourism, contacts, going out, telephone numbers, weather forecasts and much else.

Dubai Duty Free (💻 www.ddf-uae.com) – the site of 'one of the top airport retail operations in the world'.

Emirates.org (💻 www.emirates.org) – 'the most comprehensive site about UAE on the internet', with a range of items, including news and a photo gallery.

Go Dubai (💻 www.godubai.com) – covers everything to do with Dubai, including job vacancies, cinema guides, competitions and other things.

Khaleej Times (💻 www.khaleejtimes.co.ae) – the site of 'the number one English-language daily newspaper published from Dubai', with extensive local and international news, plenty of classifieds.

Ministry of Information and Culture (💻 www.uaeinteract.com) – the Ministry's official website, with plenty of information and news about all aspects of the UAE.

UAE.ac (💻 www.uae.ac) – an interactive meeting place and resource for those after information, services and links about the UAE.

UAE Kid's Web (💻 www.uaekidsweb.com) – a site designed to be fun, informative and educational for children.

UAE News (💻 www.uaenews.com) – has plenty of regional and global news, information and links.

UAE Pages (💻 www.uae.org) – offers information about all aspects of the UAE, including tourist and business information.

Yellow Pages (💻 www.uaeyellowpages.com) – local business directory.

APPENDIX D: WEIGHTS & MEASURES

The Gulf states use the metric system of measurement. Those who are more familiar with the imperial system of measurement will find the tables on the following pages useful. Some comparisons shown are only approximate, but are close enough for most everyday uses. In addition to the variety of measurement systems used, clothes sizes often vary considerably with the manufacturer (as we all know only too well). Try all clothes on before buying and don't be afraid to return something if, when you try it on at home, you decide it doesn't fit (most shops will exchange goods or give a refund).

Women's Clothes

Continental	34	36	38	40	42	44	46	48	50	52
UK	8	10	12	14	16	18	20	22	24	26
USA	6	8	10	12	14	16	18	20	22	24

Pullovers

	Women's						Men's					
Continental	40 42 44 46 48 50						44 46 48 50 52 54					
UK	34 36 38 40 42 44						34 36 38 40 42 44					
USA	34 36 38 40 42 44						sm med lar xl					

Men's Shirts

Continental	36	37	38	39	40	41	42	43	44	46
UK/USA	14	14	15	15	16	16	17	17	18	

Men's Underwear

Continental	5	6	7	8	9	10
UK	34	36	38	40	42	44
USA	sm	med		lar	xl	

Note: sm = small, med = medium, lar = large, xl = extra large

Children's Clothes

Continental	92	104	116	128	140	152
UK	16/18	20/22	24/26	28/30	32/34	36/38
USA	2	4	6	8	10	12

Children's Shoes

Continental	18	19	20	21	22	23	24	25	26	27	28	29	30	31	32
UK/USA	2	3	4	4	5	6	7	7	8	9	10	11	11	12	13

Continental	33	34	35	36	37	38
UK/USA	1	2	2	3	4	5

Shoes (Women's and Men's)

Continental	35	36	37	37	38	39	40	41	42	42	43	44
UK	2/3	3	4	4	5	5/6	6/7	7	8	8	9	9/10
USA	4	5	5	6	6	7	8	9	9	10	10	11

Weight

Avoirdupois	Metric	Metric	Avoirdupois
1oz	28.35g	1g	0.035oz
1lb*	454g	100g	3.5oz
1cwt	50.8kg	250g	9oz
1 ton	1,016kg	500g	18oz
2,205lb	1 tonne	1kg	2.2lb

Length

British/US	Metric	Metric	British/US
1in	2.54cm	1cm	0.39in
1ft	30.48cm	1m	3ft 3.25in
1yd	91.44cm	1km	0.62mi
1mi	1.6km	8km	5mi

Capacity

Imperial	Metric	Metric	Imperial
1 UK pint	0.57 litre	1 litre	1.75 UK pints
1 US pint	0.47 litre	1 litre	2.13 US pints
1 UK gallon	4.54 litres	1 litre	0.22 UK gallon
1 US gallon	3.78 litres	1 litre	0.26 US gallon

Area

British/US	Metric	Metric	British/US
1 sq. in	0.45 sq. cm	1 sq. cm	0.15 sq. in
1 sq. ft	0.09 sq. m	1 sq. m	10.76 sq. ft
1 sq. yd	0.84 sq. m	1 sq. m	1.2 sq. yds
1 acre	0.4 hectares	1 hectare	2.47 acres
1 sq. mile	2.56 sq. km	1 sq. km	0.39 sq. mile

Temperature

°Celsius	°Fahrenheit	
0	32	(freezing point of water)
5	41	
10	50	
15	59	
20	68	
25	77	
30	86	
35	95	
40	104	
50	122	

Notes: The boiling point of water is 100°C / 212°F.

Normal body temperature (if you're alive and well) is 37°C / 98.4°F.

Temperature Conversion

Celsius to Fahrenheit: multiply by 9, divide by 5 and add 32. (For a quick and approximate conversion, double the Celsius temperature and add 30.)

Fahrenheit to Celsius: subtract 32, multiply by 5 and divide by 9. (For a quick and approximate conversion, subtract 30 from the Fahrenheit temperature and divide by 2.)

Oven Temperatures

Gas	Electric	
	°F	°C
-	225–250	110–120
1	275	140
2	300	150
3	325	160
4	350	180
5	375	190
6	400	200
7	425	220
8	450	230
9	475	240

Air Pressure

PSI	Bar
10	0.5
20	1.4
30	2
40	2.8

APPENDIX E: MAP

The map below shows the Gulf states and Saudi Arabia in relation to their neighbouring countries in the Middle East and East Africa.

INDEX

A

B

C

F

N

O

P

Q

R

S

T

U

V

W

LIVING AND WORKING SERIES

Living and Working books are essential reading for anyone planning to spend time abroad, including holiday-home owners, retirees, visitors, business people, migrants, students and even extraterrestrials! They're packed with important and useful information designed to help you **avoid costly mistakes and save both time and money.** Topics covered include how to:

- Find a job with a good salary & conditions
- Obtain a residence permit
- Avoid and overcome problems
- Find your dream home
- Get the best education for your family
- Make the best use of public transport
- Endure local motoring habits
- Obtain the best health treatment
- Stretch your money further
- Make the most of your leisure time
- Enjoy the local sporting life
- Find the best shopping bargains
- Insure yourself against most eventualities
- Use post office and telephone services
- Do numerous other things not listed above

Living and Working books are the most comprehensive and up-to-date source of practical information available about everyday life abroad. They aren't, however, boring text books, but interesting and entertaining guides written in a highly readable style.

Discover what it's *really* like to live and work abroad!

Order your copies today by phone, fax, mail or e-mail from: Survival Books, PO Box 146, Wetherby, West Yorks. LS23 6XZ, United Kingdom (☎/▤ +44 (0)1937-843523, ✉ orders@ survivalbooks.net, ▱ www.survivalbooks.net).

BUYING A HOME SERIES

Buying a Home books are essential reading for anyone planning to purchase property abroad and are designed to guide you through the jungle and make it a pleasant and enjoyable experience. Most importantly, they're packed with vital information to help you **avoid the sort of disasters that can turn your dream home into a nightmare!** Topics covered include:

- Avoiding problems
- Choosing the region
- Finding the right home and location
- Estate agents
- Finance, mortgages and taxes
- Home security
- Utilities, heating and air-conditioning
- Moving house and settling in
- Renting and letting
- Permits and visas
- Travelling and communications
- Health and insurance
- Renting a car and driving
- Retirement and starting a business
- And much, much more!

Buying a Home books are the most comprehensive and up-to-date source of information available about buying property abroad. Whether you want a detached house, townhouse or apartment, a holiday or a permanent home, these books will help make your dreams come true.

Save yourself time, trouble and money!

Order your copies today by phone, fax, mail or e-mail from: Survival Books, PO Box 146, Wetherby, West Yorks. LS23 6XZ, United Kingdom (☎/🖹 +44 (0)1937-843523, ✉ orders@ survivalbooks.net, 🖳 www.survivalbooks.net).

ORDER FORM

ALIEN'S GUIDES / BEST PLACES / BUYING A HOME / DISASTERS / WINES

Qty.	Title	Price (incl. p&p)*			Total
		UK	Europe	World	
	The Alien's Guide to Britain	£5.95	£6.95	£8.45	
	The Alien's Guide to France	£5.95	£6.95	£8.45	
	The Best Places to Buy a Home in France	£13.95	£15.95	£19.45	
	The Best Places to Buy a Home in Spain	£13.45	£14.95	£16.95	
	Buying a Home Abroad	£13.45	£14.95	£16.95	
	Buying a Home in Britain	£11.45	£12.95	£14.95	
	Buying a Home in Florida	£13.45	£14.95	£16.95	
	Buying a Home in France	£13.45	£14.95	£16.95	
	Buying a Home in Greece & Cyprus	£13.45	£14.95	£16.95	
	Buying a Home in Ireland	£11.45	£12.95	£14.95	
	Buying a Home in Italy	£13.45	£14.95	£16.95	
	Buying a Home in Portugal	£13.45	£14.95	£16.95	
	Buying a Home in Spain	£13.45	£14.95	£16.95	
	How to Avoid Holiday & Travel Disasters	£13.45	£14.95	£16.95	
	Maintaining & Restoring Your French Home	Autumn 2003			
	Rioja and its Wines	£11.45	£12.95	£14.95	
	The Wines of Spain	£15.95	£18.45	£21.95	
				Total	

Order your copies today by phone, fax, mail or e-mail from: Survival Books, PO Box 146, Wetherby, West Yorks. LS23 6XZ, UK (☎/▤ +44 (0)1937-843523, ✉ orders@survivalbooks.net, 💻 www.survivalbooks.net). If you aren't entirely satisfied, simply return them to us within 14 days for a full and unconditional refund.

Cheque enclosed/Please charge my Amex/Delta/MasterCard/Switch/Visa* card

Card No.   __ __ __ __   __ __ __ __   __ __ __ __   __ __ __ __

Expiry date _____   Issue number (Switch only) _____

Signature _____   Tel. No. _____

NAME _____

ADDRESS _____

_____

_____

* Delete as applicable (price includes postage – airmail for Europe/world).

ORDER FORM

LIVING & WORKING SERIES / RETIRING ABROAD

Qty.	Title	Price (incl. p&p)*			Total
		UK	Europe	World	
	Living & Working Abroad	£16.95	£18.95	£22.45	
	Living & Working in America	£14.95	£16.95	£20.45	
	Living & Working in Australia	£14.95	£16.95	£20.45	
	Living & Working in Britain	£14.95	£16.95	£20.45	
	Living & Working in Canada	£16.95	£18.95	£22.45	
	Living & Working in the Far East	Winter 2003			
	Living & Working in France	£14.95	£16.95	£20.45	
	Living & Working in Germany	£16.95	£18.95	£22.45	
	Living & Working in the Gulf States & Saudi Arabia	£16.95	£18.95	£22.45	
	Living & Working in Holland, Belgium & Luxembourg	£14.95	£16.95	£20.45	
	Living & Working in Ireland	£14.95	£16.95	£20.45	
	Living & Working in Italy	£16.95	£18.95	£22.45	
	Living & Working in London	£11.45	£12.95	£14.95	
	Living & Working in New Zealand	£14.95	£16.95	£20.45	
	Living & Working in Spain	£14.95	£16.95	£20.45	
	Living & Working in Switzerland	£14.95	£16.95	£20.45	
	Retiring Abroad	£14.95	£16.95	£20.45	
				Total	

Order your copies today by phone, fax, mail or e-mail from: Survival Books, PO Box 146, Wetherby, West Yorks. LS23 6XZ, UK (☎/📠 +44 (0)1937-843523, ✉ orders@survivalbooks.net, 💻 www.survivalbooks.net). If you aren't entirely satisfied, simply return them to us within 14 days for a full and unconditional refund.

Cheque enclosed/Please charge my Amex/Delta/MasterCard/Switch/Visa* card

Card No. _ _ _ _   _ _ _ _   _ _ _ _   _ _ _ _

Expiry date ________ Issue number (Switch only) ________

Signature ________ Tel. No. ________

NAME ________

ADDRESS ________

____

____

* Delete as applicable (price includes postage – airmail for Europe/world).

OTHER SURVIVAL BOOKS

Survival Books publishes a variety of books in addition to the *Living and Working* and *Buying a Home* series (see previous pages). These include:

The Alien's Guides: *The Alien's Guides to Britain* and *France* provide an 'alternative' look at life in these popular countries and will help you to avoid the most serious gaffes and to appreciate more fully the peculiarities (in both senses) of the British and French.

The Best Places to Buy a Home: *The Best Places to Buy a Home in France* and *Spain* are the most comprehensive and up-to-date sources of information available for anyone wanting to research the property market in France and Spain and will save you endless hours choosing the best place for your home.

How to Avoid Holiday and Travel Disasters: This book is essential reading for anyone planning a trip abroad and will help you to make the right decisions regarding every aspect of your travel arrangements and to avoid costly mistakes and the sort of disasters that can turn a trip into a nightmare.

Retiring Abroad: This is the most comprehensive and up-to-date source of practical information available about retiring to a foreign country and will help to smooth your path to successful retirement abroad and save you time, trouble and money.

Wine Guides: *Rioja and its Wines* and *The Wines of Spain* are required reading for lovers of fine wines and are the most comprehensive and up-to-date sources of information available on the wines of Spain and of its most famous wine-producing region.

Broaden your horizons with Survival Books!

Order your copies today by phone, fax, mail or e-mail from: Survival Books, PO Box 146, Wetherby, West Yorks. LS23 6XZ, United Kingdom (☎/▤ +44 (0)1937-843523, ✉ orders@ survivalbooks.net, ▭ www.survivalbooks.net).

NOTES

NOTES

NOTES

NOTES